Religion, Spirituality,
and Positive Psychology

Religion, Spirituality, and Positive Psychology

UNDERSTANDING THE PSYCHOLOGICAL FRUITS OF FAITH

Thomas G. Plante, PhD, Editor

PRAEGER

AN IMPRINT OF ABC-CLIO, LLC
Santa Barbara, California • Denver, Colorado • Oxford, England

Library of Congress Cataloging-in-Publication Data

Religion, spirituality, and positive psychology : understanding the psychological fruits of faith / Thomas G. Plante, editor.

    p. cm.

Includes bibliographical references and index.

ISBN 978–0–313–39845–2 (hardcopy : alk. paper) — ISBN 978–0–313–39846–9 (ebook) 1. Psychology, Religious. 2. Well-being—Religious aspects. 3. Fruit of the Spirit. I. Plante, Thomas G.

BL53.R4357   2012

200.1′9—dc23   2012014836

ISBN: 978–0–313–39845–2
EISBN: 978–0–313–39846–9

16 15 14 13 12   1 2 3 4 5

This book is also available on the World Wide Web as an eBook.
Visit www.abc-clio.com for details.

Praeger
An Imprint of ABC-CLIO, LLC

ABC-CLIO, LLC
130 Cremona Drive, P.O. Box 1911
Santa Barbara, California 93116-1911

This book is printed on acid-free paper ∞

Manufactured in the United States of America

For all those who have been lead to use spiritual and religious experiences, practices, and beliefs to help make the world a more humane, just, compassionate, and loving place for all.

Contents

Preface

Few topics receive the kind of constant media attention, debate, and expression of strong emotions as religion and spirituality. While many claim that religion and spirituality are inspiration for great good in the world (e.g., charity, love, kindness), many others would claim they provide motivation for much that is wrong in the world (e.g., hate, prejudice, intolerance, warfare). Religion and spirituality seem to bring out the very best and the very worst in people and have done so for centuries. In more recent years, academic scholarship has begun to address these issues and has tried to determine, using the very best that methodological and statistical techniques can offer, if religion and spirituality make us better people. The integration of behavioral and medical sciences with spiritual, religious, and theological approaches has unfolded with collaborative projects, programs, and institutes being developed at a rapid pace.

The purpose of this book is to bring together some of the best minds on this topic in order to offer thoughtful and evidence-based reflections about the potential benefits of religious and spiritual engagement. The book is a companion to several earlier edited books on this topic published by Praeger/Greenwood/ABC-CLIO that include *Contemplative Practices in Action: Spirituality, Meditation, and Health* (2010) and *Spirit, Science and Health: How the Spiritual Mind Fuels Physical Wellness* (2007).

We have used a centering and guiding theme of "fruit of the spirit" referred to in sacred scriptures. As mentioned in the Christian New Testament, *"But the fruit of the Spirit is love, joy, peace, patience, kindness, goodness, faithfulness, gentleness, self-control"* (Galatians 5:22).

Our project tries to examine the empirical research evidence that is available to see if engagement in religious and spiritual activities does result in more love, joy, peace, patience, and so forth. Thus, the project is perhaps one of the first to closely examine the relationship between positive psychology and spirituality to reflect on the psychological fruits of faith and the spirit.

Acknowledgments

Many people other than the author or editor assist in the completion of a book project. Some contribute in a direct way, while others help in a more supportive manner. I would like to acknowledge the assistance of the people who worked to make this book idea a reality.

First and foremost, I would like to thank the contributors to this volume. They include some of the leading scholars in the field and have been an all-star team to provide the reader with state-of-the-art reflection and scholarship. Second, it is important to recognize the wonderful people at ABC-CLIO who published this book. Most especially, many thanks go to editor Debbie Carvalko for her many efforts, not only with this book project but also with many other book projects that I have published with her assistance during the past decade. Finally, I would like to thank my wife, Lori, and son, Zach, who are daily reminders that life is good and sacred and that I am blessed beyond words to have them both in my life.

Foreword

This important book breaks new ground on a topic that concerns all of us as citizens: How do spirituality and religion affect our individual and collective well-being? Dr. Plante and his colleagues at the Spirituality and Health Institute, all leading experts in their fields, take us on a reader-friendly and scientifically well-grounded tour of relevant empirical research. The book's title, of course, alludes to a famous passage in the Christian bible on *"the fruit of the spirit"* (Galatians 5:22). Similar passages can be found in other scriptures (e.g., *Bhagavad Gita* 13:7).

The present team of authors investigates many of the most important "fruits" reputed to emerge from engagement with spirituality and religion. Separate chapters discuss evidence that spiritual engagement affects—primarily favorably—a person's propensity to manifest strengths such as hope, forgiveness, gratitude, and ethical comportment. As these authors point out, much evidence links most of these qualities to better physical health. Other chapters examine direct evidence that various forms of spiritual engagement may foster recovery from addictions or serve as a force for social justice. Still other chapters discuss effects from specific spiritual practices such as meditation and how these may be integrated into psychotherapy or rehabilitation. Religious groups, too, may benefit from recovering their own legacies of spiritual practice: A very personal chapter by Dr. Carl Thoresen, a leading figure in spirituality and health research, discusses how he helped his own United Methodist congregation, including several pastors, to recover a commitment to meditating on inspired texts.

For individuals, the evidence discussed here may encourage recommitment to personal spiritual practices or beliefs. But what does such evidence mean for the larger society? Health is one apparent fruit of spiritual engagement. In response, should health professionals and educators find ways to support patient spirituality while respecting patients' beliefs? Other apparent benefits include cultivating virtues related to social involvement and civic engagement, such as forgiveness and ethical comportment. Should higher educators, in both religious and secular settings, seek to familiarize students with a range of spiritual practices that can foster such qualities? In public education, could such skills be fostered in a nonsectarian manner, respectful of diverse student backgrounds and beliefs?

With regard to health, clear moves toward reintegration have recently occurred. Nearly two decades ago, medical educator David Barnard and his colleagues pointed out in the pages of *Academic Medicine* that modern Western medicine, "shorn of every vestige of mystery, faith, or moral portent, is actually an aberration in the world scene." Since that time, more than one third of U.S. medical schools have introduced courses that address spirituality. Furthermore, hospitals and other healthcare organizations are required to maintain the capacity to conduct spiritual assessments—a requirement introduced in 2001 by the Joint Commission on Accreditation of Healthcare Agencies. Large public healthcare agencies, such as the Veterans Administration, have also used spiritual assessments. The University of Michigan, a public university, has introduced a spiritual meditation practice requirement for graduation from one of its degree programs (Ed Sarath has nicely described how its music school requires students to formally declare not only a musical instrument but also a form of spiritual practice).

Are these steps in the right direction? As Dr. Plante and his colleagues remind us, effects from spirituality and religion are not uniformly positive, although the balance generally appears to be strongly positive. As citizens, we should be concerned that any reintegration of spirituality into other sectors of society be done with sensitivity to our constitution and to our fellow citizens who believe differently than us. As citizens, therefore, we must become informed. Citizens must ponder these issues from the type of broad and pluralistic perspectives offered in this book. Of course, for both individuals and societies, renewal and healing can be a prolonged process. As the Greek philosopher Epictetus observed, "No thing great is created suddenly, any more than a bunch of grapes or a fig. . . . Let it first blossom, then bear fruit, then ripen."

We must begin where we are. To inform our journeys, this invaluable book familiarizes us with basic issues. It focuses our attention on key evidence for a diverse range of spiritual fruits and alerts us to what is unknown at the frontiers. This too is helpful, for, as the poet Rainer Rilke once advised, "Be patient toward all that is unsolved in your heart and try to love the questions themselves. . . . Live the questions now. Perhaps you will then gradually, without noticing it, live along some distant day into the answer."

Doug Oman, PhD
School of Public Health
University of California, Berkeley

Section I

The Fruit of the Spirit

1

Fruit of Faith, Fruit of the Spirit

Thomas G. Plante

> *But the fruit of the Spirit is love, joy, peace, patience, kindness, good-ness, faithfulness, gentleness, self-control.*
>
> —Galatians 5:22

This quote from the Christian New Testament states that there are many positive psychological and behavioral results when one is attentive to and perhaps filled with God's spirit. As contemporary behavioral scientists living and working within an often secular, scientific, and empirically focused world as well as being affiliated with rigorous academic institutions and research programs, we wonder if the fruits of the spirit have any empirical and scientific basis. Does engagement with religion and spirituality make us better people or make us worse?

Perhaps the answer to this question is both. We are certainly well aware of the horrific behaviors that some people engage in stating that they are doing so due to their religious beliefs and practices. Some choose to kill and abuse others in the name of their religion, for example. Some discriminate against others and treat others with contempt, justifying their behavior and attitudes through their religious beliefs and affiliations. For centuries and perhaps millennia, people chose to treat others horrifically in the name of God. Religion can bring out the worst in people.

However, the opposite also appears true. Many people behave admirably, nobly, and selflessly in the name of their religious traditions, beliefs, and practices. People show remarkable love, restraint, charity, compassion, and other admirable qualities. Religion and spirituality clearly appear to bring out the very best in people. So religion appears to play a role in turning out Mother Teresas as well as suicide bombers, both saints and sinners.

If one only hears about religious behavior and traditions from reading the daily news, the average person would likely have a very negative view of religion. Intolerant extremists, suicide bombers, and zealots of all kinds fill the news with behaviors that result in murder, torture, and hate. In contemporary years, perhaps many have come to believe that all Muslims are terrorists, all Catholic priests are pedophiles, and all Evangelical Christians hate homosexuals and believe that those not closely associated with their beliefs and practices will surely go to hell. Sadly, negative and appalling stereotypical behavior can emerge when overgeneralizing from these news reports. It is no wonder that the now-popular and well-known "new atheists" (e.g., Sam Harris, Christopher Hutchins, Richard Dawkins) have little respect or admiration for God or religious traditions. In some circles, it has become fashionable to be an atheist and a religion basher. Perhaps they read the news but don't experience or witness the fruits of the Spirit in the religious and spiritual institutions and organizations that never make the headlines. Love, compassion, charity, self-sacrifice, soup kitchens, and so forth really never make news, while violence, hate, and intolerance certainly make headlines.

During recent decades, an enormous amount of research has been published on the relationship between religious and spiritual engagement, broadly defined, and psychological health and well-being. Overall, these studies have found that more often than not, religious and spiritual engagement is good for both physical and mental health.[1–23] People who are affiliated and actively engaged with a religious and spiritual tradition tend to be more optimistic, happy, satisfied with their lives and with their loved ones and are less likely to be depressed, anxious, stressed, alcoholic, physically and mentally ill, and less likely to engage in health-damaging behaviors like cigarette smoking, drug abuse, unprotected sexual behavior, and violence. In fact, on average, research suggests that people tend to live seven years longer if engaged with religious and spiritual practices than those who are not engaged. For African Americans, the average additional longevity is 14 years.[11]

The purpose of this book project is to highlight what is currently known about how religious and spiritual engagement makes us better people. Does participation in religious and spiritual traditions, practices, and beliefs make us more loving, kind, compassionate, forgiving, humble, hopeful, grateful, good, and so forth? Does the Spirit, in other words, produce the fruit referred to in the quotation at the beginning of the chapter? Additionally, chapters in the book look at application of this research for a number of important health areas such as in cancer treatment, addiction treatment, and social justice in healthcare. Finally, one chapter offers a reflection on integrating spiritual and religious virtues into a long-running men's group.

Leading scholars, researchers, and thinkers, primarily in the psychology field, agreed to review the research that examines these fruits of the spirit. This book project is the fruit of this collaborative project among these remarkable colleagues.

Notes

1. Bormann, J. E., Gifford, A. L., Shively, M., Smith, T. L., Redwine, L., Kelly, A., Becker, S., Gershwin, M., Bone, P., & Belding, W. (2006). Effects of spiritual mantram repetition on HIV outcomes: A randomized controlled trial. *Journal of Behavioral Medicine, 29*, 359–376.

2. Hackney, C. H., & Sanders, G. S. (2003). Religiosity and mental health: A meta-analysis of recent studies. *Journal for the Scientific Study of Religion, 42*, 43–55.

3. Hill, T. D., Ellison, C. G., Burdette, A. M., & Musick, M. A. (2007). Religious involvement in a healthy lifestyles: Evidence from the survey of Texas adults. *Annals of Behavioral Medicine, 34*, 217–222.

4. Kendler, K. S., Gardner, C. O., & Prescott, C. A. (1996). Religion, psychopathology, and substance use and abuse: A multi-measure, genetic-epidemiologic study. *American Journal of Psychiatry, 154*, 322–329.

5. Koenig, H. G., McCullough, M. E., & Larson, D. B. (2001). *Handbook of religion and health*. New York: Oxford.

6. Leigh, J., Bowen, S., & Marlatt, G. A. (2005). Spirituality, mindfulness, and substance abuse. *Addictive Behavior, 30*, 1335–1341.

7. Marks, L. (2005). Religion and bio-psycho-social health: A review and conceptual model. *Journal of Religion and Health, 44*, 173–186.

8. Marsden, P., Karagianni, E., & Morgan, J. F. (2007). Spirituality and clinical care in eating disorders: A qualitative study. *International Journal of Eating Disorders, 40*, 7–12.

9. Masters, K. S., Spielmans, G. I., & Goodson, J. T. (2006). Are there demonstrable effects of distant intercessory prayer? A meta-analytic review. *Annals of Behavioral Medicine, 32*, 337–342.

10. McClain, C., Rosenfeld, B., & Breitbart, W. (2003). Effect of spiritual well-being on end-of-life despair in terminally ill cancer patients. *Lancet, 361*, 1603–1607.

11. McCullough, M. E., Hoyt, W. T., Larson, D. B., Koenig, H. G., & Thoresen, C. E. (2000). Religious involvement and mortality: A meta-analytic review. *Health Psychology 19*, 211–221.

12. Michalak, L., Trocki, K., & Bond, J. (2007). Religion and alcohol in the U.S. National Alcohol Survey: How important is religion for abstention and drinking? *Drug and Alcohol Dependence, 87*, 268–280.

13. Miller, L., Warner, V., Wickramaratne, P., & Weissman, M. (1997). Religiosity and depression: Ten-year follow-up of depressed mothers and offspring. *Journal of the American Academy of Child and Adolescent Psychiatry, 36*, 1416–1425.

14. Oman, D., Shapiro, S. L., Thoresen, C. E., Plante, T. G., & Flinders, T. (2008). Meditation lowers stress and supports forgiveness among college students: A randomized controlled trial. *Journal of American College Health, 56*, 569–578.

15. Pardini, D., Plante, T. G., Sherman, A., & Stump, J. E. (2000). Religious faith and spirituality in substance abuse recovery: Determining the mental health benefits. *Journal of Substance Abuse Treatment, 19*, 347–354.

16. Plante, T. G., & Sherman, A. S. (Eds.). (2001). *Faith and health: Psychological perspectives*. New York: Guilford.

17. Plante, T. G., & Thoresen, C. E. (Eds.). (2007). *Spirit, science and health: How the spiritual mind fuels physical wellness*. Westport, CT: Praeger/Greenwood.

18. Powell, L., Shahabi, L., & Thoresen, C. E. (2003). Religion and spirituality: Linkages to physical health. *American Psychologist, 58*, 36–52.

19. Seeman, T. E., Dubin, L. F., & Seeman, M. (2003). Religiosity/spirituality and health: A critical review of the evidence for biological pathways. *American Psychologist, 58*, 53–63.

20. Shreve-Neiger, A. K., & Edelstein, B. A. (2004). Religion and anxiety: A critical review of the literature. *Clinical Psychology Review, 24*, 379–397.

21. Siegrist, M. (1996). Church attendance, denomination, and suicide ideology. *Journal of Social Psychology, 136*, 559–566.

22. Stewart, C. (2001). The influence of spirituality on substance abuse of college students. *Journal of Drug Education, 31*, 343–51.

23. Worthington, E. L., Kurusu, T. A., McCullough, M. E., & Sandage, S. J. (1996). Empirical research on religion and psychotherapeutic processes and outcomes: A ten-year review and research prospectus. *Psychological Bulletin, 119*, 448–487.

2

Gratitude

Robert A. Emmons and Anjali Mishra

Gratitude is much admired. A small sampling of recent quotes reveals the power and potential of this virtue. "Whatever you are in search of—peace of mind, prosperity, health, love—it is waiting for you if only you are willing to receive it with an open and grateful heart," writes Sarah Breathnach in the *Simple Abundance Journal of Gratitude*. Elsewhere, she refers to gratitude as "the most passionate transformative force in the cosmos." Another popular treatment of the topic refers to it as "one of the most empowering, healing, dynamic instruments of consciousness vital to demonstrating the life experiences one desires."[1] Lock-and-key metaphors are especially common; gratitude has been referred to as "the key that opens all doors," that which "unlocks the fullness of life," and the "key to abundance, prosperity, and fulfillment."[2–3]

Feelings of gratitude can be powerful, overcoming their possessor with an intensity that rivals any other human emotion. It was this feeling of being overwhelmed with gratitude that the Catholic Saint, Ignatius of Loyola, was well familiar with. His prayer life was said to be so intense that during Mass, he often had to pause as his eyes filled with tears and he could not see. After a while, the constant tearing began to adversely affect his eyes. He sought a special papal dispensation to relieve him of some devotional duties so that his health might be preserved. In his spiritual diary, he wrote, "because of the violent pain that I felt in one eye as a result of the tears, this thought came to me: If I continue saying Mass, I could lose this eye, whereas it is better to keep it."[4]

How do these extraordinary claims regarding the power and promise of gratitude fare when scientific lights are shone on them? Can gratitude live up to its billing? In this chapter, we review the growing database on gratitude and well-being, explore mechanisms by which gratitude elevates well-being, and close by presenting what we consider important issues for the science of gratitude to address in future research.

What Is Gratitude?

Gratitude has a dual meaning: a worldly one and a transcendent one. In its worldly sense, gratitude is a feeling that occurs in interpersonal exchanges when one person acknowledges receiving a valuable benefit from another. Much of human life is about giving, receiving, and repayment. In this sense, it, like other social emotions, functions to help regulate relationships, solidifying and strengthening them. There is an energizing and motivating quality to gratitude. It is a positive state of mind that gives rise to the "passing on of the gift" through positive action. As such, gratitude serves as a key link in the dynamic between receiving and giving. It is not only a response to kindnesses received, but it is also a motivator of future benevolent actions on the part of the recipient.

Gratitude's other nature is ethereal, spiritual, and transcendent. Philosophies and theologies have long viewed gratitude as central to the human–divine relationship. As long as people have believed in a Supreme Being, believers have sought ways to express gratitude and thanksgiving to this Being, their ultimate giver. In monotheistic traditions, God is conceived of as a personal being that is the source of goodness and the first giver of all gifts, to whom much is owed. In these traditions, gratitude is a quite likely a universal religious emotion, manifested in the thank offerings described in ancient scriptures to the daily ceremonies and rituals of Native Americans to the contemporary praise and worship music of the evangelical tradition.

Though the concept of a personally transcendent God is not relevant in nontheistic traditions, gratitude retains its spiritual nature. This fundamental spiritual quality to gratitude that transcends religious traditions is aptly conveyed by Frederick Streng: "in this attitude people recognize that they are connected to each other in a mysterious and miraculous way that is not fully determined by physical forces, but is part of a wider, or transcendent context."[5] This spiritual core of gratefulness is essential if gratitude is to be not simply a tool for narcissistic self-improvement. True gratefulness rejoices in the other. It has as its ultimate goal reflecting back the goodness that one has received by creatively seeking opportunities for giving. The motivation for doing so resides in the grateful appreciation that one has lived by the grace of others. In this sense, the spirituality of gratitude is opposed a self-serving belief that one deserves or is entitled to the blessings that he or she enjoys. Rather, it is knowing the grace by which one lives, which is itself a profound spiritual realization.

Findings from the Science of Gratitude

Examinations of gratitude in the history of ideas come from a number of perspectives—philosophy, theology, and political economy, to name a few. Each of these is valid and valuable in its own right. However, only a scientific perspective can provide an evidence-based approach to understanding how and in what ways gratitude brings benefits into the life of the practitioner. Recently, the tools and techniques of modern science have been brought to bear on understanding the nature of gratitude and why it is important for human health and happiness.

Gratitude is foundational to well-being and mental health throughout the life span. From childhood to old age, accumulating evidence documents the wide array of psychological, physical, and relational benefits associated with gratitude. In the past few years, there has been a tremendous increase in the accumulation of scientific evidence showing the contribution of gratitude to psychological and social well-being.[6–7] Gratitude has been shown not only contribute to an increase in positive affect but also to a decrease in negative affect, as demonstrated in diverse samples such as among patients with neuromuscular disease[7] and early adolescents.[8]

Based on Erika Rosenberg's hierarchical levels of affective experience,[9] gratitude has been identified as a trait, emotion, and mood. The grateful disposition can be defined as a stable affective trait that would lower the threshold of experiencing gratitude. As an emotion, gratitude can be understood as an acute, intense, and relatively brief psychophysiological reaction to being the recipient of a benefit from another. Lastly, as a stable mood, gratitude has also been identified to have a subtle, broad, and longer-duration impact on consciousness.[10] Gratitude is not just a transient emotion but also a virtue. Grateful people are more prone to the emotion, are prone to respond with gratitude to a wider range of beneficent actions, and are more likely to notice beneficence on the part of others—in particular more likely to respond to it with the emotion of gratitude rather than with alternative emotions like resentment, shame, or guilt. Grateful people are likely to agree with statements such as "It's important to appreciate each day that you are alive," "I often reflect on how much easier my life is because of the efforts of others," and "For me, life is much more of a gift than it is a burden." Items such as these come from personality questionnaires designed to measure trait levels of gratitude—in other words, to identify people who are by nature grateful souls.

Both state and dispositional gratitude have been shown to enhance overall psychological, social, and physical well-being. For example, gratitude involves and encourages more positive social interactions, in turn making people better adjusted and accepted by people around them, and finally leading to well-being.[6] Since the emergence of gratitude research in the past few years, the two main measures that have been widely administered to measure dispositional gratitude are the six-item Gratitude Questionnaire[11] and the 44-item Gratitude Resentment and Appreciation Test or the GRAT.[12] Dispositional gratitude is a generalized tendency to first recognize and then emotionally respond with thankfulness after attributing benefits received through benevolence to an external moral agent.[13] The 44-item GRAT includes the three dimensions of trait gratitude: resentment, simple appreciation, and social appreciation.[12] Other measures to assess gratitude, in recent years, have mainly included personal interviews,[14] rating scales[15] and other self-report measures such as free response,[16] and personal narratives.[17]

Dispositional gratitude has been shown to uniquely and incrementally contribute to subjective well-being[18–19, 10]and contribute to benefits above and beyond general positive affect.[20] Dispositional gratitude has also been found to be positively associated with prosocial traits such as empathy, forgiveness, and willingness to help others.[11] For example, people who rated themselves as having a grateful disposition perceived themselves as having more prosocial characteristics, expressed by their empathetic behavior, and emotional support for friends within the last month. Similar associations have been found between state gratitude and well-being.

People with stronger dispositions toward gratitude tend to be more spiritually and religiously minded. Not only do they score higher on measures of traditional religiousness, but they also scored higher on nonsectarian measures of spirituality that assess spiritual experiences (e.g., sense of contact with a divine power) and sentiments (e.g., beliefs that all living things are interconnected) independent of specific theological orientation. All measures of public and private religiousness in the Emmons and Kneezel study were significantly associated with both dispositional gratitude and grateful feelings assessed on a daily basis.[21] Although these correlations were not large (ranged from $r = .28$ to $r = .52$), they suggest that spiritually or religiously inclined people have a stronger disposition to experience gratitude than do their less spiritual/religious counterparts. Watkins and colleagues found that trait gratitude correlated positively with intrinsic religiousness and negatively with extrinsic religiousness. The authors suggest that the presence of gratitude may be a *positive* affective hallmark of religiously and spiritually engaged people, just as an absence of depressive symptoms is a *negative* affective hallmark of spiritually and religiously engaged people. They likely see benefits as gifts from God, "as the first cause of all benefits."[18]

Additional research has examined trait gratitude in religious contexts or gratitude felt toward God. A nationwide survey found that people who have no religious preference or who have not attended church services recently are twice as likely to skip traditional Thanksgiving holiday observances compared to people who are active religiously.[22] Krause found that gratitude felt toward God reduced the effect of stress on health in late-life adults.[23] Using data from a longitudinal nationwide survey, Krause and colleagues further uncovered a linkage between "congregational cohesiveness" and gratitude toward God.[24] Gratitude toward God was measured by modifying the Gratitude Questionnaire[11] to make reference to God (e.g., "I have so much in life to be thankful to God for"; "I am grateful to God for all he has done for me"). Perceptions of cohesiveness (a belief that personal values are shared by church members) predicted an increase in feelings of gratitude toward God over time, leading the researchers to conclude that church attendance influences gratitude indirectly through congregation-based emotional support. Using the same data set, Krause found that gratitude toward God mediated the effect of financial strain on depression in late-life adults.[25] Financial stress had a greater impact on depression for older adults lower in gratitude, whereas the negative effects of financial strain on depressive symptoms were eradicated for older adults who were more grateful. Gratitude directed toward God adds unique variance in predicting happiness and life satisfaction above and beyond general trait gratitude.[26]

Another empirical approach to religious gratitude is to examine themes of thankfulness and gratitude in personal prayer content. In a study of prayer in the lives of college students, prayers of thanksgiving were the second most common type of prayer, following petitionary appeals.[27] Another study looking at prayer found that prayers of thanksgiving were negatively related to depression and anxiety and positively related to greater hope in patients with rheumatoid arthritis.[28] In a study examining the link between prayer and coping, prayers of praise and thankfulness were rated as the second most effective form of prayer in coping with personal difficulties.

Experimental Studies of Gratitude

In one of the first studies examining the benefits of experimentally induced grateful thoughts on psychological well-being in daily life, the experimenters focused on gratitude in relation to three conditions: gratitude-provoking experiences, hassles, and neutral life events.[7] As expected, the gratitude condition lead to overall well-being, as revealed by fewer health complaints, and a more positive outlook toward life. Participants in the gratitude condition also reported fewer physical health problems and also rated their life to be better compared to participants in the hassles and neutral conditions. Furthermore, in a study examining the contribution of gratitude in daily mood over 21 days, gratitude was strongly associated with spiritual transcendence and other positive affective traits (e.g., extraversion).[10] In the past few years, a number of laboratory- and research-based intervention studies have also been examining the positive impact of gratitude-induced activities (e.g., the gratitude visit, gratitude letter) on psychological well-being.[29–30, 10, 31, 32]

In these studies, participants in the gratitude condition are given the following instructions: "We want to focus for a moment on benefits or gifts that you have received in your life. These gifts could be simple everyday pleasures, people in your life, personal strengths or talents, moments of natural beauty, or gestures of kindness from others. We might not normally think about these things as gifts, but that is how we want you to think about them. Take a moment to really savor or relish these gifts, think about their value, and then write them down every night before going to sleep." A wide range of experiences sparked gratitude: cherished interactions, awareness of physical health, overcoming obstacles, and simply being alive, to name a few. This instructional set was in contrast with comparison conditions asking those in other randomly assigned groups to chronicle their daily travails or hassles or to reflect on ways in which they were better off than others.

In daily studies of emotional experience, when people report feeling grateful, thankful, and appreciative, they also feel more loving, forgiving, joyful, and enthusiastic. These deep affections appear to be formed through the discipline of gratitude. In this regard, it is interesting that the Greek root of the word *enthusiasm, entheos*, means "inspired by or possessed by a god." Importantly, these data showing that gratitude is correlated with beneficial outcomes are not limited to self-reports. Notably, the family, friends, partners, and others that surround them consistently report that people who practice gratitude seem measurably happier and are more pleasant to be around. Grateful people are rated by others as more helpful, more outgoing, more optimistic, and more trustworthy.[11]

The benefits of gratitude were further confirmed in another study that compared the efficacy of five different interventions that were hypothesized to increase personal happiness and decrease personal depression.[31] In a random-assignment, placebo-controlled Internet study, a gratitude intervention (writing and delivering a letter of thankfulness to someone who had been especially helpful but had never been properly thanked) was found to significantly increase happiness and decrease depression for up to one month following the visit. Results indicated that "participants in the gratitude visit condition showed the largest positive changes in the whole study." Thus, the benefits of gratitude do not appear to be limited to the self-guided journal-keeping methodology utilized by Emmons and McCullough.[7]

Why Is Gratitude Good? Exploring Mechanisms

How does one account for the psychological, emotional, and physical benefits of gratitude? Gratitude implies a recognition that it is possible for other forces to act toward us with beneficial, selfless motives. A number of possible explanations have been suggested; however, not all of them have been fully investigated. In the next section, we examine five explanations for the relationship between gratitude and well-being.

Gratitude increases spiritual awareness. Many world religions commend gratitude as a desirable human trait,[33–34] which may cause spiritual or religious people to adopt a grateful outlook. Upon recognition of God's provision of benefits, humans respond with grateful affect, and gratitude is one of the most common religious feelings that believers in virtually all spiritual traditions are encouraged to develop. When contemplating a positive circumstance that cannot be attributed to intentional human effort, such as a miraculous healing or the gift of life, spiritually inclined people may still be able attribute these positive outcomes to a human or nonhuman agent (viz., God or a higher power) and, thus, experience more gratitude. Third, spiritually inclined people also tend to attribute positive outcomes, but not negative ones, to God's intervention.[35–36] As a result, many positive life events that are not due to the actions of another person (e.g., pleasant weather, avoiding an automobile accident) may be perceived as occasions for gratitude to God, although negative events (e.g., a long winter, an automobile accident) would likely *not* be attributed to God. This attributional style, then, is likely to magnify the positive emotional effects of pleasant life events. Being grateful to a Supreme Being and to other people is an acknowledgment that there are good and enjoyable things in the world to be enjoyed in accordance with the giver's intent. Good things happen by design. If people believe in the spiritual concept of grace, they believe that there is a pattern of beneficence in the world that exists quite independently of their own striving and even their own existence. Gratitude thus depends upon receiving what we do not expect to receive or have not earned or receiving more than we believe we deserve. This awareness is simultaneously humbling and elevating to those with a spiritual worldview.

Gratitude Promotes Physical Health

Some of the benefits of gratitude for mental health may result from gratitude's ability to enhance physical health functioning. A small number of studies have reported physical health benefits of gratitude, and these relations have been largely independent of trait negative affect.[37] Gratitude interventions have been shown to reduce bodily complaints, increase sleep duration and efficiency, and promote exercise.[7, 19] Experimental research suggests that discrete experiences of gratitude and appreciation may cause increases in parasympathetic myocardial control[38] and lower systolic blood pressure[39] as well as improvements in more molar aspects of physical health such as everyday symptoms and physician visits.[7] McCraty and colleagues found that appreciation increased parasympathetic activity, a change thought to be beneficial in controlling stress and hypertension, as well as "coherence" or entrainment across various autonomic response channels.[38] Therefore, there might be some direct physiological benefits to frequently experiencing grateful emotions. These findings provide a link between positive emotions and increased physiological efficiency, which may partly explain the growing number of correlations documented between positive emotions, improved health, and increased longevity.

Gratitude Maximizes Pleasure

Gratitude maximizes enjoyment of the pleasurable in our lives. A well-established law in the psychology of emotion is the principle of adaptation. People adapt to circumstances, both pleasant and unpleasant. Our emotion systems like newness. Unfortunately for personal happiness, adaptation to pleasant circumstances occurs more rapidly than adaptation to unpleasant life changes. This is why even a major windfall, such as a huge pay raise, tends to impact happiness for only a mere few months. Once the glow fades, we return to the same happiness level we had before. Psychologists call this phenomenon hedonic adaptation. The only thing that can change it and prolong the increase in happiness is gratitude. Gratitude promotes the savoring of positive life experiences and situations so that the maximum satisfaction and enjoyment are derived from one's circumstances. In helping people not take things for granted, gratitude may recalibrate people's "set points" for happiness—our baseline levels of happiness that appear to be primarily innate, driven by our genes.

Gratitude Protects against the Negative

Gratitude also mitigates toxic emotions and states. Nothing can destroy happiness more quickly than envy, greed, and resentment. The German moral philosopher Balduin Schwarz identified the problem when he said, "the ungrateful, envious, complaining man ... cripples himself. He is focused on what he has not, particularly on that which somebody else has or seems to have, and by that he tends to poison his world."[40] Grateful people tend to be satisfied with what they have and so are less susceptible to such emotions as disappointment, regret, and frustration. Moreover, in the context of material prosperity, by maintaining a grateful focus, a person may avoid disillusionment and emptiness. The sense of security that characterizes grateful people makes them less susceptible to needing to rely on material accomplishments for a stable sense of self.

Gratitude Strengthens Relationships

Perhaps most important of all is that gratitude strengthens and expands social relationships. It cultivates a person's sense of interconnectedness. An unexpected benefit from gratitude journaling, one that I did not predict in advance, was that people who kept gratitude journals reported feeling closer and more connected to others, were more likely to help others, and were actually seen as more helpful by significant others in their social networks. Gratitude is the "moral memory of mankind," wrote noted sociologist Georg Simmel. One just needs to try to imagine human relationships existing without gratitude. By way of contrast, ingratitude leads inevitably to a confining, restricting, and "shrinking" sense of self. Emotions like anger, resentment, envy, and bitterness tend to undermine happy social relations. But the virtue of gratitude is not only a firewall of protection against such corruption of relationships; it contributes positively to friendship and civility, because it is both benevolent (wishing the benefactor well) and just (giving the benefactor his due, in a certain special way). We also have evidence that people who are high on dispositional gratitude, the chronic tendency to be aware of blessings in life, have better relationships, are more likely to protect and preserve these relationships, are more securely attached, and are less lonely and isolated. People who have an easier time conjuring up reasons to be grateful are less likely to say that they lack companionship or that no one really knows them well. Our innate longing for belonging is strengthened when we experience and express heartfelt gratitude. Gratitude takes us outside ourselves, where we see ourselves as part of a larger, intricate network of sustaining relationships, relationships that are mutually reciprocal.

Cultivating Gratitude

Despite all of the benefits that living a grateful life can bring, gratitude can be hard and painful work. It does not come easily or naturally to many. At least initially, it requires discipline. So this is the paradox of gratitude: While the evidence is clear that cultivating gratitude, in our lives and in our attitudes to life, makes us happier and healthier people, more attuned to the flow of blessings in our lives, it is still difficult. Practicing gratitude is easier said than done. A number of evidence based-strategies, including journaling and letter writing, have proven effective in creating sustainable gratefulness. At this point, we step back to see what general features these strategies share. In many respects, then, gratitude can be thought of as a mindfulness practice that leads to a greater experience of being connected to life and awareness of all of the benefits available.[41–42]

One of the first steps is attention. Attention is noticing and becoming aware of blessings that we normally take for granted. It is tuning in to the many reasons for gratitude that already exist in our lives. Simultaneously, directing our attention this way in a focused manner blocks thoughts and perceptions that are inimical to gratitude, such as feelings of exaggerated deservingness or perceptions of victimhood. Focusing techniques that enhance attentiveness (such as mindfulness meditation) will be effective in increasing one's appreciation for the simple blessings of life and in banishing incompatible thoughts from consciousness.

Finally, there is remembering. Grateful people draw upon positive memories of being the recipients of benevolence. This is why religious traditions are able to so effectively cultivate gratitude—litanies of remembrance encourage gratitude, and religions do litanies very well. The scriptures, sayings, and sacraments of faith traditions inculcate gratefulness by drawing believers into a remembered relationship with a Supreme Being and with the members of their community. There is a French proverb that states that gratitude is the memory of the heart—it is the way that the heart remembers. The memory of the heart includes the memory of those we are dependent on just as the forgetfulness of dependence is unwillingness or inability to remember the benefits provided by others.

Gratitude brings benefits. Yet much remains unknown. We have several suggestions for future research involving gratitude interventions.

Mechanisms

What are the active ingredients in gratitude interventions? It is not known whether the effects of these activities are relatively specific (e.g., increases in happiness alone) or are more general (e.g., increases in perceived physical health and decreases in negative mood). In addition, no research has attempted to examine the effects of these activities in the context of participants' levels of dispositional gratitude, an established individual difference that may modulate the positive effects of activities aimed at increasing gratitude in one's life.[11] The active ingredients may relate to processes of reflecting on things for which one is grateful or recording these in some way, or expressing them. Until it is known which of these is essential, we cannot state why these exercises work, and it is difficult to make informed recommendations about how they might be used.

Trait Moderators

Several dispositional factors may moderate the effectiveness of gratitude interventions. Of these, trait affect and dispositional gratitude are obvious candidates for consideration. It seems a reasonable prediction that persons high in positive affect (PA) may have reached an "emotional ceiling" and, thus, are less susceptible to experiencing gains in well-being. People lower in PA, however, may need more positive events—like expressing gratitude to a benefactor—to "catch up" to the positive experiences of their peers.

Froh and colleagues examined whether individual differences in positive affective style moderated the effects of a gratitude intervention in which youth were instructed to write a letter to someone to whom they were grateful and deliver it in person.[43] Eighty-nine children and adolescents were randomly assigned to the gratitude intervention or a control condition. Findings indicated that youth low in PA in the gratitude condition, compared with youth writing about daily events, reported greater gratitude and PA at posttreatment and greater PA at the two-month follow-up. Children and adolescents low in PA in the gratitude condition, compared with the control group, reported more gratitude and PA at two later time points, at three-week and two-month follow-ups. This is an important study because it is the first known randomized controlled trial of a gratitude intervention study in children and adolescents and the first paper to reinterpret the gratitude intervention literature, arguing to carefully consider control groups when concluding the efficacy of gratitude interventions. Furthermore, when considering both youth and adult populations, it is also the first known attempt at investigating a moderator, namely PA, with this gratitude intervention.

Then there is dispositional gratitude. Can we expect gratitude inductions to be more effective in increasing the well-being of grateful individuals? Grateful individuals would be more susceptible to recognizing when others are being kind to them and more open to perceiving benefits more generally. One could even postulate a gratitude schema[19] as an interpretive bias on the part of dispositionally grateful individuals prone to making benevolent appraisals. Alternatively, gratitude interventions might also be more efficacious for individuals low on trait gratitude since they may have more room for improvement. No published studies have examined dispositional gratitude as a moderator of state gratitude interventions.

Trait gratitude might also interact with trait affect. Froh and colleagues found that, compared to the control group, individuals in the gratitude group who were low on positive affect benefited the most from the gratitude intervention.[43] Therefore, given the recent evidence on the contribution of positive affect as a moderator, it might also be reasonable to examine the possibility of a curvilinear relationship between trait gratitude and well-being. For example, individuals at the extreme ends of the gratitude distribution might extract the fewest benefits from gratitude interventions.

Given the other-oriented focus of gratitude, humility might also cultivate greater gratitude. Since gratitude requires opening oneself to a vulnerable position, humble people might be more susceptible toward attributing
the attainment of lot of their life's gifts (tangible or intangible) to other
people. Indirect evidence for the possible relationship between humility
and gratitude might also be interpreted by the suggested inverse relationship between gratitude and narcissism.[44] In all, humility might promote
gratitude by first facilitating a more objective and realistic perspective of
one's achievements, success, and good qualities. Subsequently, a humble
person may feel more gratitude by perceiving success as a product of
multiple forces external to the self.

The Effect of Instructional Set

The blessings-counting gratitude intervention guides participants to reflect
on and record benefits in their lives. Participants generally focus on the
presence of good things in their lives that they currently enjoy. Yet a recent
study found that people's affective states improve more after mentally subtracting positive events from their lives than after thinking about the presence of those events.[45] People wrote about why a positive event might
never have happened and why it was surprising or why it was certain to
be part of their lives and was not at all surprising. The results showed that
the way in which people think about positive life events is critical, namely
whether they think about the presence of the events (e.g., "I'm grateful
that I was in Professor Peabody's class") or the absence of the events
(e.g., "imagine I had never met Professor Peabody!"). The latter impacted
positive affect more than did the former. Inasmuch as most previous studies adopted the former approach, asking participants to think about the
presence of positive events, the effects of gratitude on well-being may
have been underestimated. The researchers adduce that thinking about
how events might have not happened triggers surprise, and it is surprise
that amplifies the event's positivity. Along these lines, another recent study
found that the uncertainty of an event intensifies felt reaction, such that
outcomes that are uncertain produce greater emotional reactions.[46]
Another recent study found that focusing on an experience's ending could
enhance one's present evaluation of it.[47] Future gratitude interventions
could capitalize on these three studies by giving participants explicit

instructions to include in their journals events or circumstances that might not have happened, could have turned out otherwise, where the initial outcome may have been uncertain, or increasing an awareness that the experience is soon ending.

Dose–effect Relationship

More than two decades ago, an influential psychotherapy review article reported that by eight sessions of psychotherapy, approximately half of patients show a measureable outcome improvement, and that by 26 sessions, this number increases to 75%.[48] Is there an equivalent dose–response relationship for gratitude interventions? Interventions have ranged from every day to a few times a week to once a week for 10 weeks. While some differences have been reported across these studies, an insufficient number of studies have yet to be conducted such that recommendations could be made with confidence. The definition of a dose itself is up for debate. Should a dose be considered a single session of writing in a gratitude journal? Should a minimum time be set for participants to write in their journals each session? We would expect that the greater the degree of elaboration over a simple listing or counting of blessings, the greater would be the potential payoff. But a systematic comparison of the relevant variables that "gratitude dosages" vary on has yet to be conducted.

How Unique Are Gratitude Interventions?

An important issue to be addressed in future research concerns the unique contributions that gratitude interventions make to well-being outcomes that distinguish them, say, from related happiness interventions. The uniqueness of these interventions could be compared with other positive psychological constructs such as forgiveness and hope, both of which have been shown to contribute to well-being.[49–50] What's different about gratitude? First, the underlying prosocial and relational nature of gratitude, subsequently leading to social bonds, might facilitate unique pathways to well-being, unlike many other positive emotions that tend to be relatively independent of social interactions. Second, gratitude has a fulfillment aspect to it, unlike hope, that might facilitate extraction of benefits via mindful appreciation of both present and past received benefits. For example, given that hope is a positive motivational state driven by goal-directed energy and planning toward reaching future goal(s),[51] it probably reaches its fruition only in a prospective fashion in the *absence* of a desired goal—a goal that may or may not be attained. Gratitude has also been shown to be activated strongly by first focusing on absence of benefits.[45] However, unlike hope, gratitude is almost always felt in retrospection, thereby facilitating a positive cognitive framework toward an already-present benefit. Furthermore, gratitude may be extracted from immediate or present life circumstances (e.g., "I am grateful for all the benefits that I received today"), and also from the past (e.g., "I am grateful for the love and support that I received when I was sick two years back"), promoting a much more expanded positive emotional experience. Besides the retrospective recognition of benefits, gratitude also drives future prosocial motivations (e.g., "I want to return benefits to my benefactors and help other people").

Conclusion

Gratitude is held in high esteem by virtually everyone, at all times, in all places. From ancient religious scriptures through modern social science research, gratitude is upheld as a desirable human characteristic with a capacity for making life better for oneself and for others. Aside from a few harsh words from a small handful of cynics, nearly every thinker has viewed gratitude as a sentiment with virtually no downside. As Comte-Sponville pointed out, gratitude is "the most pleasant of the virtues, and the most virtuous of the pleasures."[52] It is virtuously pleasant because experiencing it not only uplifts the person who experiences it, but it edifies the person to whom it is directed as well. But the fact that people typically consider gratitude a virtue and not simply a pleasure also points to the fact that it does not always come naturally or easily. Gratitude must, and can, be cultivated. And by cultivating the virtue, it appears that people may get the pleasure of gratitude, and all of its other concomitant benefits, thrown in for free.

Notes

1. Richelieu, F. (1996). Gratitude: Its healing properties. In L. L. Hay (Ed.), *Gratitude: A way of life*. Carlsbad, CA: Hay House.

2. Emmons, R. A., & Hill, J. (2001). *Words of gratitude: For mind, body, and soul.* Philadelphia: Templeton Foundation Press.

3. Hay, L. L. (1996). *Gratitude: A way of life.* London, UK: Hay House Inc.

4. Meissner, W. W. (1999). *To the greater glory: A psychological study of Ignatian spirituality.* Milwaukee, WI: Marquette University Press.

5. Streng, F. J. (1989). Introduction: Thanksgiving as a worldwide response to life. In J. B. Carman & F. J. Streng (Eds.), *Spoken and unspoken thanks: Some comparative soundings* (pp. 1–9). Dallas, TX: Center for World Thanksgiving.

6. McCullough, M. E., Kilpatrick, S. D., Emmons, R. A., & Larson, D. B. (2001). Is gratitude a moral affect? *Psychological Bulletin, 127,* 249–266.

7. Emmons, R. A., & McCullough, M. E. (2003). Counting blessings versus burdens: An experimental investigation of gratitude and subjective well-being in daily life. *Journal of Personality and Social Psychology, 84,* 377–389.

8. Froh, J. J., Sefick, W. J., & Emmons, R. A. (2008). Counting blessings in early adolescents: An experimental study of gratitude and subjective well-being. *Journal of School Psychology, 46,* 213–233.

9. Rosenberg, E. L. (1998). Levels of analysis and the organization of affect. *Review of General Psychology, 2,* 247–270.

10. McCullough, M. E., Tsang, J., & Emmons, R. A. (2004). Gratitude in intermediate affective terrain: Links of grateful moods to individual differences and daily emotional experience. *Journal of Personality and Social Psychology, 86,* 295–309.

11. McCullough, M. E., Emmons, R. A., & Tsang, J.-A. (2002). The grateful disposition: A conceptual and empirical topography. *Journal of Personality and Social Psychology, 82,* 112–127.

12. Watkins, P. C., Grimm, D. L., & Hailu, L. (1998, June). *Counting your blessings: Grateful individuals recall more positive memories.* Presented at the 11th Annual Convention of the American Psychological Society, Denver, CO.

13. Emmons, R. A., McCullough, M. E., & Tsang, J. (2003). The assessment of gratitude. In S. J. Lopez & C. R. Snyder (Eds.), *Positive psychological assessment: A handbook of models and measures* (pp. 327–341). Washington, DC: American Psychological Association.

14. Liamputtong, P., Yimyam, S., Parisunyakul, S., Baosoung, C., & Sansiriphun, N. (2004). When I become a mother!: Discourses of motherhood among northern Thai women. *Women's Studies International Forum, 27*, 589–601.
15. Saucier, G., & Goldberg, L. R. (1998). What is beyond the Big Five? *Journal of Personality, 66*, 495–524.
16. Sommers, S., & Kosmitzki, C. (1988). Emotion and social context: An American–German comparison. *British Journal of Social Psychology, 27*, 35–49.
17. Kashdan, T. B., Mishra, A., Breen, W. E., & Froh, J. J. (2009). Gender differences in gratitude: Examining appraisals, narratives, the willingness to express emotions, and changes in psychological needs. *Journal of Personality. 77*, 691–730.
18. Watkins, P. C., Woodward, K., Stone, T., & Kolts, R. L. (2003). Gratitude and happiness: Development of a measure of gratitude, and relationships with subjective well-being. *Social Behavior and Personality, 31*, 431–452.
19. Wood, A. M., Joseph, S., & Maltby, J. (2008). Gratitude uniquely predicts satisfaction with life: Incremental validity above the domains and facets of the five factor model. *Personality and Individual Differences, 45*, 49–54.
20. Bartlett, M. Y., & DeSteno, D. (2006). Gratitude and prosocial behavior: Helping when it costs you. *Psychological Science, 17*, 319–325.
21. Emmons, R. A., & Kneezel, T. E. (2005). Giving thanks: Spiritual and religious correlates of gratitude. *Journal of Psychology and Christianity, 24*, 140–148.
22. Hargrove, T., & Stempel, G. H. III. (2004, November 17). 13 percent don't plan to celebrate thanksgiving [Web article]. Retrieved from http://www.newspolls.org/articles/19586.
23. Krause, N. (2006). Gratitude toward God, stress, and health in late life. *Research on Aging, 28*, 163–183.
24. Krause, N., & Ellison, C. G. (2009). The doubting process: A longitudinal study of the precipitants and consequences of religious doubt in older adults. *Journal for the Scientific Study of Religion, 48*, 293–312.

25. Krause, N. (2009). Religious involvement, gratitude, and change in depressive symptoms over time. *International Journal for the Psychology of Religion, 19*, 155–172.

26. Rosmarin, D. H., Pirutinsky, S., Cohen, A. B., Galler, Y., & Krumer, E. J. (2011). Grateful to god or just plain grateful? A comparison of religious and general gratitude. *Journal of Positive Psychology, 6*, 389–396.

27. McKinney J. P., & McKinney, K. G. (1999). Prayer in the lives of late adolescents. *Journal of Adolescence, 22*, 279–290.

28. Laird, S. P., Snyder, C. R., Rapoff, M. A., & Green, S. (2004). Measuring private prayer: Development, validation, and clinical application of the multidimensional prayer inventory. *International Journal for the Psychology of Religion, 14*, 251–272.

29. Bono, G., Emmons, R. A., & McCullough, M. E. (2004). Gratitude in practice and the practice of gratitude. In P. A. Linley & S. Joseph (Eds.), *Positive psychology in practice* (pp. 464–481). New York: Wiley.

30. Lyubomirsky, S., Sheldon, K. M., & Schkade, D. (2005). Pursuing happiness: The architecture of sustainable change. *Review of General Psychology, 9*, 111–131.

31. Seligman, M. E. P., Steen, T. A., Park, N., & Peterson, C. (2005). Positive psychology progress: Empirical validation of interventions. *American Psychologist, 60*, 410–421.

32. Watkins, P. C. (2000, August). *Gratitude and depression: How a human strength might mitigate human adversity*. Paper presented at the 109th Annual Convention of the American Psychological Association, San Francisco, CA.

33. Carman, J. B., & Streng, F. J. (Eds.). (1989). *Spoken and unspoken thanks: Some comparative soundings*. Cambridge, MA: Harvard University Press.

34. Emmons, R. A., & Crumpler, C. A. (2000). Gratitude as a human strength: Appraising the evidence. *Journal of Social and Clinical Psychology, 19*, 56–67.

35. Lupfer, M. B., De Paola, S. J., Brock, K. F., & Clement, L. (1994). Making secular and religious attributions: The availability hypothesis revisited. *Journal for the Scientific Study of Religion, 33*, 162–171.

36. Lupfer, M. B., Tolliver, D., & Jackson, M. (1996). Explaining life-altering occurrences: A test of the "god-of-the-gaps" hypothesis. *Journal for the Scientific Study of Religion, 35*, 379–391.

37. Wood, A. M., Joseph, S., Lloyd, J., & Atkins, S. (2009). Gratitude influences sleep through the mechanism of pre-sleep cognitions. *Journal of Psychosomatic Research, 66*, 43–48.

38. McCraty, R., & Childre, D. (2004). The grateful heart: The psychophysiology of appreciation. In R. A. Emmons & M. E. McCullough (Eds.), *The psychology of gratitude* (pp. 230–255). New York: Oxford University Press.

39. Shipon, R. W. (2007). *Gratitude: Effect on perspectives and blood pressure of inner-city African-American hypertensive patients.* Dissertation Abstracts International: Section B: The Sciences and Engineering, 68(3-B), 1977.

40. Schwarz, S. (1999). *Values and human experience: Essays in honor of the memory of Balduin Schwarz.* New York: P. Lang.

41. Brown, K. W., Ryan, R. M., & Creswell, J. D. (2007). Mindfulness: Theoretical foundations and evidence for its salutary effects. *Psychological Inquiry, 18*, 211–237.

42. Kristeller, J. L., & Johnson, T. (2005). Science looks at spirituality: Cultivating loving-kindness: A two-stage model of the effects of meditation on empathy, compassion, and altruism. *Zygon, 40*, 391–410.

43. Froh, J. J., Kashdan, T. B., Ozimkowski, K. M., & Miller, N. (2009). Who benefits the most from a gratitude intervention in children and adolescents? Examining positive affect as a moderator. *Journal of Positive Psychology. 4*, 408–422.

44. Emmons, R. A. (2007). *Thanks! How the new science of gratitude can make you happier.* Boston: Houghton-Mifflin.

45. Koo, M., Algoe, S. B., Wilson, T. D., & Gilbert, D. T. (2008). It's a wonderful life: Mentally subtracting positive events improves people's affective states, contrary to their affective forecasts. *Journal of Personality and Social Psychology, 95*, 1217–1224.

46. Bar-Anan, Wilson, T. D., & Gilbert D. T. (2009). The feeling of uncertainty intensifies affective reactions. *Emotion, 9*, 123–127.

47. Kurtz, J. L. (2009). Looking to the future to appreciate the present: The benefits of perceived temporal scarcity. *Psychological Science, 19*, 1238–1241.

48. Howard, K. I., Kopta, S. M., Krause, S. M., & Orlinsky, D. E. (1986). The dose–effect relationship in psychotherapy. *American Psychologist, 41*, 159–164.

49. Bono, G., McCullough, M. E., & Root, L. M. (2008). Forgiveness, feeling connected to others, and well-being: Two longitudinal studies. *Personality and Social Psychology Bulletin, 34*, 182–195.

50. Snyder, C. R., Rand, K. L., & Sigmon, D. R. (2002). Hope theory: A member of the positive psychology family. In C. R. Snyder & S. J. Lopez (Eds.), *Handbook of positive psychology* (pp. 257–276). New York: Oxford University Press.

51. Snyder, C. R. (2000). Hypothesis: There is hope. In C. R. Snyder (Ed.), *Handbook of hope: Theories, measures, and applications* (pp. 3–21). Orlando, FL: Academic Press.

52. Comte-Sponville, A. (2001) *A small treatise of the great tirtues.* (C. Temerson, Translator). New York: Metropolitan Books.

3

Humility

Richard A. Bollinger and Peter C. Hill

When stepped on, a worm doubles up. That is clever. In that way he lessens the probability of being stepped on again.
—In the language of morality: humility.[1]

To Friedrich Nietzsche, the author of the quotation above, humility was a great barrier against humanity's progress. He saw humility as a self-protective instinct by the weak, poor, and powerless. Since these less fortunate individuals cannot attain the power and resources needed to obtain happiness, they twist their powerlessness into a virtue and proclaim it as a desired end in itself. In this way, the weak try to stymie the strivings of the strong by proclaiming that humility, not power, should be the desired goal. When cast as a virtue, argued Nietzsche, humility keeps those who are capable (i.e., the strong and powerful) from reaching the fullness of their potential. From this he concluded that humility is based on the lie that it is virtuous to not fully achieve one's potential to be as great as possible. And he suggested that the most influential proclaimers of this lie are the great religions of the world and their followers. Similar to more modern atheistic writers, Nietzsche saw religion as primarily having a negative impact on society and the world.

Many scholars have sharply disagreed with Nietzsche, suggesting that humility should be conceptualized as the realistic acceptance that individuals (including the self) are limited, that a world exists that transcends the individual, and that discovering one's part in this greater existence rather than the misleading pursuit of one's own great existence can help establish a sense of well-being and happiness. In short, humility is the willingness to see the self accurately and the propensity to put oneself in perspective.[2]

The great religious and spiritual traditions of the world encourage this form of humility, not Nietzsche's. Humility is encouraged because it helps to facilitate self-transcendence, which is a direct or indirect focus of many religious and spiritual traditions. By shifting one's primary focus from the self to something greater beyond the self, the process of transcending self-interest helps develop specific character traits, one of which is humility. Humility then allows the individual to embrace a worldview similar to the one outlined above. The health implications of developing a humble character include but are not limited to self-acceptance, empathic relations with others, and a broad perspective and worldview. Humility then serves as an organic source for virtuous behavior. Religious and spiritual traditions provide the soil within which humility develops.

Recognizing that Nietzsche was correct in his propagation that religion encourages humility, we wish to explicitly detail the relationships between humility, religion and spirituality, and positive well-being. After providing a conceptual alternative to Nietzsche's understanding of humility, we will explore how religion and spirituality foster humility and will conclude by considering some concrete benefits and liabilities of being a humble person.

Humility Defined

Humility can be considered as both a trait and a state. While most of us can think of some people who are more or less humble than others, there are certainly conditions under which a state of humility may be induced even among the most arrogant—receiving forgiveness from somebody we have wronged, a failure on an exam, or a poor performance on the playing field are a few examples that come to mind. However, Nietzsche was concerned with humility as a disposition, and this will be our focus here.

In her groundbreaking article, Tangney illustrated six components of humility, which together capture the essence and complexity of this virtue.[3] They are: (a) a willingness to see the self accurately, (b) an accurate perspective of one's place in the world, (c) an ability to acknowledge personal mistakes and limitations, (d) openness, (e) low self-focus, and (f) an appreciation of the value of all things. Each of these components will be briefly explored.

The foundation of dispositional humility appears to be the willingness to see oneself accurately. Humility is not prideful boasting, nor is it self-deprecating pleading. C. S. Lewis described what humility *is not* when he wrote that the humble person "will not be a sort of greasy, smarmy person, who is always telling you that, of course, he is nobody."[4] Lewis counters this picture with another of a humble person as someone who is "so free from any bias in his own favour that he can rejoice in his own talents as frankly and gratefully as in his neighbour's talents, or in a sunrise, an elephant, or a waterfall" (p. 59).[4] Peterson and Seligman contended that what is most important in accurate self-knowledge is not necessarily a fully accurate self-portrait, but rather a *willingness* to see the self accurately.[5] One may never fully arrive at the point of full, accurate self-knowledge, but a humble person desires to know him- or herself accurately.

Accurate self-assessment then would necessarily imply that one could recognize and acknowledge one's limits and weaknesses. These two factors, logically, appear to be inseparable. Embedded in acknowledging one's weaknesses is the presupposition that every human has weaknesses and limitations. This belief about human nature is key to humility being understood as a virtue, not a vice, and is the point at which Nietzsche and Lewis part ways. If one had no weakness or limits, then humility would be unnecessary and, if present, ego-dystonic.[6]

The acceptance of weakness appears to be a precursor to another component of humility: openness. An open person recognizes that his or her knowledge and ability have limits and that others have valuable knowledge and ability from which to learn. However, the acceptance of personal limitations does not necessarily result in humility or openness. Someone who accepts personal limitations and weaknesses may just as likely become despondent and defensive. It appears that a securely held, positive self-esteem that enables an individual to see and accept weakness without feeling threatened by their lack moderates the relationship between accurate self-assessment, the recognition of limits, and openness.[2, 7] It follows then that a posture of openness develops if one accepts personal limits but does not feel threatened by them.

The final two components of humility, as outlined by Tangney,[3] are a low self-focus and an accurate perspective of one's place in the world. These two components are mutually enhancing: As one grows, so does the other. Furthermore, it is the characteristic of openness that augments each component. When a person contemplates the magnificence of the universe and the important contributions of others to this magnificence, he or she is less likely to focus exclusively on the self. C. S. Lewis further fleshes out his conceptualization of humility in *Mere Christianity* when he casts humility as self-forgetfulness, describing a humble person as someone who "will not be thinking about humility: he will not be thinking about himself at all" (p. 114).[4] A humble person is one who is not focused on himself or herself, but is freely, openly, and genuinely absorbed in the well-being of others around. As an individual looks outward, that person will soon discover that there is a vast world of otherness to behold, a world much greater than the self. If the individual allows this realization to shape self-understanding and become a part of him or her, the focus and life-direction will become increasingly directed to this greater perspective. Inherently, then, one's focus on the self lessens, and as this happens, one's ability to focus outwardly increases. When this dialectic takes place, one is characteristically humble.

As already noted, it is the attitude of openness that facilitates an accurate worldview and a low self-focus. However, openness can also simply lead to a continual quest for more knowledge and experience to continue to bolster the self, a motivation diametrically opposed to humility as conceived here. What then predicts whether openness leads to more or less self-focus? Perhaps one likely candidate is transcendence. Understood as a state of being beyond the limits of normal experience, such as a larger vision or sense of purpose beyond what is materially perceptible, transcendence enhances the ability to lessen one's self-focus. Perhaps nowhere is transcendence more explicitly articulated and experienced than through religious and spiritual domains and functions of life.

In summary, humility is the desire for an accurate view of the world and the self that includes an embrace of limitations and weaknesses. The acceptance of these limits and the desire for accurate assessment enable a posture of openness to the good in all things. As one opens to the vastness of existence, an outward orientation grows and the self-orientation diminishes.

Religion and Humility

Although Nietzsche's view of humility stands in stark contrast to the view espoused here, his claim that humility as a concept was propagated by religious traditions is quite sound. Humility has been an important concept within many religious traditions and, therefore, has been a relatively commonplace term in Western and Eastern culture for centuries. Common to many religious and spiritual understandings is the emphasis on the grandness of existence, which often is translated through two central components: (a) the essence of this greater reality, and (b) how one should align with that reality in order to experience fulfillment. Almost without exception, the world's most long-standing religious traditions have emphasized the personality characteristic of humility as a crucial characteristic needed to align oneself with this higher reality. Two traditions, one from the East and one from the West, will be utilized as an example of humility's role in the transcendental experience.

In the Eastern tradition of Buddhism, adherents are encouraged to let go of the self and to embrace truth in order to pursue the path of enlightenment. The self is filled with cravings for a certain type of existence that ultimately bring suffering and leave one unfulfilled. The pathway out of these cravings is the Noble Eightfold Path, which encourages an alignment of the self with the true nature of life. Each one of the eight paths embraces the "right" (i.e., correct or proper) wisdom, ethical conduct, or mental discipline needed to see the true nature of reality. As one moves further along the path of enlightenment, the attachment to the self and its cravings lessens and the desire to see the world and self as they truly are increases. Hence, humility—the reduction of self-focus, seeing the self and world accurately, and seeing the greater picture—is formed and transcendence is acheived.[2, 8]

An explication of the Christian notion of humility can be found in Andrew Murray's short work titled *Humility*.[9] Murray places humility as the foundation of all other virtues because in Christianity, as in Buddhism, humility is considered the alignment of the self with the truth of existence. The truth of existence as laid out by Christianity is that God is good, creation (including humans) was good but is now fallen, and only God can redeem (or put right) creation. Therefore, humanity needs to open itself to the power of God to bring about transformation in people so that they can live virtuous lives. Humility, within the Christian view, is essentially the process of recognizing God's totality and humanity's limited capacity for goodness and allowing one's being to be occupied and transformed by God. Since all virtues exist in people only because of God's indwelling presence, humility is then, quite literally, the root of all other virtues. Within the Bible, writers such as David (Psalms 45:4), Solomon (Proverbs 15:33), and Paul (Colossians 3:12) describe humility as desirable. The gospel writer Matthew tells that Jesus invoked himself as being humble (Matthew 11:29). In both Christianity and Buddhism, humility is accurate self-knowledge, an acknowledgment of one's limitations and weaknesses, and opening oneself to the greater reality.

Humility and Well-being

Finally, we turn to humility's relationship with well-being. The empirical evidence linking humility with well-being is in its infancy. This scarcity is not due to a lack of interest in humility; rather, it is due to the difficulty with measuring and assessing humility. Two factors are primary reasons for this difficulty. First, humility is a composite trait. As reflected in the definition, there are several core components to humility, including willingness to see the self accurately, low self-focus, and seeing oneself as part of a greater perspective. Although these are interconnected, and when present simultaneously represent humility, they each need to be measured uniquely. Creating a measure to ascertain all of these factors has proven difficult.

Second, self-reports are the primary method of measurement in psychology. Measuring humility presents problems on both ends of the humility spectrum. For those low in humility, the very definition implies that these individuals may self-enhance, or inflate their positive qualities. Since humility is considered a positive virtue,[10] the likelihood that individuals low in humility would self-enhance and inflate their humility score is high. Alternatively, individuals high in humility may be subject to a modesty effect, where they report lower levels of humility due to an increased tendency to moderate the presentation of their strengths.[11] The result is a decrease in variability, since low scores may tend to be higher than they should be and high scores may be lower than they really are. However, these effects can be partially controlled through the administration of a measure of social desirability, which can remove some of the impact of low humility individuals self-enhancing.

Studies with a Composite Measure of Humility

Self-report Measures

Although difficult, attempts at studying humility through self-report have been made. One relatively recent study conducted by Krause has directly linked religion, humility, and health.[12] The hypothesis that humility may predict higher levels of health is rooted, according to the author, in two areas of current knowledge: coping with life stressors and competition. The coping literature demonstrates that two major predictors of whether one copes well with a stressor are (a) the ability to accurately discern the cause of the stressor and (b) how to respond to reduce or eliminate the stressor. Often, one plays some role in the onset of a stressor (e.g., fired due to poor job performance), and therefore, the ability to accurately assess one's possible contribution to the stressor is essential to adequately recover and adjust to the stressor. Therefore, true humility should predict overall coping capacity, which is highly predictive of health. Second, highly competitive individuals generally exhibit lower levels of health. Humility, and its lowered focus on the self and acceptance of its limited place in the world, should reduce competition and increase health. Humility in this study was measured as a composite of four items drawn from Peterson and Seligman.[5]

Krause found that church attendance was found to be predictive of spiritual support, self-reported humility, and self-reported health. Similarly, spiritual support predicted self-reported humility and self-reported health. Finally, self-reported humility also directly predicted higher physical health. A major limitation of this study, however, is the likelihood that social desirability impacted the study. No measure of social desirability was utilized, and the constructs were measured explicitly (i.e., individuals were asked directly how humble they were, how often they went to church, and how healthy they were). Potentially, individuals who attended church more frequently would have a self-serving bias to present themselves as more humble and potentially as healthier. Regardless, though, the study still presents an initial link between religiosity, humility, and health that will hopefully fuel greater interest and study.

The current, most widely utilized self-report measure of humility is one factor of a revised measure, known as HEXACO, of the Big Five personality characteristics. Honesty/Humility, defined as "the tendency to be fair and genuine in dealing with others, in the sense of cooperating with others even when one might exploit them without suffering retaliation" (p. 156), was added as a sixth factor.[13] The Honesty/Humility factor significantly predicted integrity and ethical decision-making ability, correlated positively with supervisor ratings of overall job performance in caregivers, and correlated with low hierarchy (greater equality) orientation. Although these are indicators that link humility to other virtues, the Honesty/Humility measure is considered relatively limited given its rather narrow and unique definition. The questions used to measure this factor seem to emphasize primarily issues of low self-focus and modesty, which, although they are either a component of or closely related to humility, are not equivalent to the robustness of the humility construct presented here. Therefore, other methods will be considered.

The Dispositional Humility Scale (DHS) is composed of three factors measuring the major components of humility: worldview, appreciation and recognition of limits, and low self-focus.[14] This three-factor model of humility exhibited a negative relationship with measures of narcissism and unforgiveness. In a study designed to assess the validity of the measure, the low self-focus factor predicted a more accurate assessment of a situation, which was designed to elicit strong feelings of self-consciousness. Individuals with a low self-focus were able to more accurately assess the situation than individuals who were more prone to get caught up in their own experience of the situation.

Humility has also been measured as a religious construct in terms of a "holier-than-thou" effect.[15] That is, to the extent that an individual reported greater (or lesser) adherence to Biblical commands than others, the greater (or lesser) the holier-than-thou effect—a reflection of less (more) humility. The authors found that the higher the intrinsic religiosity, the higher the holier-than-thou effect. A major limitation in this study is the failure to actually assess the behavior of the participants to ascertain the accuracy of their statements. If individuals have a higher internal, personal motivation to be religious, it might follow that they then would strive for and perhaps achieve greater adherence to Biblical commands than their less intrinsically motivated peers. Studies such as these are enlightening and potentially valuable, but they underscore the difficulty of assessing the complexity of the humility construct.

Implicit Assessments of Humility

One team of researchers has sought to circumvent the difficulties of self-report humility measures by developing an Implicit Association Test (IAT) of humility.[16, 17] The Humility IAT gauges how individuals subconsciously associate words that describe humility with themselves. Humble individuals are those individuals who more quickly associate humility-related words with the self than arrogance-related words. The researchers found that the Humility IAT corresponded in expected directions with various self-report measures of narcissism and humility. The Humility IAT did not correspond with reports of participants' humility from informants (friends and family of the participants). The IAT is dependent upon the notion that a person's subconscious beliefs about him- or herself are potentially more accurate than their conscious beliefs. This proposition is disputable since if a person lacks humility, he or she may not realize this on either a conscious or subconscious level.

Relational Humility Scale

A final approach to the measure of humility is a relational approach.[10] Here, humility is conceptualized as a personality judgment made within the context of a specific relationship. Relational humility then is the degree to which an observer describes a target person as other-oriented, as able to regulate self-focused emotions (e.g., pride and shame), and as one who maintains an accurate view of self. The relational humility scale is unique in that it relies entirely on an observer's judgments regarding the target person's levels of humility. This method is thought to circumvent the difficulties of self-reporting humility and is based on the proposition that humility manifests itself in specific, recognizable behavior, a sustainable assertion. The scale has been shown to correlate positively with traits of gratitude, empathy, and forgiveness. The unsolved issue with this measure is the question of validity; that is, to what extent are observers able to accurately gauge humility as a dispositional trait?

Studies Involving Components of Humility

It should now be clear that measuring humility as a composite trait is a difficult venture, though some headway has been made. However, various components of humility have been studied in depth. Several of these components will be outlined and their relationship to greater well-being highlighted.

Self-accuracy

It is not clear whether accurate self-assessment is good for one's health or well-being. What we do know is that most people, at least in theory, desire to be self-accurate, even if means receiving potentially negative feedback. However, we also know that when faced with an immediate self-evaluative situation, people often utilize self-enhancement strategies to protect self-esteem. Other components of humility, such as having an accurate perspective of one's place in the world and low self-focus, are relevant here as well. One implication, yet to be empirically tested, is that individuals who are able to maintain perspective of purpose behind an evaluation (i.e., an emphasis on accuracy) are better able to tolerate negative feedback. Those unable to keep the greater purpose of evaluation in mind are more likely to focus on the immediate experience and will be more concerned with preserving self-esteem than with receiving accurate feedback (i.e., an emphasis on self-enhancement).

Though humility is more than simply the absence of self-enhancement, research on self-enhancement has important implications for the study of humility. Research has demonstrated that some forms of self-enhancement, conceptualized as the natural motivation to positively present oneself and to hold a positive self-concept,[18] are associated with negative well-being. Virtually all people, no matter how humble or arrogant, are motivated to feel good about themselves and to project a positive image to those around them. We would expect humble people, however, to self-enhance within the limits of what they know to be true regarding themselves and to be less averse to negative feedback than nonhumble people. Self-enhancement then only becomes "problematic" when a gap exists between what is presented and what is accurate regarding the self, as the following studies indicate.

A five-year study demonstrated that self-enhancers (persons with the largest discrepancies between self-reports of personality and friend and family reports of their personality) were rated more negatively than were non–self-enhancers.[19] When placed in observed social situations, observers rated self-enhancers as having a greater likelihood of exhibiting socially maladaptive skills. If self-enhancement is associated with maladaptive skills, a reasonable question would be why is it so prevalent. The prevailing hypothesis is that self-enhancement provides an immediate boost to self-esteem. This hypothesis was strengthened by a subsequent finding that individuals tended to self-enhance even when it is not necessary to impress others, indicating that the benefits extend beyond social presentation. Those who tended to self-enhance more on a given task tended to feel better about themselves in regard to the task, hence increasing task-specific positive affect.[20] In a follow-up study by the same researchers, data were collected from a cohort of students over the entirety of their college career. Self-enhancers (as measured by discrepancy in perceived and actual ability as measured by GPA and SAT) upon entering college also showed higher levels of narcissism and self-serving attributions. Over time, self-enhancers became more disengaged with school than did non–self-enhancers, perhaps to protect positive illusions about themselves. Self-enhancers also saw a gradual decline in self-esteem as well as overall well-being during their time in college. Self-enhancement may show some initial benefit but appears to have negative long-term consequences. The finding that self-enhancement appears to have negative long-term consequences carries with it implications, though not yet empirically tested, that accurate self-assessment has potential positive consequences for well-being.

Recognition of Weakness

Recognition of one's own weaknesses and limitations is a critical predictor in the facilitation of forgiveness. At the core of forgiveness is the ability to develop empathy for the perpetrator by recognizing one's own need for forgiveness.[21] One who can identify and openly admit identification with a transgressor is one who has—to some extent—accepted her or his own limitations and weaknesses by being able to admit that she or he too is flawed. Therefore, unforgiveness is given greater license for the individual who cannot or will not recognize his or her own capacity to commit wrongdoings. With humility comes the recognition and ownership that just as the other committed wrongdoing, so too has (at some time) the transgressed upon. With reflection on one's own transgressions comes the desire to experience mercy; hence, when coupled with empathy, one finds the capacity to extend mercy and forgiveness to others.[22]

Research has shown that focusing on one's transgressions appears to increase forgiveness through two primary pathways.[23] First, it was found that focusing on one's past transgressions helped make the transgression more understandable to the participant, increasing the empathy for the transgressor, which in turn made forgiveness more likely. Second, focusing on one's transgressions also reduced the perceived severity of the transgression in the eyes of the participant, enabling forgiveness to be granted more easily. Interestingly, aside from focusing on one's past transgressions, the more similarity the participants saw between themselves and the transgressor, the greater empathy they had for the transgressor and, therefore, the more likely they were to forgive.

Low Self-focus

Excessive self-interest appears to be at the root of both narcissism and shame, two characteristics linked with poor well-being. Entitlement occurs when the holier-than-thou principle, whether rooted in religious beliefs or not, becomes a stable part of one's personality. Entitled persons have demonstrated a pattern of self-serving beliefs and patterns that lead to such diverse attitudes and behaviors as lowered empathy, taking more candy from children, and interpersonal aggression.[24]

Shame involves a global assessment of the self, often leading to a preoccupation with the self in one's desire to hide it from others. Shame has been found to predict higher levels of self-oriented personal distress.[25] Shame-prone individuals tend to engage in self-rumination, defined as a "neurotic category of self-attentiveness [characterized by] recurrent thinking or ruminations about the self prompted by threats, losses, or injustices to the self (p. 292)."[25] Research has shown that rumination over how an individual was hurt due to an interpersonal transgression increased unforgiveness, with anger as a mediating emotion.[19] Excessive self-focus thus appears to be a contributing factor in decreasing one's likelihood to forgive. This finding corresponds with other research showing that self-rumination over one's wrongdoings leads to an increase in one's shame, thus resulting in difficulty to forgive oneself. Excessive self-focus either on how one was wronged or on how one wrongs predicts unforgiveness, either of the self or others.[26]

Liabilities of Being Humble

One can, at this point, rightfully question our ability to objectively analyze humility given what appears to be an uncritically positive conception. Do we have an implicit utopian vision of a society consisting entirely of humble individuals? We admit that we are tempted to say that if all people were humble according to the conception provided here, the world would likely be a better place. However, we are also aware that despite its association with several aspects of greater well-being, humility brings with it some liabilities as well.

Perhaps the most serious issue is the sheer complexity of the construct, especially in terms of actual human experience. Does humility, as presented here, involve a precarious balance between the dual abysses of self-denial and self-enhancement? Does a slight lean too much in one direction result in a fall that requires, much like Humpty-Dumpty, that the pieces be put back together again? And how does the person even know if he or she is teetering successfully on the brink? That is, while humility is complex in terms of its conceptualization and other cognitive considerations, it is perhaps even more complex experientially. Admittedly, it is true that any of the components of humility presented here can be manifested in less than healthy ways: a preoccupation with the self in the name of self-accuracy, a sense of failure or low self-esteem resulting from acknowledgement of weaknesses, an openness to new understandings that lead to self-differentiation without integration, or a low self-focus that borders on self-neglect. However, these concerns, which should be taken seriously, merely point to the complexity of the dispositional nature of human existence and complexity, which in and of itself is no reason to question the validity of or avoid a concept.

Second, somewhat related is the inherent tension in the juxtaposition of several of the individual components of humility as outlined here. For example, the ability to see the self accurately may be compromised by one's willingness to acknowledge limitations and weaknesses; that is, the humble person may overemphasize the limitations to the point that the self-concept is distorted. Furthermore, to see oneself accurately may require considerable self-focus such that one who questions the wisdom of self-focus may have less self-insight. While certainly the components of humility described here are not necessarily working in opposition to each other, it is indeed possible that one can be emphasized to the extent that it works against the realization of another component.

Third, humility can be deceptive, even to oneself. For example, admitting weakness may be a convenient substitute for not putting forth effort to improve. Similarly, a low self-focus may disguise an unwillingness to behave responsibly for the betterment of one's group. Such tendencies can be easily masked by a misguided sense of humility.

How might these concerns play out in ordinary living? Humble individuals may be less likely to bring about social change. The proclivity to accept reality coupled with the tendency to see good in all could lead to a passive acceptance of all reality, including injustice and poverty. Similarly, the tendency to maintain an accurate perspective of one's place in the world may result in an underestimation of what one can accomplish. Yet another liability involves the tendency to not emphasize enough a focus on the self; that is, completely losing oneself in something greater than the self may lead to a loss of individual identity (or where individual identity pales in significance) such as what is sometimes seen in group psychology. In these occasions, humble individuals may be more prone to conformity pressure that is sometimes unhealthy.

These potential liabilities merely point out what we already know about any dispositional tendency—it is neither wholly good nor wholly bad. The specific benefits and liabilities of being humble are far from understood and have been empirically neglected. As such, they present fertile ground for empirical research.

Conclusion

Nietzsche saw humility as a great entrapment for humanity set by the religious establishment to convince people of the lie that they are limited and to prevent them from achieving the fullness of their potential. The great religious traditions do indeed encourage an understanding of humility that humans are limited, that they should recognize and accept their limitations, and that they should embrace a transcendent reality greater than self-interest. Empirical research testing the claims of religion is limited. Early returns from research that are available, however, indicate that humility, as defined here, does indeed correlate with greater well-being, greater forgiveness and higher self-esteem and is a characteristic viewed positively in the self and in others. Ironically then, humility may be, despite Nietzsche's insistence otherwise, the pathway to experiencing one's fullest potential.

Notes

1. Nietzsche, F. (1976). Twilight of the idols (31). In Walter Kaufmann (Trans.), *The portable Nietzsche* (p. 471). New York: Penguin Books, 1976.
2. Morris, J. A., Brotheridge, C. M., & Urbanski, J. C. (2005). Bringing humility to leadership: Antecedents and consequences of leader humility. *Human Relations, 58*, 1323–1350.
3. Tangney, J. P. (2000). Humility: Theoretical perspectives, empirical findings and directions for future research. *Journal of Social and Clinical Psychology, 19*(1), 70–82.
4. Lewis, C. S. (1996). *Mere Christianity.* New York: Simon and Schuster. (Original work published 1952).
5. Peterson, C., & Seligman, M. E. P. (2004). *Character strengths and virtues: A handbook and classification.* Washington, DC: American Psychological Association.
6. Bauer, J. J., & Wayment, H. A. (2008). The psychology of the quiet ego. In J. J. Bauer & H. A. Wayment (Eds.), *Transcending self-interest: Psychological explorations of the quiet ego* (pp. 7–19). Washington DC: American Psychological Association.

7. Worthington, E. L. (2007). *Humility: The quiet virtue*. Philadelphia: Templeton Foundation Press.

8. Rahula, W. (1974). *What the Buddha taught*. New York: Grove Press.

9. Murray, A. (1896). *Humility: The journey toward holiness*. London: Nisbet.

10. Exline, J. J., & Geyer, A. (2004). Perceptions of humility: A preliminary study. *Self and Identity, 3*, 95–114.

11. Davis, D. E., Worthington, E. L., Jr., & Hook, J. N. (2010). Humility: Review of measurement strategies and conceptualization as personality judgment. *Journal of Positive Psychology, 5*, 243–252.

12. Krause, N. (2010). Religious involvement, humility, and self-rated health. *Social Indicators Research, 98*, 23–39.

13. Ashton, M., & Lee, K. (2007, May). Empirical, theoretical, and practical advantages of the HEXACO model of personality structure. *Personality and Social Psychology Review, 11*, 150–166.

14. Bollinger, R. A. (2010). *Humility: An integrative analysis and validation of a dispositional measure* (Unpublished dissertation). Biola University.

15. Rowatt, W. C., Ottenbreit, A., Nesselrode, K. P., Jr., & Cunningham P. A. (2002). On being holier-than-thou or humbler than thee: A social-psychological perspective on religiousness and humility. *Journal for the Scientific Study of Religion, 41*, 227–237.

16. Rowatt. W. C., Powers, C., Targhetta, V., Comer, J., Kennedy, S., & Labouff, J. (2006). Development and initial validation of an implicit measure of humility relative to arrogance. *Journal of Positive Psychology, 1*(4), 198–211.

17. Powers, C., Nam, R. K., Rowatt, W. C., & Hill, P. C. (2007). Associations between humility, spiritual transcendence, and forgiveness. *Research in the Social Scientific Study of Religion, 18*, 75–94.

18. Sedikides, C., & Strube, M. J. (1997). Self evaluation: To thine own self be good, to thine own self be sure, to thine own self be true, and to thine own self be better. In M. P. Zanna (Ed.), *Advances in experimental social psychology*, Vol. 29 (pp. 209–269). San Diego, CA: Academic Press.

19. Colvin, C. R., Block, J. B., & Funder, D. C. (1995). Overly positive self-evaluations and personality: Negative implications for

mental health. *Journal of Personality and Social Psychology, 68*, 1152–1162.

20. Robins, R. W., & Beer, J. S. (2001). Positive illusions about the self: Short-term benefits and long-term costs. *Journal of Personality and Social Psychology, 80*, 340–352.

21. McCullough, M. E., Worthington, E. L. Jr., & Rachal, K. C. (1997, August). Interpersonal forgiving in close relationships. *Journal of Personality and Social Psychology, 73*, 321–336.

22. Worthington, E. L. (1998). An empathy-humility-commitment model of forgiveness applied within family dyads. *Journal of Family Therapy, 20*, 59–76.

23. Exline, J. J., Baumeister, R. F., Zell, A. L., Kraft, A. J., & Witvliet, C. V. O. (2008). Not so innocent: Does seeing one's own capability for wrongdoing predict forgiveness? *Journal of Personality and Social Psychology, 94*, 495–515.

24. Campbell, W. K., Bonacci, A. M., Shelton, J., Exline, J. J., & Bushman, B. J. (2004). Psychological entitlement: Interpersonal consequences and validation of a self-report measure. *Journal of Personality Assessment, 83*, 29–45.

25. Trapnell, P. D., & Campbell, J. D. (1999). Private self-consciousness and the five factor model of personality: Distinguishing rumination from reflection. *Journal of Personality and Social Psychology, 76*, 284–304.

26. Joireman, J. (2004). Empathy and the self-absorption paradox II: Self-rumination and self-reflection as mediators between shame, guilt, and empathy. *Self and Identity, 3*, 225–238.

4

Hope

David B. Feldman and Maximilian M. Kubota

Hope is difficult to cover in a single chapter because of its deep history and powerful legacy, especially regarding its connection with religion and spirituality. Though well known as one of the three theological virtues in Catholicism (along with faith and charity), hope was important in religious worldviews long before the advent of Christianity. One of the earliest and most famous references to hope appears in the ancient Greek myth of Pandora, recorded by Hesiod around the year 700 B.C. This story, which bears a striking resemblance to the Old Testament's Garden of Eden narrative, begins with the creation of Pandora, the first woman on earth. Formed by Hephaestus out of earth and water, she was gifted with beauty, intelligence, and talent. Unfortunately, the gods gave Pandora one additional gift—a box that she was warned never to open. Pandora's curiosity got the better of her, of course, and as she opened the box, untold evils were unleashed upon the world. All the maladies that now afflict humankind were suddenly thrust upon us—war, disease, poverty, hatred, tyranny. Horrified, Pandora slammed the lid shut and grasped the box tightly to her. But as she held it, she realized that it still had weight; one thing was left deep in its recesses—hope. To the ancient Greeks, then, hope was one of the most powerful psychological and spiritual assets. It was what remained with humanity, allowing us to cope and even thrive in a world that confronts us with setbacks, misfortune, and tragedy.

Nonetheless, hope has not always been viewed as such an important asset. In American culture, a much less powerful perspective seems to have taken hold. Anecdotally, hope often seems to be treated as a comforting yet essentially powerless feeling, a kind of "consolation prize" that makes us feel better when we really have lost. Many sayings portray this powerless view of hope, including "Even when you've failed, at least you still have your hope," "Hope for the best, but plan for the worst," and "Cross your fingers and hope for the best." If we were to accept these sayings as true, we would never dare to make plans based on hope; after all, it has little more power than crossing two small appendages.

Personally, we cast our lot with the ancient Greeks. We believe that hope is a powerful psychological asset that not only comforts us in the face of misfortune but also allows us to actively build meaningful lives.[1] But we are speaking in generalities. Although myths and sayings provide valuable cultural reference points, they do not help us to understand precisely what hope is, how it affects our lives, how it is related to spirituality, or how it can be nurtured. These are the purposes of the present chapter.

What Is Hope?

The definition of hope used throughout this chapter is based on C. R. Snyder's "Hope Theory."[1] Accordingly, hope is conceptualized as a cognitive process through which individuals actively accomplish their goals. Hope is not something needed only to provide comfort in the face of unsolvable ills, but also to improve one's life in the absence as well as presence of problems.

According to Hope Theory, hopeful thinking includes three components: goals, pathways thinking, and agency thinking. Goals are hoped-for ends. They are anything that an individual desires to get, do, be, experience, or create. Of course, goals are subjective and often very personal. Some individuals may spend their lives pursuing career goals by meeting monthly sales quotas or climbing corporate ladders, whereas others may be more interested in pursuing social and even spiritual goals by striving to be a more loving partner or more faithful Christian, Jew, Muslim, Hindu, or Buddhist.

What a goal is is not as important as what a goal does. Goals serve to anchor deliberate behavior.[2, 3, 4] In other words, virtually everything that we do is directed toward achieving some goal. We say that actions are successful when they bring us closer to achieving our goals and unsuccessful when they move us further away. Thus, goals are at the heart of our emotional life, because our success or failure at goal pursuits is one of the major determinates of how we feel. We experience positive emotions when we achieve our goals or believe we are progressing toward achieving them but experience negative emotions when we fail to achieve our goals or believe that we are in the process of failing. Prior to engaging in any goal-directed behavior, however, the final two components of hope come into play—pathways and agency thinking.

A pathway is a plan or strategy.[2] Thus, we engage in pathways thinking whenever we consider how to reach our goals. Because some of these plans may not succeed when put into motion, hopeful people may produce many pathways in order to circumvent possible obstacles to goal accomplishment.[3] Such pathways will not lead to goal attainment, however, without the last component of hope—agency thinking.

Agency is composed of "the thoughts that people have regarding their ability to begin and continue movement on selected pathways toward those goals."[4] As in Watty Piper's *The Little Engine That Could*, agency thoughts such as "I think I can" are the fuel that powers the goal-pursuit engine.[5] It is through such mobilizing thoughts that people are motivated to do the hard work of pursuing goals.

Although pathways and agency thinking are distinct components of hope, they constantly influence one another, such that an increase or decrease in one will correspondingly change the other.[3] If one begins pursuing a goal with high agency but cannot develop effective pathways, one's initially upbeat agency thoughts (e.g., "I can do this," "I am capable of accomplishing this goal") will soon sour as his or her hope begins to stagnate. Likewise, if one has generated a number of possible pathways to a goal but is unable to conjure sufficient levels of motivating agentic thought, he or she will likely begin rejecting these pathways, believing that they are not workable. Thus, hope is a reciprocal combination of pathways and agency thinking. It does not fully exist unless both of these components are present.

The Benefits of Hope

Research demonstrates robust connections between hope and a number of positive outcomes. In this section, we discuss the roles that hope plays across the life span.

The "birth" of hope may be traceable to one's relationship or "attachment" with primary caregivers. John Bowlby wrote that hope is established at least in part through a strong bond with one's early caregivers.[6] In this vein, one study found that attachment was strongly predictive of hope and that individuals with secure attachment had higher levels of both agency and pathways compared to those with insecure attachments.[7] Research also has found that children with higher hope had overall greater positive affect, lower depression, lower anxiety, and higher self-esteem when compared to those with lower hope.[7, 8]

As children age, hope may play an important role in school performance. Higher-hope students appear not to let failures affect their self-worth as much as lower-hope students. Instead, they are more likely to attribute failure to insufficient effort or not identifying appropriate studying or test-taking strategies.[9] Perhaps as a result of this greater emphasis on effort and strategy, grade school children with higher hope have better scores on achievement tests than their lower-hope counterparts.[8]

As individuals move into adulthood, they increasingly look to the future by setting and pursuing life goals. In one study, researchers Feldman, Rand, and Kahle-Wrobleski asked college students to nominate seven goals that they wished to accomplish within a three-month period and complete a measure of hope for each goal.[10] Three months later, hope's agency component not only predicted greater goal progress but also appeared to be a better predictor than students' evaluations of how important the goals were to them. Perhaps related to this heightened goal achievement, high-hope college students enjoy better grades, higher graduation rates, and better sports performance than do their low-hope counterparts.[11, 12] They also report feeling less depressed and less anxious, and perceiving that their lives have greater meaning and purpose.[13]

As individuals continue to age, hope may be an important factor in coping with the difficulties that often arise. For instance, higher hope is associated with the tendency to grow from adverse circumstances.[14] A number of studies also lend credence to the notion that hope affords greater functioning in the face of painful health conditions. Elliot, Witty, Herrick, and Hoffman surveyed 57 individuals with paralysis due to spinal cord injury and found an interaction between hope and time since injury.[15] Soon after the injury, higher agency was associated with better psychosocial functioning. As time progressed, however, greater pathways thinking was associated with higher levels of psychosocial functioning. In other words, agency may have helped individuals immediately following injury, whereas pathways aided in longer-term adjustment. Moreover, a study conducted on lung cancer patients found that those with higher hope had lower reported levels of pain, fatigue, and coughing as well as lower levels of depression than patients with lower hope, even after controlling for cancer stage.[16] Another study examined the role of hopeful thinking in older adults three months after surviving a stroke, finding that low-hope stroke survivors experience more depressive symptoms than high-hope survivors.[17] Moreover, those with higher hope reported higher levels of physical functioning, memory, and communication.

Hope for the Sacred

In addition to the aforementioned research regarding its associations and effects, Snyder, Sigmon, and Feldman have suggested that Hope Theory offers a useful lens through which to examine the effects of spirituality and religion on mental and physical health.[18] In particular, they suggest that religion offers "a prepackaged matrix of goals, pathways for accomplishing those goals, and agency thoughts for applying those pathways" (p. 235).

In Western religions, there seem to be six general classes of goals: (1) unity, harmony, or relationship with the divine; (2) supernatural assistance in establishing a peaceful, happy life; (3) a place in heaven or equivalent afterlife; (4) social support; (5) an understanding of truth; and (6) an increased comprehension of one's purpose in life. Eastern religions such as Buddhism and Hinduism share many of these goals with Western religion, though the prescribed pathways to their accomplishment may differ. Many of these goals, of course, are difficult to attain and require a lifetime of pursuit. Therefore, religion also offers important pathways to aid in their pursuit.

Recall that individuals with high hope are more confident than their low-hope counterparts that they can generate pathways to desired goals.[19] Pathways are often composed of "subgoals," smaller steps along the way to one's larger objective. Although this larger goal may require years or decades to achieve, these subgoals can be accomplished on a daily basis, providing feedback that one is moving in the right direction.[2] Examples of religious subgoals include performing rites or rituals, practicing virtues, reading scripture, meditating, and praying, among others. Most religious systems assert that a "good life" can be attained by those who pursue such subgoals. For instance, Hinduism offers four major paths to the attainment of spiritual liberation—the paths of devotion, ethical action, knowledge, and mental concentration—each of which is associated with particular religious practices (i.e., subgoals).[20] Similarly, Buddhism offers the Noble Eightfold Path, consisting of eight important subgoals—right view, right intention, right speech, right action, right livelihood, right effort, right mindfulness, and right concentration.[21] Moreover, religious pathways can include secular subgoals like remaining drug free, exercising regularly, helping a friend in need, or giving to charity.

Religion also offers believers agency to motivate goal pursuit. According to Snyder, Sigmon, and Feldman, such religious agency can be "a result of both specific religious beliefs and supportive resources inherent in most religious communities" (p. 237).[18] Religious literature, in particular, can provide powerfully motivational beliefs. In the New Testament, for instance, one finds the agentic verse, "I can do all things through him who strengthens me" (Philippians 4:13 NRSV). Religious and spiritual communities can provide another contributor to agency, social support. In fact, research demonstrates associations between social support and hope.[22, 23]

In summary, religion offers its practitioners a set of goals, pathways, and agentic motivations. We are not implying, however, that all goals and pathways (religious or otherwise) are equally beneficial. Some goals may be healthier than others and some pathways may be more effective at leading to goals than others. From the perceptive of Hope Theory, the degree to which adherence to the tenets of a particular religion leads to concrete benefits may be due to variations in the adaptiveness of particular religious goals and the functionality of particular religious pathways.

Nurturing Hope

Given hope's links with so many positive outcomes, an important question concerns whether hope can be nurtured and increased. Fortunately, several studies demonstrate that hope is malleable through the use of therapeutic techniques. In one study, we randomly assigned 39 adults with a variety of mental illness diagnoses to either eight sessions of hope-based group therapy or an eight-week waiting list.[24] In this relatively brief time, hope therapy participants showed significant increases in agency thinking and marginally significant increases in both overall hope and pathways thinking. Moreover, group participants showed significant increases in their self-esteem and sense of life purpose, as well as significant decreases in anxiety. Similar results for hope-based therapies have been demonstrated in older adults with depression, older adults with suicidal ideation, adult survivors of traumatic brain injury, children in residential care, and college students.[25, 26, 27, 28, 29]

Although the aforementioned hope-based therapies make use of many different techniques, certain commonalities emerge. In the remainder of this chapter, we offer four "lessons" extracted from some of these interventions.

Do Not Be Afraid to Hope

People often are afraid to hope. Many have been warned by well-meaning parents or teachers, "don't get your hopes up." Thus, when discussing goal setting, the topic of "false hope" invariably arises. Scholars have pro posed that hope may be maladaptive under three circumstances: (1) goals are inappropriately lofty or difficult, (2) expectations are based on illusions rather than reality, or (3) poor strategies are used to pursue goals.[30, 31, 32, 33] Notably, when reviewing the empirical research, Snyder, Rand, King, Feldman, and Woodward pointed out the lack of convincing empirical evidence that hope is damaging to mental health under any of these circumstances.[34] Of course, this lack of evidence may be due to the fact that empirical investigation of this phenomenon is in its infancy. Nonetheless, it appears that getting one's hopes up does not *necessarily* expose oneself to greater failure or disappointment than had one not allowed hope to flourish. In contrast, as mentioned previously, hopeful thinking appears to increase the probability of successfully accomplishing goals.[10] To link this notion to religion, in the books of Psalms and Proverbs, the Jewish and Christian traditions offer similar instruction not to surrender hope—"For the needy shall not always be forgotten, nor the hope of the poor perish forever" (Psalms 9:18 NRSV), "Hope deferred makes the heart sick, but a desire fulfilled is a tree of life" (Proverbs 13:12 NRSV), and "Surely there is a future, and your hope will not be cut off" (Proverbs 23:18 NRSV).

Set Meaningful Goals

A first step in nurturing hope is to set goals. Hope Theory suggests that hope thrives when individuals set meaningful goals in multiple areas of life.[2] According to McDermott and Snyder, setting multiple goals in diverse domains helps ensure that if a particular goal fails, there will be others on which to fall back.[35] Moreover, at least some goals should be personally meaningful. So often, people pursue goals that are important to others— bosses, family members, friends—but fail to set goals that are personally significant. This can be accomplished by reflecting on the values and beliefs that one holds dear, using these as guides for brainstorming goals. As discussed earlier in this chapter, values derived from one's spiritual or religious beliefs can be important sources of goals for many people.[18] Research suggests that, in general, such values-concordant goals are more motivating and lead to greater increases in well-being than nonconcordant goals.[36, 37]

Break Complex Goals Into Subgoals

An important skill regarding pathways thinking involves breaking down goals into a set of manageable steps called subgoals. Some versions of hope therapy have made use of a pathways mapping exercise to aid in this process.[24, 29, 35] Participants draw a vertical line on a sheet of paper; at the top, they write their final goal, and at the bottom they write "now." They then brainstorm various subgoals and ultimately arrange them along the line in chronological order, writing approximate dates by each subgoal. These dates, of course, are not set in stone; rather, they are guidelines to aid in planning. In our experience, many people enjoy this exercise because it allows for a great deal of creativity. We recall the diagram of one woman in hope group therapy for depression. As she unfurled her several-foot-long diagram (it was on old perforated computer paper), the other group members applauded.

Allow Yourself to Daydream

An important way to bolster agency involves mental rehearsal or "structured daydreaming."[24, 29, 35] Mental rehearsal has long been used to increase success in a variety of domains, including sports, musical performance, teaching, and work skill acquisition.[38, 39, 40, 41, 42] In hope-based structured daydreaming, participants are asked to envision themselves pursuing each subgoal on their pathways map. Over the course of 10 to 20 minutes, they are to see themselves working on and succeeding at each subgoal, one at a time, then eventually accomplishing their final goal. The key to this exercise is realism; this is not a fantasy, but rather a visualization that attempts to foresee a realistically positive goal-pursuit process. For instance, participants are encouraged to anticipate obstacles that may interfere with their attainment of any of the subgoals and see themselves encountering and circumnavigating them with alternative plans. As can be readily discerned, this is no ordinary daydream. Though spontaneous, unstructured daydreaming appears to decrease the likelihood of goal achievement, people who engage in a particular combination of fantasy and realistic planning similar to what we are advocating here are *more* likely to achieve their desires.[43, 44]

Conclusion

In this chapter, we've attempted to show that hope is just as relevant in our modern lives as it was for the ancient Greeks. It is an essential spiritual and psychological asset, allowing us to build a meaningful and satisfying existence despite life's inevitable setbacks. Modern research confirms what followers of various faith traditions have believed for millennia: Hope is a virtue worth cultivating.

Notes

1. Snyder, C. R., Harris, C., Anderson, J. R., Holleran, S. A., Irving, L. M., Sigmon, S. T., Yoshinobu, L., Gibb, J., Langelle, C., & Harney, P. (1991). The will and the ways: Development and validation of an individual-differences measure of hope. *Journal of Personality and Social Psychology, 60,* 570–585.

2. Snyder, C. R. (1994). *The psychology of hope: You can get there from here*. New York: Free Press.

3. Snyder, C. R. (2002). Hope theory: Rainbows in the mind. *Psychological Inquiry, 13*, 249–275.

4. Snyder, C. R., Michael, S. T., & Cheavens, J. S. (1999). Hope as a psychotherapeutic foundation of nonspecific factors, placebos, and expectancies. In M. A. Huble, B. Duncan, & S. Miller (Eds.), *Heart and soul of change* (pp. 205–230). Washington, DC: American Psychological Association.

5. Piper, W. (1978). *The little engine that could*. New York: Grosset & Dunlap.

6. Bowlby, J. (1980). *Attachment and loss, Vol. 3. Loss, sadness, and depression*. New York: Basic Books.

7. Shorey, H. S., Snyder, C. R., Yang, X., & Lewin, M. R. (2003). The role of hope as a mediator in recollected parenting, adult attachment, and mental health. *Journal of Social and Clinical Psychology, 22*(6), 685–715.

8. Snyder, C. R., Hoza, B., Pelham, W. E., Rapoff, M., Ware, L., Danovsky, M. et al. (1997). The development and validation of the Children's Hope Scale. *Journal of Pediatric Psychology, 22*, 399–421.

9. Snyder, C. R., McDermott, D., Cook, W., & Rapoff, M. (2002). *Hope for the journey: Helping children through the good times and bad*. Clinton Corners, NY: Percheron Press.

10. Feldman, D. B., Rand, K. L., & Khale-Wrobleski, K. (2009). Hope and goal attainment: Testing a basic prediction of hope theory. *Journal of Social and Clinical Psychology, 28*(4), 479–497.

11. Snyder, C. R., Shorey, H. S., Cheavens, J., Pulvers, K. M., Adams, V., & Wiklund, C. (2002). Hope and academic success in college. *Journal of Educational Psychology, 94*, 820–826.

12. Curry, L. A., Snyder, C. R., Cook, D. L., Ruby, B. C., & Rehm, M. (1997). Role of hope in academic and sport achievement. *Journal of Personality and Social Psychology, 73*(6), 1257–1267.

13. Feldman, D. B., & Snyder, C. R. (2005). Hope and the meaningful life: Theoretical and empirical associations between goal-directed thinking and life meaning. *Journal of Social and Clinical Psychology, 24*, 401–421.

14. Tennen, H., & Affleck, G. (1999). Finding benefits in adversity. In C. R. Snyder (Ed.), *Coping: The psychology of what works* (pp. 279–304). New York: Oxford Press.

15. Elliott, T. R., Witty, T. E., Herrick, S., & Hoffman, J. (1991). Negotiating reality after physical loss: Hope, depression, and disability. *Journal of Personality and Social Psychology, 4*, 608–613.

16. Berendes, D., Keefe, F. J., Somers, T. J., Kothadia, S. M., Porter, L. S., & Cheavens, J. S. (2010). Hope in the context of lung cancer: Relationships of hope to symptoms and psychological distress. *Journal of Pain and Symptom Management, 40*(2), 174–182.

17. Gum, A., Snyder, C. R., & Duncan, P. W. (2006). Hopeful thinking, participation and depressive symptoms three months after stroke. *Psychology & Health, 21*(3), 319–334.

18. Snyder, C. R., Sigmon, D. R., & Feldman, D. B. (2003). Hope for the sacred and vice versa: Positive goal-directed thinking and religion. *Psychological Inquiry, 13*, 234–238.

19. Snyder, C. R. (1994). *The psychology of hope: You can get there from here.* New York: Free Press.

20. Tarekeshwar, N., Pargament, K. I., & Mahoney, A. (2003). Measures of Hindu pathways: Development and preliminary evidence of reliability and validity. *Cultural Diversity and Ethnic Minority Psychology, 9*, 316–332.

21. Bodhi, B. (2005). *In the Buddha's words: An anthology of discourses from the Pali canon.* Somerville, MA: Wisdom Publications.

22. Glass, K., Flory, K., Hankin, B. I., Kloos, B., & Turecki, G. (2009). Are coping strategies, social support, and hope associated with psychological distress among Hurricane Katrina survivors? *Journal of Social and Clinical Psychology, 28*, 779–795.

23. Horton, T. V., & Wallender, J. L. (2001). Hope and social support as resilience factors against psychological distress of mothers who care for children with chronic physical conditions. *Rehabilitation Psychology, 46*, 382–399.

24. Cheavens, J. S., Feldman, D. B., Gum, A., Michael, S. T., & Snyder, C. R. (2006). Hope therapy in a community sample: A pilot investigation. *Social Indicators Research, 77*, 61–78.

25. Klausner, E. J., Clarkin, J. F., Spielman, L., Pupo, C., Abrams, R., & Alexopoulos, G. S. (1998). Late-life depression and functional disability: The role of goal-focused group psychotherapy. *International Journal of Geriatric Psychiatry, 13*, 707–716.

26. Lapierre, S., Dube, M., Bouffard, L., & Alain, M. (2007). Addressing suicidal ideations through the realization of meaningful personal goals. *Crisis, 28*, 16–25.

27. Wilbur, R. C., & Parente, R. (2008). A cognitive technology for fostering hope. *International Journal of Cognitive Technology, 13*, 24–29.

28. McNeal, R., Handwerk, M. L., Field, C. E., Roberts, M. C., Soper, S., Huefner, J. C., & Ringle, M. A. (2006). Hope as an outcome variable among youths in a residential care setting. *American Journal of Orthopsychiatry, 76*, 304–311.

29. Feldman, D. B., & Dreher, D. (2011). *Can hope be changed in 90 minutes? Testing the efficacy of a single-session goal-pursuit intervention for college students.* Unpublished manuscript.

30. Rule, W. R. (1982). Pursuing the horizon: Striving for elusive goals. *Personnel and Guidance Journal, 61*, 195–197.

31. Beavers, W. R., & Kaslow, F. W. (1981). The anatomy of hope. *Journal of Marital and Family Therapy, 7*, 119–126.

32. Callan, D. B. (1989). Hope as a clinical issue in oncology social work. *Journal of psychosocial oncology, 7*, 31–46.

33. Kwon, P. (2002). Hope, defense mechanisms, and adjustment: Implication for false hope and defensive hopelessness. *Journal of Personality, 70*, 207–231.

34. Snyder, C. R., Rand, K., King, E., Feldman, D. B., & Woodward, J. T. (2002). "False" hope. *Journal of Clinical Psychology, 58*, 1003–1022.

35. McDermott, D., & Snyder, C. R. (1999). *Making hope happen: A workbook for turning possibilities into reality.* Oakland, CA: New Harbinger Publications.

36. Sheldon, K. M. (2001). The self-concordance model of healthy goal striving: When personal goals correctly represent the person. In P. Schmuck & K. Sheldon (Eds.), *Life goals and well-being: Towards a positive psychology of human striving* (pp. 18–36). Ashland, OH: Hogrefe & Huber Publishers.

37. Sheldon, K. M., & Elliot, A. J. (1999). Goal striving, need satisfaction, and longitudinal well-being: The self-concordance model. *Journal of Personality and Social Psychology, 76*, 482–497.

38. Feltz, D. L., & Landers, D. M. (1983). The effects of mental practice on motor skill learning and performance: A meta-analysis. *Journal of Sport Psychology, 5*, 25–57.

39. Murphy, S. M. (1990). Models of imagery in sport psychology: A review. *Journal of Mental Imagery, 14*, 153–172.

40. Lim, S., & Lippman, L. G. (1990). Mental practice and memorization of piano music. *Journal of General Psychology, 118*, 21–30.

41. Romeo, F. (1985). Observational learning procedures applied to the supervision of student teaching. *Education, 105*, 423–426.

42. Wohldmann, E. L., Healy, A. F., & Bourne, L. E., Jr. (2008). A mental practice superiority effect: Less retroactive interference and more transfer than physical practice. *Journal of Experimental Psychology: Learning, Memory, and Cognition, 34*, 823–833.

43. Oettingen, G., & Wadden, T. A. (1991). Expectations, fantasy, and weight loss: Is the impact of positive thinking always positive? *Cognitive Therapy and Research, 15*, 167–175.

44. Oettingen, G., & Mayer, D. (2002). The motivating function of thinking about the future: Expectations versus fantasies. *Journal of Personality and Social Psychology, 83*, 1198–1212.

5

Forgiveness

Everett L. Worthington, Jr., Don E. Davis, Joshua N. Hook,
Jon R. Webb, Loren Toussaint, Steven J. Sandage,
Aubrey L. Gartner, and Daryl R. Van Tongeren

The major world religions each have doctrines, beliefs, rituals, and other structures that encourage forgiveness under certain circumstances.[1] Thus, religion and spirituality (R/S) play a strong role in many people's experiences of forgiveness. R/S may influence the likelihood of forgiveness to occur, whether in a facilitative or inhibitive fashion. That is, forgiveness may be more likely to occur, for instance, if one believes that receiving God's forgiveness is a basis for forgiving others. Alternatively, it may be less likely to occur if one is angry with God. Research has begun to accumulate that empirically links R/S to forgiveness.[2]

In this chapter, we address an important question: What (if anything) does R/S add to the experience of forgiving? Most ethical claims that encourage specific behaviors are supported by one of two basic arguments. Deontological arguments suggest that a behavior is right in and of itself, whereas consequentialist arguments suggest that one behavior is better than another because it produces better outcomes. Although most religions draw upon both arguments to encourage forgiving, we will focus primarily on the empirical evidence (i.e., consequentialist support) regarding the benefits of forgiveness and how R/S may enhance these benefits.

We first define religion, spirituality, and forgiveness. Second, we review evidence supporting the beneficial effects of forgiveness. Third, we consider possible ways that R/S may enhance forgiveness. Fourth, we briefly present a theoretical model for understanding how R/S may *fluidly* enhance forgiveness. Lastly, we consider implications for research and practice.

Definitions

Religion and Spirituality

We adopt Hill and colleagues' definition of *religion* as adherence to a faith-based, organized belief system in which there is general agreement about what is believed and practiced.[3] In contrast, *spirituality* can be defined as a more general feeling of closeness and connectedness to the sacred. The object one views as sacred is often a socially influenced perception of either (a) a divine being or object or (b) a sense of ultimate reality or truth.[3] Many people experience their spirituality in the context of religion (i.e., *religious spirituality*), but not all do. As such, scholars have identified *secular spirituality* and have described three categories based on the type of scared object.[4] *Humanistic spirituality* involves a particular sense of purpose and meaning in and/or closeness and connection to humankind. *Nature spirituality* involves such experience in the context of a particular aspect of the environment or nature (e.g., sunset(s) or the Grand Canyon). *Transcendent spirituality* involves the broader context of creation, the natural order, or things beyond normal life (e.g., magnificence and vastness of the universe or existence). Importantly, many religious people consider themselves both spiritual and religious, and fewer people tend to view themselves as spiritual but not religious.[5] We know very little about the association between nonreligious spiritualities and forgiveness.

Forgiveness

Forgiveness refers to a victim's reduction of negative thoughts, emotions, motivations, and behaviors toward an offender, as well as the promotion of positive thoughts, emotions, motivations, and behaviors toward an offender.[6] Forgiveness can be measured as both a trait (called forgivingness) and a state. *Forgivingness* refers to a person's tendency to forgive across relationships and situations, whereas *state forgiveness* refers to forgiveness of a specific offense. Forgiveness can involve a variety of targets (e.g., self, others, and God) and methods (e.g., offering, seeking, and feeling).[7] McCullough, Fincham, and Tsang have argued that because most definitions of forgiveness imply changes over time, the construct should be studied longitudinally.[8]

Benefits of Forgiveness

Scientific research on forgiveness has proliferated recently, partly due to consistent evidence of the benefits of forgiveness for repairing relationships as well as for mental and physical health.[9] Worthington proposed a stress-and-coping theory of forgiveness that helps explain the benefits of forgiveness.[6] This model treats unforgiveness as a stress response to a transgression (i.e., the stressor). The consequences of this stress response include negative effects on physical health, mental health, relationships, and R/S.

Accordingly, forgiveness has been found to mitigate these negative effects. The *Handbook of Forgiveness* includes overviews of the benefits of forgiveness in a variety of contexts.[10] Webb, Toussaint, and Conway-Williams provide an updated review of 54 recent studies in which salutary associations were observed in health-related categories of physical, mental, substance abuse (see Pearce & Wachholtz, this volume), and spirituality.[11] Consistent with a model of the direct effect of forgiveness on health proposed by Worthington, Berry, and Parrott,[12] these effects are mostly explained by reductions of stress due to (un)forgiveness.[7] Worthington and colleagues also proposed that forgiveness is indirectly related to health through the *distinct* mediating variables of health behavior, social support, and interpersonal functioning.[12]

Most empirical studies on forgiveness have been (a) cross-sectional and (b) focused on forgiveness of others. Of studies including multiple aspects of forgiveness, emerging evidence suggests that relationships may be nuanced based on each unique dimension of forgiveness and specific health conditions under consideration. For example, in reviewing research on forgiveness and alcohol problems, Webb, Hirsch, and Toussaint concluded that forgiveness of self may be more important than forgiveness of others and feeling forgiven by God.[13]

Does R/S Enhance the Benefits of Forgiveness?

As reviewed above, the research evidence has been consistent in showing the harmful effects of unforgiveness and the benefits of forgiveness for physical and mental health. Research findings have also been consistent in describing the physical and mental health benefits of R/S.[14] If R/S promotes forgiveness, forgiveness may be one avenue by which R/S improves physical and mental health. Indeed, the aforementioned model regarding the effect of forgiveness on health is actually one component of a larger, more complex model of the relationship between religion and health proposed by Worthington and colleagues,[12] wherein forgiveness may operate as a mechanism in the larger model. Research testing this indirect effect hypothesis directly has been mixed. Lawler-Row provided evidence from three studies that forgiveness did act as an indirect mechanism between R/S and health.[15] Strenthal, Williams, Musick, and Buck, on the other hand, found that although forgiveness was related to health, it did not function as an indirect mechanism linking R/S and health.[16] In this section, we describe a model for how R/S might positively affect physical and mental health via forgiveness. That is, R/S might positively affect physical and mental health via forgiving in one of two ways: consistently or fluidly.

Consistent Forgiveness

First, R/S may enhance physical and mental health by making people more consistently forgiving across situations and relationships. Because many religions promote forgiveness as a virtue and provide religious individuals with rituals to promote forgiveness, perhaps religious individuals are simply better at forgiving others across relationships and situations. The vast majority of research on R/S and forgiveness has focused on this question.[2, 9, 17]

McCullough and Worthington conducted a qualitative review of the empirical literature on R/S and forgiveness.[17] They found that religious people consistently reported being more forgiving (as a trait), yet in studies that measured forgiveness of specific offenses, the relationship was less consistent. In these studies, religious individuals were not consistently more forgiving than nonreligious individuals. To explain this discrepancy, they discussed several possible explanations. First, religious individuals may report that they are more forgiving because this virtue is valued in religious communities, but they are not actually more forgiving. Second, individuals are likely to recall transgressions that have not been forgiven, making it appear as though they are unforgiving. Third, religion is often measured as a trait whereas forgiveness is measured as a state, and this may act to suppress relationships between the two.

More recently, two meta-analyses have examined the relationship between R/S and forgiveness more definitively.[9, 2] Fehr and colleagues examined the relationship between R/S and state forgiveness—they estimated the correlation at .19.[9] Davis and colleagues provided a more detailed examination of the relationship between R/S and forgiveness. The estimated overall correlation between R/S and trait forgivingness ($k = 64$; $N = 99,164$) was .19, whereas the overall correlation between R/S and state forgiveness was .14 (predicting only 2% of the variance in forgiveness scores). When R/S and forgiveness were both measured at the state level, however, the correlation was .33 (predicting around 11% of the variance in forgiveness scores).[2] Indeed, state measures of R/S, such as appraising the transgression as a desecration, are conceptually very different from general measures of R/S such as religious commitment. Someone's degree of R/S involvement may not influence forgiveness as much as how he or she spiritually experiences a transgression because transgressions involve aspects of human experience that can deviate from many religious ideals.

Fluid (Efficient) Forgiveness

A second way that R/S may affect physical and mental health via forgiving may be through involvement in R/S communities, thereby enhancing a person's ability to know when and how to forgive. According to McCullough's theorizing regarding the evolutionary development of forgiveness, forgiveness and justice are two opposing processes that regulate cooperation in one's relationships.[18] It may not be adaptive for a person to forgive immediately and statically every transgression because this strategy may result in others taking advantage of the rigidly forgiving individual. The emotions of unforgiveness motivate people to learn from prior experiences of exploitation so that they can set appropriate boundaries. The most adaptive strategy may be for a person to benefit from such learning with minimal strain from the stress of unforgiveness—quickly and appropriately adjusting his or her relationship with the offender in order to restore a sense of security and safety in the relationship.

There are many ways that involvement in religious communities may help fine-tune a person's ability to forgive. First, religious communities often provide doctrine and guidelines on when and how a person should forgive. For example, the Christian faith promotes a general norm of forgiving offenders but also provides (a) a course of action for confronting undesirable behavior and (b) a series of punishments and boundaries for continued undesirable behavior (e.g., removal from faith community). These beliefs and rituals should not be considered static across a religion (e.g., Christians) or even a denomination (e.g., Pentecostals). Rather, congregations, as well as subgroups within them, have unique beliefs and rituals related to the interpretation and application of forgiveness and repair of relationships after transgressions.

Second, the belief in a Divine being that cares about when and how one forgives increases the emotional intensity of these beliefs and rituals. Religious individuals may want to adhere to community beliefs and rituals related to forgiveness in order to remain in good standing in their relationship with God, or, in a more altruistic sense, to emulate God. Conversely, there is some empirical evidence that intense anxiety about one's relationship with God is negatively associated with forgiving others.[4, 19]

Third, religious communities are often communal and collectivistic. Thus, beliefs and rituals related to forgiveness gain social power and serve to regulate communal boundaries. Religious belief systems identify in-groups and out-groups, thereby strengthening relationships within the in-group due to the similarity of the group identity. This strengthening of relationships should make relationships more valued and thus enhance forgiveness within the in-group but, conversely, might impede forgiveness of out-group members.[18]

Fourth, involvement in a religious community helps identify when it is acceptable not to forgive. Religious communities identify which aspects of life are valued and sacred versus evil. Consequently, viewing an offender and/or behavior in a justifiably negative valence may lead a person to distance him- or herself from that relationship while at the same time maintaining status within the religious community (because the religious community supports this viewpoint). Because the unforgiveness is validated within the context of the religious community, it may be an efficient (i.e., involving less stress) strategy of decreasing conflict.

Fifth, religious communities influence who is considered a good citizen of the community, as well as who should be avoided or perhaps even shunned. Religious communities often establish norms for initiating repair of a relationship. For example, in some Jewish communities, to restore good standing with the victim, as well as the greater religious community, the offender is expected to repent, which involves offering an apology as well as restitution for the transgression. If the offender shows humility (see Bollinger & Hill, this volume) by following these norms, then the burden for forgiveness then shifts to the victim (i.e., the victim must forgive). From the standpoint of the community, theological doctrines may promote the view that God expects the victim to be willing to forgive. This capacity of religious groups to take away someone's good standing with the community exists even in religions (e.g., Christianity) that teach that one should forgive unconditionally (i.e., without requiring apology or restitution).

We propose that such R/S adaptations can often enhance forgiveness. For example, consider a woman whose husband is unfaithful. The victim— as well as the entire community—may view the transgression as a desecration. The community expects the offender to sacrifice greatly (e.g., see a Christian counselor, follow recommendations of religious leaders) in order to indicate a desire to repair the relationship. If the offender refuses, the religious leader and community may inflict costs on the reputation of the offender. Still, the offender refuses. Within a relatively short period of time, the victim can decide not to try to repair the relationship with the blessing of the religious community. This may actually speed along the grieving process for the victim and limit the potential for repeated transgressions within the relationship. The norms and rituals of the religious community—as well as the social pressure of the group— helped push the relationship toward repair or disintegration more quickly. This streamlining may benefit the group, because stability is restored. It can also benefit the individual, because less energy was expended (i.e., less stress and unforgiveness occurred). One downside of this process could be a religious system in which a particular "offender" is scapegoated while the spouse or others in that relational system are not challenged toward growth.

Similarly, religious communities may have fluid norms and rituals related to forgiveness that increase the adaptability of the community to the social context. For example, religious communities in urban areas of the United States may tend to have more fluid beliefs and rituals that promote greater tolerance and cohesion among diverse cultural identities. Conversely, cities in areas entrenched in violent political conflicts that are expressly supported by religious ideology (e.g., Middle East) may have norms and rituals that streamline forgiveness of in-group members that express loyalty to the group but that swiftly enact justice against out-group members and quickly remove or distance the person from further harming the community.

In summary, prior research has been focused on the extent to which R/S makes people more forgiving, but it has not considered the more nuanced question of how some forms of R/S may help individuals forgive more efficiently and effectively (i.e., experience less stress) than nonreligious individuals while other forms of R/S might impede forgiveness.

Model of Forgiveness and Relational Spirituality

Despite some comprehensive theoretical models of forgiveness in general, the field lacks a widely accepted organizing model that connects R/S with forgiveness. Below, we draw on an integration of theology and psychology by Shults and Sandage involving relational spirituality.[20] We extend this model to the study of forgiveness by suggesting there are a variety of ways of relating to the Sacred even within a single spiritual or religious tradition; moreover, these differing forms of relational spirituality demonstrate different patterns of association with forgiveness.[4, 19] Our newly developed model of the R/S-forgiveness link is depicted in Figure 5.1. The triangular base of the model involves the victim, the offender, and the transgression, as well as the relationships among them. These secular aspects of the situational context of a transgression have been heavily studied in prior research. We are especially interested in the vertical dimension of the model—the Sacred and its relationship with the victim, offender, and

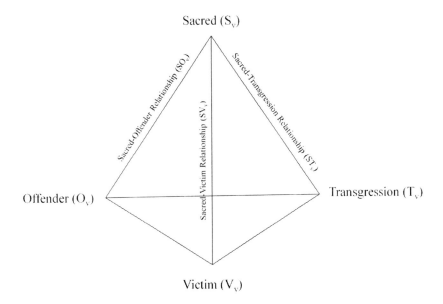

Figure 5.1   Model of Psychology and Theology Integration

transgression. For each of the following constructs, we focus on the victim's point of view.

Characteristics of the Sacred (S)

Victims differ in their understanding of what the Sacred is like, and this may influence the likelihood of forgiveness. For example, Exline and colleagues found that differences in ways people perceive the Sacred (e.g., viewing God as active or passive, just or merciful) affected whether people became angry with God. Furthermore, victims differ in what they believe the Sacred requires regarding forgiveness.[21] For example, if the victim believes that God does not require forgiveness until the offender apologizes and offers restitution, this may thwart forgiveness until such apology or restitution occurs. Viewing the Sacred as incorporating *samsaric circularity* (a wheel of suffering) that is driven by *karma* (unrelenting justice) and *dharma* (holy duty) might make some victims indifferent to suffering. Other victims may view endurance of suffering as a compassionate duty;

they may see forgiveness as a benevolent act that moves them closer to *anatta* (release from suffering).[1] Other victims may believe that the Sacred requires unilateral forgiveness that can motivate them to try to forgive quickly and thoroughly, but if they fail, they may feel guilt or shame that may impede forgiveness. Those in Animistic religions may believe that ancestral spirits will not forgive them unless they perform sacred rituals of forgiveness.

Relationship between the Sacred and the Victim (SV)

Victims also appraise the ongoing status of their relationship with the Sacred, which may influence the likelihood of forgiveness. Feeling intimately connected with the Sacred will likely enhance the salience of any R/S beliefs or rituals related to forgiveness. On the other hand, feeling disconnected from the Sacred may motivate some victims to try to repair their relationship with an offender in order to restore a sense of spiritual peace. Others who feel disconnected from the Sacred may disengage from any R/S rituals or coping strategies that they have learned to deal with transgressions. Indeed, there are a variety of ways one might conceptualize this relationship between the Sacred and the victim. One conceptualization is secure attachment to God, which has been found to be positively related to forgiveness.[4]

Relationship between the Sacred and the Offender (SO)

Victims also appraise the offender's relationship with the Sacred—which can influence the likelihood of forgiveness. For example, victims might assess the similarity of the offender's spirituality to their own. Wohl and Branscombe have examined this systematically: The more similar the offender and victim are regarding group identity, the more hurt the victim will feel by a given betrayal.[22] Worthington hypothesized that despite this greater hurt, victims are more likely to forgive a spiritually similar offender than a spiritually different offender.[6] In direct tests of the model, Davis and colleagues provided supporting evidence that the victim's perception of the similarity of the offender's spirituality to his or her own was positively related to forgiveness.[23]

Relationship between the Sacred and the Transgression (ST)

The victim also appraises the relationship between the Sacred and the transgression. An example is the degree to which the victim views the transgression as a defilement or desecration of something sacred (e.g., body, sexuality, marriage, country). Pargament and Mahoney showed that such appraisals are particularly associated with negative and stressful outcomes.[24] In direct tests of the model, Sacred loss and desecration consistently predicted less forgiveness.[4, 23]

Implications for Research and Practice

Implications for Future Research

We offer several recommendations for future research and practice. For researchers interested in exploring the relationship between R/S, forgiveness, and physical and mental health, we believe that it is time for researchers to explore more nuanced hypotheses about the relationships between these variables. Several studies have shown positive associations between (a) R/S and health, (b) R/S and forgiveness, and (c) forgiveness and health. As such, it may be that forgiveness is an intervening mechanism that goes between R/S and health. We offer a very tentative hypothesis. We suggest—and urge strict testing of this hypothesis—that the relationships between R/S and health might be described as a mediated moderation. Namely, for people who are high in R/S, forgiveness might mediate the relationship with health. But for people moderate to low in R/S, forgiveness does not mediate the relationship. Although the majority of research has supported positive relationships among these variables, the evidence is mixed about the extent to which forgiveness acts as a mechanism between R/S and health, thus the need for strict testing of our hypothesis.

There is also a need for more research on forms of R/S, such as spiritual grandiosity, that might be negatively associated with forgiveness. Furthermore, we believe that research on the relationship between R/S and forgiving should move beyond examining cross-sectional correlations between these variables.

We offer three next steps for this area of research. First, more research must be conducted on how R/S affects forgiveness over time. How do the R/S constructs described in the model of relational spirituality and forgiveness affect the unfolding of forgiveness over time? Likewise, are some forms of forgiveness easier to achieve and thus more likely to occur before others? There is some evidence that those with an avoidant style of attachment with God might rapidly deactivate the emotions of unforgiveness in ways that might represent pseudoforgiveness rather than healthy forgiveness.[25]

Second, research could be conducted evaluating our assertion that R/S helps a person to be more efficient in forgiving. We offered five methods by which R/S improves forgiveness efficiency, and each could be tested empirically.

Third, while continuing to examine forgiveness of others, it will be important to focus on additional targets and methods of forgiveness in order to gain a more complete understanding of the relationship between forgiveness and health. Similarly, understanding the possible interactions between such dimensions of forgiveness and dimensions of spirituality will likely be useful. For example, future studies might explore the role of differentiation of self in promoting forgiveness across spiritual differences.

Implications for Practice

We also offer several recommendations for practitioners who are addressing forgiveness issues with their clients. As is recommended in ethical guidelines, practitioners are advised to conduct a sufficient assessment of clients' R/S. Richards and Bergin describe such an assessment as involving questions regarding whether the client believes R/S might play a part in the problem and whether the client would like to pay attention to R/S in psychotherapy.[26] For R/S individuals dealing with forgiveness issues, it may be helpful to explore the client's beliefs about the intersection of R/S and forgiveness. For example, what is the client's understanding regarding what his or her religion teaches about forgiveness? Does the client agree with, believe, and adhere to these teachings? Should forgiveness be offered unequivocally? Does forgiveness require some level of apology or restitution on the part of the perpetrator? What is the balance between forgiveness and justice? What is the relationship between forgiveness and reconciliation in one's religious community? What role (if any) does the religious community play in the process of forgiveness or reconciliation? Are there R/S strategies or rituals that might be helpful in the individual's process of forgiveness? Are some dimensions of forgiveness more achievable for the individual (although some may be easier than others, which may also have a facilitative effect on those that are more difficult)? Has the client felt coerced to forgive by R/S leaders? Lastly, it is important for the clinician to be aware of his or her biases with regard to addressing R/S and forgiveness with clients.

Conclusions

The experiences of R/S and forgiveness are intertwined for many individuals. Both R/S and forgiveness appear to have positive influences on physical and mental health, although more research is needed to determine the specific links among these constructs. In the present chapter, we have provided a brief review of this research, as well as proposed important hypotheses to explore regarding the more nuanced relationships among these variables. Although previous work has addressed how faith and health are intertwined, our goal was to add to the extant knowledge on the importance of R/S for health, as well as provide direction for future areas of inquiry.[27] As the intricate relationship between R/S and forgiveness is more suitably explored, we expect that additional evidence for the benefits of forgiveness will continue to be discovered.

Notes

1. Rye, M. S., Pargament, K. I., Ali, M. A., Beck, G. L., Dorff, E. N., Hallisey, C., Narayanan, V., & Williams, J. G. (2000). Religious perspectives on forgiveness. In M. E. McCullough, K. I. Pargament, & C. E. Thoresen (Eds.), *Forgiveness: Theory, research, and practice* (pp. 17–40). New York: Guilford Press.
2. Davis, D. E., Worthington, E. L., Jr., & Hook, J. N. (2011). *Research on religion/spirituality and forgiveness: A meta-analytic review.*

Manuscript under editorial review. Virginia Commonwealth University.

3. Hill, P. C., Pargament, K. I., Hood, R. W., McCullough, M. E., Swyers, J. P., Larson, D. B., & Zinnbauer, B. J. (2000). Conceptualizing religion and spirituality: Points of commonality, points of departure. *Journal for the Theory of Social Behaviour, 30,* 51–77.

4. Davis, D. E., Hook, J. N., & Worthington, E. L., Jr. (2008). Relational spirituality and forgiveness: The roles of attachment to God, religious coping, and viewing the transgression as a desecration. *Journal of Psychology and Christianity, 27,* 293–301.

5. Zinnbauer, B. J., Pargament, K. I., Cole, B., Rye, M. S., Butter, E. M., Belavich, T. G., & . . . Kadar, J. L. (1997). Religion and spirituality: Unfuzzying the fuzzy. *Journal for the Scientific Study of Religion, 36*(4), 549–564. doi:10.2307/1387689

6. Worthington, E. L., Jr. (2006). *Forgiveness and reconciliation: Theory and application.* New York: Brunner-Routledge.

7. Toussaint, L., & Webb, J. R. (2005). Theoretical and empirical connections between forgiveness, mental health, and well-being. In E. L. Worthington (Ed.), *Handbook of Forgiveness* (pp. 349–362). New York: Brunner-Routledge.

8. McCullough, M. E., Fincham, F. D., & Tsang, J. (2003). Forgiveness, forbearance, and time: The temporal unfolding of transgression-related interpersonal motivations. *Journal of Personality and Social Psychology, 84,* 540–557.

9. Fehr, R., Gelfand, M. J., & Nag, M. (2010). The road to forgiveness: A meta-analytic synthesis of its situational and dispositional correlates. *Psychological Bulletin, 136,* 894–914.

10. Worthington, E. L., Jr. (Ed.). (2005). *Handbook of forgiveness.* New York: Brunner-Routledge.

11. Webb, J. R., Toussaint, L., & Conway-Williams, E. (in press). Forgiveness and health: Psycho-spiritual integration and the promotion of better healthcare. *Journal of Health Care Chaplaincy.*

12. Worthington, E. L., Jr., Berry, J. W., & Parrott, L. (2001). Unforgiveness, forgiveness, religion, and health. In T. G. Plante &

A. C., Sherman (Eds.), *Faith and health: Psychological perspectives* (pp. 107–138). New York: Guilford Press.

13. Webb, J. R., Hirsch, J. K., & Toussaint, L. (2011). Forgiveness and alcohol problems: A review of the literature and a call for intervention-based research. *Alcoholism Treatment Quarterly, 29*(3), 245–273. doi: 10.1080/07347324.2011.585922

14. Koenig, H. G., McCullough, M. E., & Larson, D. B. (2001). *Handbook of religion and health.* New York: Oxford University Press.

15. Lawler-Row, K. A. (2010). Forgiveness as a mediator of the religiosity–health relationship. *Psychology of Religion and Spirituality, 2,* 1–16.

16. Sternthal, M. J., Williams, D. R., Musick, M. A., & Buck, A. C. (2010). Depression, anxiety, and religious life: A search for mediators. *Journal of Health and Social Behavior, 51*(3), 343–359.

17. McCullough, M. E., & Worthington, E. L. Jr. (1999). Religion and the forgiving personality. *Journal of Personality, 67,* 1141–1164.

18. McCullough, M. E. (2008). *Beyond revenge: The evolution of the forgiveness instinct.* San Francisco: Jossey-Bass.

19. Sandage, S. J., & Jankowski, P. J. (2010). Forgiveness, spiritual instability, mental health symptoms, and well-being: Mediation effects of differentiation of self. *Psychology of Religion and Spirituality, 2,* 168–180.

20. Shults, F. L., & Sandage, S. J. (2006). *Transforming spirituality: Integrating theology and psychology.* Grand Rapids, MI: Baker Academic.

21. Exline, J. J., Park, C. L., Smyth, J. M., Carey, M. P. (2011). Anger toward God: Social-cognitive predictors, prevalence, and links with adjustment to bereavement and cancer. *Journal of Personality and Social Psychology, 100,* 129–148. doi: 10.1037/a0021716

22. Wohl, M. J., Branscombe, N. R., & Reysen, S. (2010). Perceiving your group's future to be in jeopardy: Extinction threat induces collective angst and the desire to strengthen the ingroup. *Personality and Social Psychology Bulletin, 36,* 898–910. doi: 10.1177/0146167210372505

23. Davis, D. E., Worthington, E. L. Jr., Hook, J. N., Van Tongeren, D. R., Green, J. D., & Jennings, D. J., II. (2009). Relational spirituality and

the development of the Similarity of the Offender's Spirituality (SOS) scale. *Psychology of Religion and Spirituality, 1*, 249–262.

24. Pargament, K. I., & Mahoney, A. (2005). Sacred matters: Sanctification as a vital topic for the psychology of religion. *International Journal for the Psychology of Religion, 15*, 179–198. doi: 10.1207/s15327582ijpr1503_1

25. Hall, T. W., Fujikawa, A., Halcrow, S. R., Hill, P. C., & Delaney, H. (2009). Attachment to God and implicit spirituality: Clarifying correspondence and compensation models. *Journal of Psychology and Theology, 27*, 227–242.

26. Richards, P. S., & Bergin, A. E. (2005). *A spiritual strategy for counseling and psychotherapy* (2nd ed.). Washington, DC: American Psychological Association.

27. Plante, T. G., & Sherman, A. C. (Eds.). (2001). *Faith and health: Psychological perspectives.* New York: Guilford Press.

6

Goodness

Thomas G. Plante

And what does the Lord require of me?
To love mercy, do justice, and walk humbly with God.

—Micah 6:8

This quote from the Hebrew Bible has been one of my favorite quotes from sacred scripture in the Judeo-Christian tradition for a very long time. It well summarizes how we should live. It well articulates how to live a good life. In this brief and simple statement in response to what God wants of us, it makes clear that there are three things that we should do throughout our lives if we want to follow the dictates of the God in the Jewish and Christian tradition. Even if one isn't affiliated with the Judeo-Christian traditions, it is still pretty good advice regarding how one should live.

First, we must love mercy, meaning to always be compassionate. Many of the various religious traditions support the view that we should treat others with compassion and mercy. For example, in the New Testament used by Christians, the Gospel of Luke states, "Be compassionate as your heavenly Father is compassionate" (Luke 6:36). Other religious traditions also support the notion that compassion is the very heart of religion.[1] In fact, the well-known author Karen Armstrong states that when closely examining all of the major religious traditions that came to fruition during the Axial Age (starting in the ninth century B.C.), compassion was the heart, soul, and point of them all. She states: "... the spirit of compassion . . . lies at the core of all our traditions" (p. 476)[1] and that "religion *was* the Golden Rule" (p. 468).[1]

Second, we must focus our attention on justice, treating everyone fairly with honor, dignity, and respect. In doing so, we strive to become more responsible and respectful and behave with integrity toward others when we treat everyone justly. Again, all of the major religious traditions highlight the need to treat others fairly and with justice. Even the most famous part of the Hippocratic Oath, although not part of our current religious traditions, regarding first doing no harm, actually reads, "I will keep them from harm and injustice."[2] Curiously, the emphasis on justice in this sentence appears to have been dropped from the public and perhaps physician radar screen, who tend to think that the sentence (erroneously) reads, "first do no harm."

Finally, we are instructed to walk *humbly* with God. In my view, *humble* is very much the operative word here. Sadly, many people who report being religious or are closely affiliated with a particular religious tradition have behaved in ways that are hardly humble at all. In fact, sometimes the word *arrogant* comes to mind. They somehow know the mind of God and are quite clear that they are correct in their views and perspectives and others are clearly wrong. Some seem to be quite confident about who is going to heaven and who is going to hell and exactly what the afterlife looks like. Some are quite clear and confident of what God thinks of people different than themselves who may come from other religious or spiritual traditions and practices or who are identified by their sexual orientation, clothing, both private and public behavior, beliefs, and so forth. They seem to know exactly what God thinks. Curiously, some seem much more confident in what the sacred scriptures mean than almost all of the scholars who study these documents (often in their original languages) as a full-time career with numerous advanced degrees in the field to prepare them. Thus, humble they are not. Yet again, at their best, all of the religious and spiritual traditions highlight the value of and support humility.

There is much to digest and reflect upon in this very brief, simple, and, may I suggest, beautiful scripture quote. In my view, behaving in a way that encourages a humble journey with God while treating others with both mercy and justice well summarizes an ethical model of how to behave in the world and how to be good. It briefly states the principles to live a life of goodness.

All of the religious and spiritual traditions offer much guidance on how one ought to live one's life. They provide principles for living and decision making. They provide ways of living an ethical and good life. The religious and spiritual traditions provide wisdom on how to be in the world. Therefore, one of the fruits of the spirit from all of the wisdom traditions found among the great religious and spiritual frameworks is ethics. While it is true that one doesn't necessarily need to be engaged in a religious or spiritual tradition to be ethical or good, these traditions offer such rich material that it would be foolish not to learn at least a few things from them.

For some examples, let us consider a few quotes from sacred scripture and religious commentary that well illustrate how the traditions offer ethical principles for living. Since I am most familiar with the Jewish and Christian traditions, most of my examples will come from these two closely related religious traditions.

Examples of Ethical Principles within Religious Scriptures and Documents

Consider these quotes from the Talmud within the Jewish tradition:
"Have you dealt honorably with your fellow man?" (Talmud Shabbat 31a).
"Respect one another" (Eleazar ben Azariah, Talmud).
"If the community is in trouble, a person must not say, 'I will go home, and eat and drink, and my soul will be at peace.' A person must share in the concerns of the community" (Talmud Ta'anit).

These are just a few of many examples in which ethical behavior (e.g., respect, integrity, and concern for others) is emphasized and encouraged.

Now consider these quotes from the Christian tradition:

"Love your enemies and pray for those who persecute you" (Matthew 5).
" . . . share with those in need" (Ephesians 4:28).
"Be devoted to one another in brotherly love. Honor one another above yourselves" (Romans 12:10).

As seen in these few examples, an emphasis on being concerned for the welfare of others is highlighted in these texts.

Both Christian and Jewish traditions endorse and support the Ten Commandments (Exodus 20:1–17), which many consider a reasonable, useful, and practical set of ethical guidelines regardless of religious tradition affiliation. In fact, during recent years, a number of conservative politicians in the United States have suggested that the Ten Commandments be posted in all public schools and other public spaces such as courthouses. Some even have boldly asserted that if the Ten Commandments were posted in public schools, there would be a decrease in many of the troubles that teens get themselves into (e.g., teen pregnancy, drug use, and violence). Whether true or not or supported by empirical research data, this perspective underscores the popularity of the Ten Commandments as a set of rules for ethical living.

The well-known and sometimes controversial German theologian Hans Kung[3] maintains that all of the major world religions endorse, support, and encourage five basic ethical principles of behavior. These include avoiding killing, lying, stealing, and behaving immorally while respecting parents and loving children. Additionally, all of the major religions of the world advocate integrity and responsibility as well as concern and as respect for others. Sadly, there are too many examples of people behaving in ways contrary to these ethical ideals in the name of their religions.

What Do We Mean by Ethics Anyway?

Ethics simply are a set of principles or guidelines that we use to decide how we ought to live.[4, 5] Several thousand years of writing and thought in the area of moral philosophy have arrived at several key principles that guide our way to make ethical decisions. They include the following approaches:

Cultural Relativism

Cultural traditions, experiences, and expectations over time create particular guidelines and rules for behavior. What might be ethical in one cultural tradition might be unethical in another. Culture can be defined as broadly taking into consideration race, ethnicity, socioeconomic level, educational level, and so forth.

Egoism

An egoism approach to ethics is often the one that most people use naturally and perhaps without much thought. It also might be the most difficult one of the list to fully understand. When faced with an ethical dilemma, most people probably consider what decision likely would benefit them the most. Egoism often can be well masked in altruism. For example, one might send money to help those in need but do so to relieve guilt, making the giver feel good that he or she has done some part to help. Someone might help a marginalized group of people in need by helping to build a house for someone poor or perhaps going to a third-world country to help out in some way. However, the motive may be to brag about the experience or perhaps include the activity on a resume that might help them to get admitted to a competitive college, for example.

Utilitarianism

The utilitarianism approach is democratic in that it approaches ethical issues by what will please the most people. Thus, voting and allowing the majority to decide an outcome would often be the utilitarian approach to an ethical issue. What results in the most happiness for the most people is considered the ethical choice using this perspective on ethics.

Absolute Moral Rules

The absolute moral rule approach to ethics states that there are specific rules for behavior that should apply in all circumstances regardless of the consequences. For example, one should always be honest, kind, respectful, generous, and so on. No one should ever be allowed to rape or torture children or animals as well. Thus, ethical rules are universal and applied at all times and in all situations.

Social Contract

The social contract approach to ethics states that in order for us to live ethically in community, we ought to use formal and informal guidelines about how to behave in order to get along. Most laws and other rules are based on this important notion. Laws provide structure and guidelines so that a group of people can live together in a safe and orderly manner.

If individuals or a group of people choose to violate an important social contract, then societal structures are in place to arrest and punish them or at least provide corrective feedback.

In addition to laws and rules, there are many informal contracts that we go along with while living with others. For example, people naturally wait in line to buy movie or subway tickets. If a child you don't know is hurt on a playground and there's no parent or guardian nearby, you'd likely try and help the child. While there is no specific law that states you must wait your turn in line at a movie, we have come to expect that this is the informal procedure to get along well with others.

Rights Approach

The rights approach to ethics suggests that every human being has certain rights that should be protected and promoted. For example, many people in America agree that people have a right to express their opinions, even if they are unpopular ones. Americans also value the right to "life, liberty, and the pursuit of happiness." Many feel that as long as you harm no one, you have the right to think and behave as you like. Some argue that every human should have the right to food, housing, a living wage, and perhaps marriage regardless of sexual orientation and gender of the partner.

Justice Approach

The justice approach focuses on treating others in a fair, reasonable, and respectful manner and holds that the rules and laws of the land apply to all regardless of position, status, power, wealth, and so forth. Thus, what is ethical is what is fair.

Common Good Approach

The common good approach to ethics states that what's in the best interest of the community is what's most ethical. Therefore, if it is in the best interest of the community to imprison child molesters, then it is ethical to take away their rights to freedom in order to protect the larger community. The common good approach might, for example, suggest that it is important to insist that drivers not drink when driving because it is in the common good to be sure that everyone drives sober.

Virtue Approach

The virtue approach to ethics suggests that there are a number of qualities or personal characteristics that we value and should all strive toward. These might include honesty, integrity, responsibility, compassion, politeness, thoughtfulness, kindness, competence, and so forth. Each person might have a list of personal characteristics that he or she strives toward in being ethical.

Most people would likely agree with a core list of virtues that we hope that all members of society would strive toward. We would hope that everyone is honest, responsible, thoughtful, caring, kind, civil, generous, loyal, friendly, courteous, and so forth. These are values that we encourage our children to adopt and that we usually seek in selecting friends, coworkers, and relationship partners.

A popular virtue approach to ethics includes the Boy Scouts' list of ethical principles.[6] These include the following characteristics to aspire to. A Scout should be:

- Trustworthy
- Loyal
- Helpful
- Friendly
- Courteous
- Kind
- Obedient
- Cheerful
- Thrifty
- Brave
- Clean
- Reverent

Most people would likely feel comfortable with following at least the majority of these characteristics. For example, most people would likely agree that being trustworthy, courteous, and kind are ethical principles worth following whether one is a Boy Scout or not.

Religion and Ethics

Religious Modeling and Observational Learning

The religious traditions not only provide guidance for ethical behavior but also models for it. The popular question "What would Jesus do?" is an excellent example. All of the religious traditions offer models of ethical behavior that people are encouraged to emulate. Jesus, the Buddha, the Dali Lama, Mother Teresa, Martin Luther King, the various saints (St. Francis, St. Ignatius, St. Dominic), Mohammad, and Gandhi, among so many others, give followers models to copy. In doing so, the religious traditions provide both guidelines for behavior as well as models of exemplary behavior for followers to emulate. Perhaps Jesus's well-known comment as quoted in the Gospel of Luke, "Go and do likewise" (Luke 10:37), well summarizes this emphasis on modeling ethical behavior by watching and repeating what exemplars do.

Bandura[7,8] articulates how modeling or observational learning must attend to four important stages for learning and behavior change to occur. Although not likely aware of the empirical social science research on observational learning, religious traditions have been using this theory for centuries. According to Bandura, the observational learning stages include *attention, retention, repetition*, and *motivation*. One must first *attend* to the desired behavior demonstrated by a model. One must watch it carefully. Then, one must *retain* the behavior by observing it repeatedly and using other methods to remember the desired target behavior in question. Then the person needs to *repeat* the behavior to be sure that he or she can do it, practice it, and work out the details that might make any new skill or behavior pattern challenging to do. Finally, one must be *motivated* to conduct the target behavior in question on an ongoing basis. Much of what religious traditions do in their use of modeling follows these principles of observational learning. By attending religious and spiritual services as well as religious community activities on a repeated basis, one has the opportunity to attend to, retain, repeat, and be inspired to engage in desired target behaviors, to obtain corrective feedback and support from others, and to better perfect the target behavior or behaviors in question.

For example, perhaps an important virtue that religious traditions typically encourage is charity. Religious services might offer sacred readings on how religious models (e.g., Jesus) behaved in a charitable manner. Religious leaders such as priests, rabbis, pastors, and other ministers might model charity in their behavior with congregants. Finally, congregants might be encouraged and reinforced to be charitable with opportunities for volunteerism and donations to causes supported by the religious community made available.

Research has demonstrated that people do learn from spiritual models, including not only famous religious figures but also family, friends, neighbors, and others. They learn to behave in a spiritual, religious, and ethical manner by observing and mimicking others.[9, 10]

Are Religious People More Ethical?

Do we need religion and spirituality to be ethical or to be good? Most moral philosophers would say no . . . but it can help.[5] People can certainly maintain ethical perspectives and subscribe to ethical principles without engagement in religious or spiritual beliefs, institutions, or practices. However, there are few secular forums that can offer the guidance, fellowship, support, models, and engagement that the religious institutions offer. These organizations have a wide variety of comprehensive services, programming, groups, readings, models, and so forth that can regularly impart and support ethical principles and guidelines to their members. The secular community just doesn't seem to have the organizational structure to do so. There are some exceptions, of course. For example, the Boy Scouts is technically a secular organization not affiliated with one particular religious tradition that offers a clear set of ethical principles that tend to use a virtue approach to ethics (e.g., Scouts are loyal, courteous, kind, thrifty, reverent, . . .). Perhaps self-help groups based on the Alcoholic Anonymous (AA) model do the same. While not affiliated with any particular religious tradition, the 12 steps of AA are spiritually focused, with numerous references to God and His will. AA offers ethical principles that highlight virtues such as honesty, integrity, and responsibility. So it appears that one doesn't have to be religious or spiritual to be ethical, but it might help to have the organizational structure that religion offers to encourage and reinforce ethical principles and behavior.

Religious engagement and practice encourages "clean living." Religious people are less likely to engage in criminal behavior, marital infidelity, alcoholism, or unprotected sexual activity as well as being more likely to engage in prosocial behaviors such as volunteerism and charity (for reviews, see notes 11–13). Thus, those who tend to report being spiritual, religious, or both tend to behave themselves better.

Conclusion

Religion and spirituality encourage ethical behavior in their sacred scripture readings, in their models or exemplars for behavior (not only well-known religious figures such as saints and founding members of religious traditions but also among religious elders, pastors, teachers, and congregants). Research suggests that religion- and spirituality-minded people behave better than those not affiliated with a religious or spiritual tradition or institution. Religious people tend to be better citizens by engaging in charity and volunteerism and not engaging in criminal and antisocial behavior that might harm others.

As stated at the beginning of this chapter, if what might be required of us is to "love mercy, do justice, and walk humbly with God" (Micah 6:8), then ethical behavior and a better world should result. And if compassion is indeed the core of all of the major religious traditions, according to scholars,[1] then the world can be a better place if these ideals are upheld by those who claim to be religious and spiritual.

Notes

1. Armstrong, K. (2006). *The great transformation: The beginning of our religious traditions.* New York: Anchor Books.
2. Von Staden, H. (1996 translation). In a pure and holy way: Personal and professional conduct in the Hippocratic Oath. *Journal of the History of Medicine and Allied Sciences, 51,* 406–408.

3. Kruger, J., & Dunning, A. (1999). *Hans Kung: New horizons for faith and thoughts*. London: SCM Press Ltd.

4. Plante, T. G. (2004). *Do the right thing: Living ethically in an unethical world*. Oakland, CA: New Harbinger.

5. Rachels, J., & Rachels, S. (2010). *The elements of moral philosophy* (6th ed.). New York: McGraw-Hill.

6. Boy Scouts of America. (2005). *Boy Scout handbook* (11th ed.). Irving, TX: Author.

7. Bandura, A. (1986). *Social foundations of thought and action*. Englewood Cliffs, NJ: Prentice Hall.

8. Bandura, A. (2003). On the psychosocial impact and mechanisms of spiritual modeling. *International Journal for the Psychology of Religion, 13*, 167–174.

9. Oman, D., Shapiro, S., Thoresen, C. E., Flinders, T., Driskill, J. D., & Plante, T. G. (2007). Learning from spiritual models and meditation: A randomized evaluation of a college course. *Pastoral Psychology, 55*, 473–493.

10. Oman, D., Thoresen, C. E., Park, C. L., Shaver, P. R., Hood, R., & Plante, T. G. (2009). How does one become spiritual? The Spiritual Modeling Inventory of Life Environments (SMILE). *Mental Health, Religion & Culture, 12*, 427–456.

11. Plante, T. G. (2009). *Spiritual practices in psychotherapy: Thirteen tools for enhancing psychological health*. Washington, DC: American Psychological Association.

12. Plante, T. G., & Thoresen, C. E. (Eds.), (2007). *Spirit, science and health: How the spiritual mind fuels physical wellness*. Westport, CT: Praeger/Greenwood.

13 Plante, T. G., & Sherman, A. S. (Eds.), (2001). *Faith and health: Psychological perspectives*. New York: Guilford.

7

Tolerance

Richard L. Gorsuch and Aubyn Fulton

Tolerance is a "fruit of the Spirit" supported by most religious groups, with numerous religiously inspired leaders being noted for their encouragement of tolerance toward others. These range from Gandhi to Jesus to the Buddha. A contemporary example is the way in which Islam serves as a uniting factor across tribal and national boundaries in the non–Israel Middle East. However, Islam's hatred of Israel as well as the support by Christian leaders for slavery in the history of the United States suggests that religions may have an Achilles' heel, producing prejudice toward others. How, then, can religions encourage tolerance toward all?

To address these questions, we will need to recognize the complexity of the definitions of *tolerance* and *prejudice*. The definition of *tolerance* is rather straightforward—acceptance of others despite differences of beliefs or customs—while "prejudice is a stereotypical prejudgment based on group membership without recognition of the individual's characteristics."[1] (While the definition allows for a positive prejudice, the general psychological practice is to consider only negative prejudgments as prejudice.)

While these definitions are clear, their applications become fuzzy. There are groups that we do feel justified is treating negatively based on a characteristic universal to that group. Consider, for example, when intolerance is strongly supported by a group. Can we be tolerant of the intolerant? Or consider a child rapist. Can we tolerate that person as a part of normal society? Can a neighbor who is a rape victim accept them as neighbors given the high risk of recidivism? Such examples show that, for many, there are basic values that lead us to accept or reject another person based on their behavior. In fact, many would add to the definitions just given, including in the definition of *tolerance* a "fair and objective" treatment of others despite our differences with them, and in *prejudice*'s definition an "unreasonable" rejection formed "without knowledge or thought." This allows for a community to jail some to protect society or to restrict them in other ways. But who defines what is fair or reasonable? Gorsuch, for example, has rejected just war theory on this issue of defining "just": both sides of a war always deems it just from their point of view.[1] There is no clear way to define and assure that "fair," "objective," and "reasonable" are indeed fair, objective, and reasonable.

A solution to the problem of intolerance toward others is to "love the sinner and hate the sin." The definition of tolerance itself implies this. For tolerance to occur, there must be an unwelcome difference. We welcome those who believe the same as we do, but we tolerate those who object to our beliefs or behave in a manner with which we disagree. So there must be some negative judgment toward those we tolerate for it to be tolerance. Without the negative judgment, we would use terms such as *acceptance* or *affirmation* or *apathy* toward the belief or behavior. And in the area of the negative judgment itself, tolerance means we may continue to strive against them on a difference (but not to the extent of denying them their civil rights, such as their freedoms to argue against us) . . .

There is still one more definitional issue that needs to be raised. Prejudice occurs when a rejection occurs based on group membership, not on an individual's characteristics. It is active. When taking the social distance measure, a prejudiced person says that all people of group X should be denied their civil rights solely because of this group membership.[2] . . . But tolerance can be inactive. The tolerant person just does nothing about the other person. The problem here is knowing if that person has an objection to the other person's beliefs or behavior or whether they just "don't care." Kerlinger examined liberal and conservative attitudes independently of each other.[3] He reports that the two most common positions are (1) those in which the person wants to help others by a mixture of both liberal and conservative approaches and (2) those who do not want to help others by either method. But the psychological research on prejudice does not distinguish between the tolerant and the apathetic. Grouped with tolerant people—who differ from another person in some significant way—are those who just do not care about the other person one way or another. Given that the apathetic have not been separated from the tolerant, all the results found for unprejudiced people may or may not be results for either apathy or tolerance.

"Loving the sinner but not the sin" is a tolerant position. It recognizes that there are differences—the sin—but that otherwise, one has a positive attitude toward the other. However, this is a difficult position for people to hold and live by. We people make wholistic judgments about others. It has long been known as "the halo effect": When we like a person on one important factor, we judge them highly on all positive factors. An example comes from student ratings of classes. Having been involved in several faculty committees on student evaluation of courses, we have seen the desire to separate different aspects of a class, such as the manner of lecturing versus the content of the lectures versus the value of the homework. Despite clear differences in item content, measures from every area correlate so highly with the single item "how did you like this class?" that they add little additional information. While it is referred to as the "halo" effect, it can also be a "horns" effect in that a major negative evaluation in one area leads us to negatively evaluate the faculty person in another area (prejudice). So how can we encourage people to separate their judgments of another to be tolerant toward one with whom we disagree on an issue?

Our plan for addressing how tolerance can be a fruit of the Spirit is to first present the relationship of religion to prejudice/tolerance and then consider ways in which prejudice can be transformed into tolerance. As almost all of the research on religion and prejudice has been done with Christians in the United States, we shall discuss these issues from that perspective. That also allows us to speak from our own religious culture, recognizing that other religious cultures also address these issues from their perspectives.

The prejudices addressed are prejudice based on race and prejudice based on sexual orientation. The former is recognized throughout U.S. contemporary mainstream culture as unjust. The goal in this case is affirmation of the person, including of the distinctive racial features. The latter, however, is seen by some as unjust and by others as just. To what extent, then, do those who claim a just reason for rejecting homosexuality separate the sin from the sinner? How can we encourage tolerance where one may reject something like homosexuality but still accept the person?

Research

Almost every modern discussion of the relationship of religion to prejudice has included the defining observation made by Gordon Allport in 1954[4] that "The role of religion is paradoxical. It makes prejudice and it unmakes prejudice." After more than a half a century of scientific research, we still see this paradoxical role of religion, and it has not yet been fully explained. Allport theorized that what he originally called mature religion was incompatible with prejudice and enhanced tolerance, while it was primarily immature religion that drove prejudice.[5] Allport's later operationalization of mature and immature religion as intrinsic (a genuine commitment to religious values and ends) and extrinsic (an exploitative use of religion as a means to some other end) as religious orientations drove much of the empirical study of religion and prejudice in the second half of the 20th century. However, whereas Allport conceptualized intrinsic (I) and extrinsic (E) as opposite ends of a continuum, the research found I and E to be uncorrelated and that E has two components: Extrinsic Personal (Ep) and Extrinsic Social (Es).[6, 7] The former describes turning to religion for relief from problems and the latter as participating in religion to develop relationships with others (although Gorsuch and McPherson[7] noted that the mean of Extrinsic Social was so low that few college students now are religious for this reason alone). Note that the items are worded that the "only reason" or "main reason" for being religious is I, Ep, or Es. If these terms are excluded, all these items correlate together. Allport's intent was to identify the master motive and not what intrinsic religious people would identify as secondary benefits.

A recent meta-analysis of all such studies published between 1964 and 2008 found a small but significant positive relationship between intrinsic religion and racial tolerance and a larger positive relationship between extrinsic religion and racial prejudice.[8] One complication to Allport's religious-orientation paradigm is evidence suggesting the existence of another orientation, labeled "Quest."[9, 10, 11] This is conceptualized as a flexible, questioning approach to religion. This is, it should be noted, uncorrelated with I, Es, and Ep; for example, there are as many high Is as low Is among those high on Quest. While some wonder if Quest should be considered a religious orientation at all, since it is defined in part by valuing exploration more than commitment, and there are some stubborn methodological problems in much of the research, there does seem to be a subset of self-identified Christians who value flexibility and openness in their religious commitments, and these appear to be among the most tolerant in the Christian population.[12]

Compared to the early research on religious orientations, two other religious variables, religious fundamentalism (RF) and right-wing authoritarianism (RWA), have been found to play a stronger and more consistent role in prejudice. The most commonly used approach to RF in relationship to prejudice has been based on the work of Altemeyer and Hunsberger,[13] who define it as the belief that there is a single set of knowable and perfectly true teachings, divinely revealed, that must be rigidly followed to fight evil forces. As formulated, this understanding of fundamentalism is intended to be distinct from any specific belief content. There are many RFs who hold to specific Christian doctrines (see, for example, Laythe, Finkey, Bringle, & Kirkpatrick[14]). Studies of RF have found very strong associations with prejudice.

The construct of RWA, rooted in classic studies of authoritarianism by Adorno and colleagues[15, 4, 5] after World War II and refined and measured by Altemeyer,[16] appears to be the most consistent and strongest variable associated with prejudice (see, for example, Laythe, Finkel, & Kirkpatrick[17]). RWA consists of three elements: conventionalism, authoritarian submission, and authoritarian aggression. The studies show these elements to be common among religious people. Some studies have shown that when RF and RWA are both controlled for, Christian belief is correlated with tolerance, or at least less correlated with prejudice.[14] This might suggest that perhaps Christian belief is the factor that unmakes prejudice, while the more toxic traits of RWA and RF are what make prejudice. Predictably, the picture is more complicated than that. In a recent study, Mavor, Louis, and Laythe[18] provide evidence that the three components of RWA are distinct and to some extent unique, with conventionalism correlating more highly with RF than the other two RWA components of aggression and submission. Their analysis showed that when this is taken into account, Christian belief reduces prejudice less than previously thought, and the usefulness of the unified construct of RWA is brought into question. This would still suggest that the two constructs of authoritarian aggression and submission, and fundamentalism/conventionalism, are responsible for much of the association between religion and prejudice. If so, it might be possible that an approach to religion that minimized these elements might also be associated with decreases in prejudice.

One problem with the earlier religious-orientation data has to do with distinguishing between the effects of religious faith on the one hand and cultural conformity on the other (note that we use the term *cultural* to refer to the society in which a person lives and *religious* or *group* to refer to the religious group with which the person participates). This was the basis of Gorsuch and Aleshire[19] noting that religion and blatant, overt prejudice were found more in the occasional church attender than in the intrinsic, frequent attender or the nonattender of that era. The casual attenders were conformist, they suggested, to a society that was both racist and Christian in name. They also noted that the curvilinear relationship found at the end of a blatantly prejudiced era would not be likely to be found in research after that era (post –970) because society was no longer so overtly, blatantly raciest. Although few have checked for a curvilinear relationship, recent work such as that of Hood, Hill, and Spilka[12] has assumed that there would be no curvilinearity for racism. However, according to Gorsuch and Alshire,[19] a curvilinear relationship would be predicted if there were a blatant, overt prejudice in a pro–Christian society, a prediction confirmed by Ponton and Gorsuch.[20] Since racial prejudice was increasingly defined as socially undesirable as the 20th century progressed, individuals who had a strong need to be seen as desirable would be more likely to deny it.[21] In that sense Extrinsic Christians, who reported more racial prejudice, might be seen as expressing their genuine attitudes even when socially undesirable. This argument is supported by findings that Intrinsic Christians tended to score higher on measures of socially desirable beliefs and behaviors.[19] Of course, it could also be true that Intrinsic Christians who sincerely attempt to live out their commitments not only have less racial prejudice but also genuinely have more other socially desirable beliefs and behavior when their religious group has a position like that of the culture.

One way of trying to get at the effect of social conformity has been to compare proscribed forms of prejudice (prejudice that is discouraged in the social group being studied) and nonproscribed prejudice (prejudice that is encouraged, or at least acceptable, in the group being studied). If decreased prejudice were actually associated with religious belief instead of social conformity, we would expect to see Christians demonstrating not just less proscribed prejudice (which could simply be conforming to the demands of their culture) but also less nonproscribed prejudice (which might require them to go against the social pressure of their culture). This has not always been the case. For example, in the 1980s, before the end of apartheid, Intrinsic (the kinds of Christians Allport thought were more genuine and mature) Afrikaners in South Africa were more prejudiced against blacks, presumably because such prejudice was a part of their religion at that time.[22] However, evidence was also found that the Intrinsic English speakers in South Africa were less prejudiced because their religion did not support the prejudice. Around the same time, Intrinsic Seventh Day Adventists in St. Croix, Virgin Islands, were found to be more negative toward Rastafarians, competitors in the religious market, who were generally viewed negatively by the local Adventist culture.[23]

By far the most common form of antipathy due to religious norms that has been studied is negative attitudes toward homosexuals.[18] For the most part, studies suggest that across a variety of religious variables, including Intrinsic, Christians have been found to have more negative attitudes toward homosexuals.[12] The fairly broad findings that Christians tend to be more tolerant with some targets but not with other targets suggests that conformity to religious group values plays at least some significant role in the relationship.

The above also suggests that Allport's view was more characterological while the data show the religion tolerance issue to be more social group oriented. In Allport's view, all Intrinsics should be the same regardless of the values of the religious group. That is not so. As the above shows, the norms of the religious group are important. As Snook and Gorsuch[22] found as well as the research on RF and on homosexuality, the direction of the correlation is determined by the nature of the religion that is internalized.

However, the difference between proscribed and nonproscribed prejudice is greater than simply the former being disapproved and the latter approved by the religious culture. Religiously nonproscribed prejudice often includes not just social conformity but also the reflection of historically and culturally plausible interpretations of religious text and doctrine.

It is possible that committed, conservative American Christians who express negative attitudes toward homosexuals are not just conforming to their subculture but are also following what they genuinely believe to be the requirements of their authoritative religious texts. However, these same Christians also believe in the commandment "Love your neighbor as yourself." If so, then we would expect to see evidence that these Christians are able to show relevant distinctions in their negative reactions to homosexuals. For example, while such Christians might express moral disapproval of homosexual behavior, they should still be willing to interact with them in normal social activities and should still be in favor of homosexuals having the same basic civil rights and privileges as heterosexuals. Fulton, Gorsuch, and Maynard[2] suggested that this kind of dissociation between morally legitimated antipathy toward homosexuals and nonmoralized civil tolerance could be seen as an index of the ability to "love the sinner and hate the sin."

Commonly used measures of antipathy against homosexuals include items that relate to both moral and nonmoral aspects and so potentially confuse the two. Fulton and colleagues[2] did report evidence for dissociation between moral and nonmoral antipathy toward homosexuals, and similar findings have been reported by other investigators.[24, 25, 26] Still, other studies have not found evidence that religious people are able to reliably distinguish between their antipathy for behavior they judge to be immoral (the "sin") and the people who engage in this behavior (the "sinners").[27, 28] As Fulton and colleagues[2] pointed out, even if logically and, occasionally, empirically demonstrated as possible, the cognitive and emotional operations required to distinguish and isolate genuinely held moral judgments of behavior from prejudicial treatment of the people who engage in that behavior are no doubt complex and demanding, and thus probably relatively rare. More research may allow better understanding of these operations and of ways of increasing them.

Another way of looking at the role of cultural conformity in the relationship between religion and prejudice has been to compare explicit versus implicit prejudice. Explicit prejudice refers to feelings about outgroups that are accessible to conscious awareness, under more voluntary control, more situationally flexible, and usually measured through self-report. Implicit prejudice is often less accessible to awareness, is more difficult to control, and is often measured through indirect behavioral measures such as reaction time.[29] Implicit attitudes are thought to result from repeated exposure to associations between the target and negative stimuli, such as might be common when brought up in a racist, sexist, or homophobic subculture. With direct measures, Intrinsic subjects reported themselves to be less aggressive than others but were not different in their experimentally observed behavior.[30, 31]

Rowat and colleagues[32, 33, 34] investigated the relationship of religion to proscribed and nonproscribed prejudice as measured by the Implicit Association Test (IAT), which is seen as reflecting automatic, unconscious attitudes. Rowatt and Franklin[32] found that RWA was the main religious variable associated with explicit prejudice against blacks (proscribed), and Rowatt, Tsang, Kelly, LaMartina, McCullers, and McKinley[34] found the same for homosexuals (nonproscribed). RWA was only found to be correlated with implicit prejudice against blacks.[32] For implicit prejudice against homosexuals, the most important variable was Intrinsic religion.[34] Similarly, implicit prejudice against another nonproscribed group (Muslims) was most associated with a measure of Christian orthodoxy.[33] These findings have been interpreted as suggesting that nonproscribed prejudicial attitudes (e.g., prejudice against homosexuals) is an "internalized implicit component" of intrinsic religion, while proscribed prejudicial attitudes are not.[12]

The investigation into religion, prejudice, and social conformity suggests that what we might call "genuine" Christian commitment (Intrinsic religion, orthodox Christian belief) is most often associated with either explicit tolerance (in the case of proscribed racial prejudice) or at least the absence of prejudice (for nonproscribed sexual orientation). Explicit tolerance does not have to be seen as nothing but the disingenuous expression of social conformity. The difference between explicit and implicit tolerance is not so much genuineness as degree of awareness and voluntary control. Genuine Christian commitments seem to do best at encourage loving (or at least discouraging hateful) attitudes toward proscribed groups—that is, the groups that Christians are most aware of their duty to be loving and kind toward. Genuine Christian commitments seem to have less impact on encouraging loving attitudes toward nonproscribed groups, who might be seen as groups that Christians are less aware of their duty to be loving and kind toward, or perhaps groups that do not activate the loving and kind schemas associated with their Christian faith. In this sense, the goal of fighting prejudice, for Christians, is to do a better job of having unfamiliar groups activate the core schemas of their faith commitments. Fulton and colleagues[2] found that Intrinsic Christians reported the desire for the same amount of social distance from sexually active homosexuals as they did from other groups who engaged in behavior they defined as sinful (such as bigots and liars), perhaps in part because being asked directly about desired social distance from target groups activated relevant schemas related to love and justice associated with their Christian faith.

While the evidence does seem to suggest that the more implicit, automatic kinds of nonproscribed prejudice are associated with even the most genuine forms of Christian commitment, the good news is that there is evidence that even these less voluntary implicit prejudicial attitudes can be controlled and minimized with higher levels of self-awareness. This would suggest that implicit prejudice can be fought, and the fight can be aided by greater familiarity with the target of the prejudice and with the principles of the Christian faith that emphasize love and justice.

The complexity of the religion–prejudice–tolerance relationship is expanded when we broaden our focus away from internal mechanisms and include intergroup effects. Hood and colleagues[12] summarize the argument, based on realistic group conflict theory,[35] that people who identify with a specific group and who perceive themselves to be in conflict with other groups tend to exhibit greater levels of intergroup tension and antipathy. This is exacerbated when the competing group is perceived to pose a threat to core values.[36] Most of the religious measures discussed above (orientation, orthodoxy, fundamentalism) are associated with stronger in-group identification, and Jackson and Hunsberger[37] found them all to be associated with more negativity toward a variety of out-groups. In this sense, religion can lead to or at least exacerbate prejudice simply by increasing in-group identification and the out-group hostility that often flows from that.

Promoting Tolerance as a Fruit of the Spirit

At this point, we must acknowledge a limitation of psychology of religion. The research is on correlates of prejudice, but there has been almost no research on how to reduce prejudice and increase tolerance. Hence, this selection must be more speculative than empirical.

From the literature review, intolerance among religious people seems to be, first, a product of right-wing authoritarianism, religious fundamentalism, and being a non–Questing person. In our judgment, all of these share two critical elements. The first element is a conviction that one is a member of a group that *already knows* what is true and good. The second element is that they have a conviction that they could not possibly be wrong, and everyone else is wrong. Classical theology would consider this the sin of pride. The problems of pride, one suspects, are the same as those of high self-esteem: devaluing others.[1] And it may be that a more contemporary philosophy that acknowledges human limitations and that there is no absolute foundation upon which to build truth might be helpful.[1] And in terms of the fruits of the Spirit, we also recommend the current project's chapter on humility.

A social psychological perspective sees these issues in terms of ethnocentrism, that is, the fact that all ethnic groups—unless there are special circumstances—look down on others. It has been found in the most nominal of groups, that is, groups that only exist momentarily and with no interaction among their members. It is so pervasive, so automatic, and yet so divisive that Gorsuch has suggested it is a good interpretation of original sin.[1] To summarize briefly, the Christian concept of original sin has Adam (the first man) and Eve (the first woman) living without sin. In that state, they walk and talk with God and do not even notice they are naked. God warns them to not eat of the fruit of a particular tree. They talk together and trust their own evaluation more than they trust God's and so eat the fruit. This is classical ethnocentric effect: Our views (Adam and Eve) are better than others' views (God's). God is then an outsider, Adam and Eve are embarrassed by their nakedness, and humans have been separated from God ever since. And we all repeat the sin of thinking our views are better than those of any other group without even noticing what we are doing.

This Christian interpretation of ethnocentrism shows that religions often have theological material that can be meaningfully related to ethnocentrism and tolerance. Religious variables such as Intrinsic and RF identify people who are strongly committed to their religious faith. Therefore, elements of their religious faith that promote tolerance may be useful for fighting ethnocentrism. As we are not experts in world religions, we shall use the religion we do know, American Protestant Christianity, to suggest some theological material that should be helpful with these people. As the religious fundamentalists have a particularly strong view of the Bible as normative, we shall use those materials as examples.

Jesus gave two great commandments: first, "you shall love the Lord your God with all your heart, mind, and soul" and then "you shall love your neighbor as yourself." The critical point for tolerance is the answer Jesus gave when he was immediately asked "Who is my neighbor?" Jesus responded with the parable of the "Good Samaritan" in which a Samaritan proves to be a good neighbor to a Jew (Luke 10: 25–37). The ethnocentrism is apparent in the title, for the Jewish audience assumed that all Samaritans would be far from "good" unless explicitly described as such. Samaritans were seen as traitors to Judaism, and no Jew was allowed to associated with such evil people. For Jesus to pick this despised group to be an example of fulfilling the Second Commandment is a clear attack on ethnocentrism. Jesus also lived with tolerance to the point that he was accused as being too much involved with outcast groups (Matt. 9:11). After Jesus, the New Testament constantly fits ethnocentrism. For example, Paul wrote, "there is neither Jew nor Greek . . . slave nor free . . . male nor female" (Gal. 3:28) to a culture where the lines of ethnocentrism were clearly drawn by these categories.

Prominent in the New Testament is also the image of God as "our father." The family is our most intimate group, and acceptance into the family is the clearest evidence for tolerance in the social distance measures often used to measure ethnocentrism and prejudice. This is the importance of Adam and Eve not noticing their nakedness when with God until they formed a group separate from God, that is, until God was no longer family. Biblically, God is seen as not just the father of Christians but of all peoples. The story is told in missionary circles of a 20th-century New Guinea man who, after being convinced that the Bible did stress that God is father to us all, remarked: "That's the first good reason anyone has given me not to eat people. You don't eat family." Instead, one accepts or tolerates family.

Theology such as the above can be used to help Christians become more tolerant toward peoples who differ due to race, national origin, and other such ethnocentric variables. But, as noted above, the Christian faith has values, and values lead to intolerance. Our contemporary example is homosexuality. Those who hold to a literal interpretation of the Bible hold that God has stated homosexuality is a sin, and there are no offsetting scriptures such as noted above regarding slavery, gender, and nationality. Can one promote tolerance in cases when a forbidden behavior is involved?

A widely used statement applicable to this situation is "Love the sinner but not the sin." Fulton and colleagues[2] and Rosik and colleagues[26] have examined this possibility. They found that Christians did, to some degree, follow this principle. When items about values favorable to homosexual behavior were removed from scales used to measure rejection of homosexuality, the Christians showed that they were more accepting of homosexuals than of homosexual behavior. So a theologically based intervention to increase tolerance of people among Christians would be to teach that we should love the sinner even if we reject the sin. Of course, the value differences between antihomosexual Christians and prohomosexuals would still remain.

While psychology of religion has not tested ideas such as those above, psychology in general has investigated some strategies for reducing prejudice. Jackson,[38] in reviewing interventions, suggests that it is the norm of tolerance that becomes effective. When groups pride themselves on including a variety of otherwise hostile ethnocentric groups, tolerance increases. This norm of tolerance and acceptance appears to be a natural outgrowth of theological intervention such as suggested above.

Jackson[38] notes that a limitation in programs that directly address the problems of rejection of a group is that the exercise itself makes the distinguishing characteristic more salient, that is, it is more likely to come to mind. Ethnocentrism only occurs when the person perceives the difference (but may not be consciously aware of the perception). The more salient the characteristic, the more often it will be perceived and ethnocentrism will result. This appears to be one reason many multicultural programs in the workplace fail. Such programs, Johnson concludes, often produce a rebound effect of more prejudice at a later time. Programs using theology as suggested above may need to include a sufficient variety of examples to, hopefully, reduce the rebound effect.

Jackson[38] reviews the contact hypothesis—that people spending time with each other reduces prejudice. That is a practice that has proven to often bring as much harm as good. Realistic group-conflict theory notes that people can be brought together when there is a strong, superordinate (interlocking) goal. Such a goal occurs when the situation is not just "win-win" but also "lose-lose" for everyone. A second condition is that people from the different groups have the skills and background to contribute on an equal basis. If these conditions are not met, contact will increase prejudice.

The research summarized by Jackson has not involved religious groups, but we can suggest some hypotheses from that work. For example, many U.S. religious groups have "mission trips" during which a group of young people, for example, goes to another section of the United States or another country to help in a project, such as working on a water system. Insomuch as the local people provide many of the skills and expertise in a project that interlocks the goals of the local people and the youth, we hypothesis that the youth will decrease in prejudice toward them.

Religious schools that are multicultural also have potential for increasing tolerance among the subcultures involved if the several groups have comparable skills. This generally occurs if the schools start at the youngest age so that each group develops comparable academic skills. Otherwise, the task will be more difficult. Religious schools do have one problem: By their nature, it is difficult to be multireligious. With tolerance including tolerance toward other religions, public schools have an inherent advantage as multiple religious groups are involved in a setting that can involve many interlocking goals.

These few suggestions are offered as starting points. The goal is to reduce the problem noted by Allport so that religions will reduce prejudice and increase tolerance more than they increase prejudice and intolerance.

Notes

1. Gorsuch, R. L. (2002). *Integrating psychology and spirituality?* Westport, CT: Praeger.
2. Fulton, A. S., Gorsuch, R. L., & Maynard, E. A. (1999). Religious orientation, antihomosexual sentiment, and fundamentalism among Christians. *Journal for the Scientific Study of Religion, 38*(1), 14–35.

3. Kerlinger, F. N. (1984). *Liberalism and conservatism: The nature and structure of social attitudes*. Hillsdale, NJ: Erlbaum.

4. Allport, G. W. (1954). *The nature of prejudice*. Cambridge, MA: Addison-Wesley.

5. Allport, G. W. (1950). *The individual and his religion*. New York: Macmillan.

6. Kirkpatrick, L. A. (1989). A psychometric analysis of the Allpot-Ross and Feagin measures of intrinsic-extrinsic religious orientations. In M. L. Lynn & D. O. Moberg (Eds.), *Research in the social scientific study of religion* (Vol. 1, pp. 1–31). Greenwich, CT: JAI Press.

7. Gorsuch, R. L., & McPherson, S. E. (1989). Intrinsic/extrinsic measurement: I/E—Revised and single-item scales. *Journal for the Scientific Study of Religion, 28*(3), 348–354. doi:10.2307/1386745

8. Hall, D. L., Matz, D. C., & Wood, W. (2010). Why don't we practice what we preach? A meta-analytic review of religious racism: Erratum. *Personality and Social Psychology Review, 14*(2) 126–139.

9. Batson, C. (1976). Religion as prosocial: Agent or double agent? *Journal for the Scientific Study of Religion, 15*(1), 29–45.

10. Batson, C. (1990). Good Samaritans—or priests and Levites? Using William James as a guide in the study of religious prosocial motivation. *Personality and Social Psychology Bulletin, 16*(4), 758–768.

11. Batson, C., Eidelman, S. H., Higley, S. L., & Russel, S. A. (2001). "And who is my neighbor?" II: Quest religion as a source of universal compassion. *Journal for the Scientific Study of Religion, 40*(1), 39–50.

12. Hood, R., Hill, P. C., & Spilka, B. (2009). *The psychology of religion: An empirical approach* (4th ed.). New York: Guilford Press.

13. Altemeyer, B., & Hunsberger, B. (1992). Authoritarianism, religious fundamentalism, quest, and prejudice. *International Journal for the Psychology of Religion, 2*, 113–133.

14. Laythe, B., Finkel, D., Bringle, R., & Kirkpatrick, L. (2002). Religious fundamentalism as a predictor of prejudice: A two-component model. *Journal for the Scientific Study of Religion, 41*, 623–635.

15. Adorno, T. W., Frenkel-Brunswik, E., Levinson, D. J., & Sanford, R. N. (1950). *The authoritarian personality*. New York: Harper & Row.

16. Altemeyer, B. (1996). *The authoritarian specter*. Cambridge, MA: Harvard University Press.

17. Laythe, B., Finkel, D., & Kirkpatrick, L. A. (2001). Predicting prejudice from religious fundamentalism and right-wing authoritarianism: A multiple-regression approach. *Journal for the Scientific Study of Religion, 40*(1), 1–10.

18. Mavor, K. I., Louis, W. R., & Laythe, B. (2011). Religion, prejudice, and authoritarianism: Is RWA a boon or bane to the psychology of religion? *Journal for the Scientific Study of Religion, 50*(1), 22–43.

19. Gorsuch, R. L., & Aleshire, D. (1974). Christian faith and ethnic prejudice: A review and interpretation of research. *Journal for the Scientific Study of Religion, 13*, 281–307.

20. Ponton, M. O., & Gorsuch, R. L. (1988). Prejudice and religion revisited: A cross-cultural investigation with a Venezuelan sample. *Journal for the Scientific Study of Religion, 27*(2), 260–271.

21. Sedikides, C., & Gebauer, J. E. (2010). Religiosity as self-enhancement: A meta-analysis of the relation between socially desirable responding and religiosity. *Personality and Social Psychology Review, 14*(1), 17–36.

22. Snook, S. C., & Gorsuch, R. L. (1985). *Religious orientation and racial prejudice in South Africa*. Paper presented at the 93rd Annual Convention of the American Psychological Association, Los Angeles, CA.

23. Griffin, G. A. E., Gorsuch, R. L., & Davis, A. L. (1987). A cross-cultural investigation of religious orientation, social norms, and prejudice. *Journal for the Scientific Study of Religion, 26*(3), 358–365. doi:10.2307/1386437

24. Ford, T. E., Brignall, T., VanValey, T. L., & Macaluso, M. J. (2009). The unmaking of prejudice: How Christian beliefs relate to attitudes toward homosexuals. *Journal for the Scientific Study of Religion, 48*(1), 146–160.

25. Mak, H. K., & Tsang, J. (2008). Separating the "sinner" from the "sin": Religious orientation and prejudiced behavior toward sexual orientation and promiscuous sex. *Journal for the Scientific Study of Religion, 47*(3), 379–392.

26. Rosik, C. H., Griffith, B. A., & Cruz, Z. (2007). Homophobia and conservative religion: Toward a more nuanced understanding. *American Journal of Orthopsychiatry, 7,* 10–19.

27. Altemeyer, B., & Hunsberger, B. (1993). Response to Gorsuch. *International Journal for the Psychology of Religion, 3,* 33–37.

28. Batson, C., Floyd, R. B., Meyer, J. M., & Winner, A. L. (1999). 'And who is my neighbor?' Intrinsic religion as a source of universal compassion. *Journal for the Scientific Study of Religion, 38*(4), 445–457.

29. Henry, P. J., & Hardin, C. D. (2006). The contact hypothesis revisited: Status bias in the reduction of implicit prejudice in the United States and Lebanon. *Psychological Science, 17*(10), 862–868.

30. Greer, T., Berman, M., Varan, V., Bobrycki, L., & Watson, S. (2005). We are a religious people; we are a vengeful people. *Journal for the Scientific Study of Religion, 44*(1), 45–57.

31. Leach, M. M., Berman, M. E., & Eubanks, L. (2008). Religious activities, religious orientation, and aggressive behavior. *Journal for the Scientific Study of Religion, 47*(2), 311–319.

32. Rowatt, W. C., & Franklin, L. M. (2004). Christian orthodoxy, religious fundamentalism, and right-wing authoritarianism as predictors of implicit racial prejudice. *International Journal for the Psychology of Religion, 14*(2), 125–138.

33. Rowatt, W. C., Franklin, L. M., & Cotton, M. (2005). Patterns and personality correlates of implicit and explicit attitudes toward Christians and Muslims. *Journal for the Scientific Study of Religion, 44*(1), 29–43.

34. Rowatt, W. C., Tsang, J., Kelly, J., LaMartina, B., McCullers, M., & McKinley, A. (2006). Associations between religious personality dimensions and implicit homosexual prejudice. *Journal for the Scientific Study of Religion, 45*(3), 397–406.

35. Sherif, M. (1966). *The psychology of social norms.* Oxford, UK: Harper Torchbooks.

36. Jackson, L. M., & Esses, V. M. (1997). Of scripture and ascription: The relation between religious fundamentalism and intergroup helping. *Personality and Social Psychology Bulletin, 23*(8), 893–906.

37. Jackson, L. M., & Hunsberger, B. (1999). An intergroup perspective on religion and prejudice. *Journal for the Scientific Study of Religion*, 38(4), 509–523.

38. Jackson, L. M. (2011). *The psychology of prejudice*. Washington, DC: American Psychological Association.

8

Loving-Kindness

Shauna L. Shapiro and Megha Sahgal

In recent years, there has been great interest in the capacity of meditative and spiritual practices to decrease illness and increase well-being.[1] The majority of the research has focused on transcendental meditation (TM) and mindfulness meditation (MM), with promising results including decreases in stress, depression, anxiety, and pain and increases in attention, satisfaction with life, positive mood, and well-being.[2] Yet very little attention has focused on the effects of loving-kindness meditation. The current chapter explores the practice of loving-kindness meditation (LKM), reviews current research on its effects, and theorizes about how LKM contributes to well-being. Future directions and implications are also discussed.

All spiritual and religious traditions advocate the cultivation of compassion and kindness. In Buddhism, a specific meditation practice called loving-kindness meditation aims intentionally at the cultivation of kindness, friendliness, and care for oneself and all beings. Loving-kindness, or Metta meditation, was first described in the 2,500-year-old Pali canon, the sacred text of various sects of Tibetan Buddhism, as a way to increase feelings of warmth and caring for oneself and for others. LKM is defined as an unconditional love, characterized by an open, friendly, accepting attention.[3] LKM focuses on cultivating positive emotions through intentionally directing the mind toward feelings of openness, friendliness, and care toward oneself and all beings.

By intentionally directing our mind in this way, we are able to directly transform an emotional landscape of negative emotions into one of positive emotions that contribute to greater life satisfaction. Of importance is that these positive emotions are generated by internal mechanisms and are independent of external circumstances. Thus, LKM offers a process of cultivating positive emotions that is unconditioned, not based on external conditions.

Loving-kindness is traditionally taught as part of a four-part meditation practice referred to as the Brahma Viharas, or four divine emotions that are believed to create positive and peaceful states of being. Compassion (Karuna), empathic joy (Mudita), and equanimity (Upekkha) comprise the remaining and complementary emotions of the Brahma Viharas.[3] Compassion is defined as the wish for others to be free from suffering; empathic joy is the ability to experience a sympathetic, appreciative joy at the sight of others' joy; and equanimity is the balanced state of mind sans aversion and craving.

The intention behind loving-kindness meditation is to cultivate an experience of positive emotions such as love and compassion during the meditation as well as in everyday life. LKM is also used as an antidote to fear, anxiety, and worry. In fact, the Buddha originally taught the forest monks the practice of LKM in part to help them overcome their fear of spending the night in the forest.[4] LKM is meant to decrease anxiety as well as to foster the development of positive emotions that lead to changes in motivation and behavior that, in turn, promote positive feelings and kindness toward oneself and others.[3] LKM is intended to help shift people's daily emotional states, shape their enduring personality traits, and increase their potential to positively transform and build personal resources and well-being.[5]

The practice of LKM traditionally involves choosing specific phrases of care and kindness, which are directed toward oneself, a benefactor, a dear friend, a neutral person, a difficult person, and eventually to all sentient beings. Examples of these phrases include, "May I be safe and protected," "May I be peaceful," "May I be healthy," or, when they are being sent to the different categories of persons, "May you be safe and protected," "May you be peaceful," "May you be healthy." Each of these different phrases and each of the different categories of people may be experienced differently. What is important is for the practitioner to stay open and present to whatever arises instead of forcing or expecting that specific emotions will arise. For example, it may be easier to send kind, caring wishes to one's grandfather than to a neutral person whom one has only met a few times at the grocery store. The intention of LKM is to help concentrate the mind with clear intentions of sending kind, caring phrases and calling to mind kind images. Eventually, as with any practice, the meditation becomes more concentrated and the capacity to feel the genuine caring for oneself and others begins to arise. What is essential is that one's intention be clear and genuinely aimed at creating greater health, ease, and well-being for oneself and others. (See Appendix A for the original instructions of Metta meditation and Appendix B for sample instructions of loving-kindness meditation.)

Summary of Current Literature

Below we highlight the pioneering research that has been done in the area of loving-kindness meditation.

In the first published study on loving-kindness meditation, Carson and colleagues[6] examined the effects of LKM intervention to treat patients who were experiencing chronic lower back pain. Forty-three participants with chronic lower back pain were randomly assigned to a LKM intervention or a standard care control group. Participants in the intervention group participated in eight weekly 90-minute group sessions and kept meditation practice diaries. Four to eight patients were placed in groups that included a practice of LKM in which they were instructed to (a) remember a time when they felt connected to a loved one and (b) focus on the love and kindness elicited from this memory while letting go of its content and (c) direct positive feelings of love and kindness to the loved one and oneself via silent mental phrases (i.e., "May this person be happy/loved") and (d) rest with a focus on the feelings of love and kindness that remained from the previous step. During subsequent weeks, patients were instructed to extend this practice to a neutral person, a person who harmed them, and, finally, to all sentient beings and were given didactic presentations (i.e., on the unhealthy effects of long-held anger), group exercises (i.e., consideration of forgiveness as a gradual process), engaged in group discussion about incorporating LKM into their daily lives, as well as supplementary practices such as body scans in which they accepted their bodies as they were in their state at the moment. Patients were also encouraged to spend 10 to 30 minutes each day practicing audiotaped LKM strategies. Participants' pain, anger, and psychological distress were assessed pre- and postintervention and at 3 months following the intervention.

Results demonstrated that the LKM group reported significant improvements in pain and psychological distress compared to the control group. Additionally, findings showed that the more time participants spent practicing loving-kindness meditation, the greater their decrease in pain that day and the less anger they experienced the next day.

One important area for future research noted by the authors is to address difficulties in participant retention that arose from participants' concern that LKM would not help with their pain. Future research will need to determine how to help motivate participants and increase their belief that LKM can be effective for the treatment of pain. One suggestion is to add an initial component to the loving-kindness intervention such as motivational interviewing[7] to strengthen participants' receptivity and readiness to participate in the LKM intervention.[6]

Another well-designed study examining the effects of LKM, conducted by Fredrickson and colleagues,[8] is the first experimental study to test the broaden-and-build theory,[9] which posits that daily experiences of positive emotions compound over time to build personal cognitive, psychological, social, and physical resources.

In this controlled longitudinal study on LKM, 139 participants were randomly assigned to a 7-week LKM intervention or a wait-list control group and provided daily web reports of their emotions. The intervention consisted of 60-minute weekly sessions with 20 to 30 participants per group. During Week 1, participants focused on practicing a meditation that directed love and compassion toward themselves. In the second week, participants added directing love and compassion toward loved ones, and in subsequent weeks, to acquaintances, strangers, and all sentient beings. Each session included 15 to 20 minutes of group meditation, 20 minutes to check in and allow for participants' questions, and 20 minutes of didactic instruction on ways to integrate the meditation into participants' lives. Participants reported meditating an average of 80 minutes per week.

Results of this research demonstrated that LKM generated positive emotions that endured even after the intervention when compared to the control condition. Specifically, the dose–response relationship of repeated

LKM practice and the experience of positive emotions *tripled* during the study.

Results also demonstrated that the practice of LKM led to a wide range of positive emotions, including love, joy, gratitude, contentment, hope, pride, interest, amusement, and awe and that these emotions were correlated with increases in personal resources, including mindful attention, self-acceptance, positive relations with others, and good physical health.[8] Further, the authors state, "These gains in personal resources were consequential: they enabled people to become more satisfied with their lives and to experience fewer symptoms of depression."[8] Fredrickson and colleagues conclude, "Positive emotions emerged as the mechanism through which people build the resources that make their lives more fulfilling."[8] What is most noteworthy is that this was the first field experiment to document that LKM increases positive emotions in the present moment and places people on "trajectories of growth, leaving them better able to ward off depressive symptoms and become ever more satisfied with life."[8]

The results of this study are promising and offer much direction for future work. Future research could build on the study by including multiple methods of assessment, for example, behavioral measures, observer reports, and physiological markers, as all data in the current study were based on self-report. Another direction for future research would be to include long-term follow-up, as the current study only assessed short-term gains. It will be helpful for future research to examine if intentionally engaging in continued LKM practice was related to continued gains.

A third study[10] investigated LKM's efficacy in increasing positivity and social connectedness toward others. The study included a total of 93 randomly assigned participants, including 45 in a LKM condition and 48 in a neutral imagery induction control group. Prior to the intervention, the authors conducted a baseline assessment of LKM's impact on explicit and implicit affective responses to six photos that included the participants, a close other, three neutral strangers (who were similar in gender, age, and ethnicity) and a control of a photograph of a nonsocial object (a lamp), per a pre-post guided visualization that was focused on one of the neutral stranger photos.

Participants in the LKM condition were instructed to complete a 7-minute LKM in which they were directed to send love to two imagined loved ones standing next to them for 4 minutes and then redirect their feelings of love and compassion to a picture of neutral stranger on a screen for 3 minutes. In the control condition, participants were told to imagine and focus on the physical appearance of two acquaintances standing next to them for 4 minutes and then look at a photo of a neutral stranger and focus their attention on his/her features and appearance for 3 minutes. All photos were matched to the participants' age, gender, and ethnicity.

Prior to the manipulation, participants indicated their current mood as either positive or negative. After the manipulation, explicit affective responses were measured by participants' indication of how connected and positive they felt toward each photograph subject. Implicit responses were evaluated by participants' judgment of one of nine positive words and one of nine negative words that followed 18 occurrences of the photographs. These responses were further evaluated by taking the difference between the average response time to positive and negative words following a particular prime (the photograph).

Results of the study showed that participants in the LKM condition experienced a marked increase in positive emotions when compared to the control group. Specifically, participants' moods in the LKM condition became more positive, while those in the control condition showed no change. Gains in explicit positivity were noted in both the LKM intervention and control, with the former showing a more pronounced increase. The LKM condition also became significantly more positive to the nontarget neutral strangers and object, underscoring the generalized shift toward positive responding. Additional findings support LKM's efficacy in cultivating participants' implicit positivity toward the target photograph while showing no change after being exposed to the neutral control condition.

Although the study shares significant findings that illustrate LKM's ability to effect positive emotional states, the authors share several limitations. First, the authors selected the neutral target as being of the same age, gender, and ethnicity as the participant, which may have already set the stage for positive bias in participants' responses. Future studies may show more substantiated efficacy if out-group members are selected as targets in the LKM and control conditions. Second, the authors acknowledge the lack of understanding of the long-term effects of manufacturing positive emotions via intentionally controlled processes.

Johnson and colleagues explore LKM's potential to enhance hope and purpose in life and reduce schizophrenia's negative symptoms such as anhedonia, avolition, and asociality.[11] In this study, three patients with schizophrenia attended 60-minute weekly LKM sessions for 6 weeks, as well as a postsession 6 weeks after the final session, while on anti-psychotic medications. The session included discussion, mindfulness skills teaching, and practice of LKM. Patients were given pre-post assessments and gave weekly self-reports. They were also encouraged to practice LKM by listening to a LKM CD and practice LKM when distressing situations arose during the week.

Results of the study varied, with patients experiencing moderate, modest, and negligible effects of reducing negative symptoms of schizophrenia. One participant, who had 1 year of prior mindfulness meditation experience and practiced LKM for 5 minutes for 5 to 7 days a week, reported significant reduction in avolition, asociality, and paranoid thoughts, as well as increased flexible thinking and connection to others. LKM helped the participant to experience an improvement in mood, which in turn helped her to turn negative perceptions into positive ones. Another participant had difficulty with racing thoughts throughout the practice of LKM but reported an improvement in mood and her anhedonia. Moreover, the group setting helped her to establish and maintain relationships as well as develop effective problem-solving skills. The third participant showed no significant improvement in mood pre- and postassessment but did feel more relaxed and able to cope with auditory hallucinations. He reported having difficulty participating in the group and difficulty concentrating on the LKM and used it 2 to 3 days each week for 10 minutes.[11]

Despite the promising initial results, several limitations of the study are highlighted. First, extensive experience in meditation has been shown to alter neural structure and affect baseline responding,[12] thereby skewing outcomes. Specifically, patients' varying levels of familiarity with mindfulness meditation contributed to more positive outcomes for the patient who had 1 year of prior mindfulness training. This outcome suggests that a previous mindfulness meditation practice could be beneficial for outcomes in future LKM studies. Second, it was noted that incongruence between a patient's recovery goals and the rationale for practicing LKM contributed to some resistance in fully engaging in the group. Thus, it is of clinical significance to align patient goals and motivation with LKM rationale (as will be discussed below). And third, the group was only 6 weeks long, which may not have served as enough time for patients to learn and imbibe teachings. Despite these limitations, the authors posit that LKM and the use of positive psychology can be most effective in treating schizophrenia when combined with concurrent cognitive approaches.

Mechanisms of Action

These pioneering studies suggest that loving-kindness meditation has great potential to benefit our health and well-being. These studies have begun to address the first-order question, "Is loving-kindness meditation helpful?" Clearly this line of research is fundamental to validating LKM as an efficacious psychological intervention, and controlled clinical trials across diverse populations should continue. However, an equally important direction for future research is to address the question, "How is loving-kindness meditation helpful?"

Investigating questions concerning the mechanisms of action underlying the transformational effects of LKM requires reflection and exploration in an attempt to understand the mysterious and complex process of LKM. Below, we offer a beginning attempt to search for common ground on which to build a more precise understanding of the primary mechanisms of action involved in LKM practice.

Positive Emotions

The most obvious mechanism through which LKM may enhance well-being is through its explicit and intentional cultivation of positive emotions. Research indicates that positive emotions contribute to important positive outcomes, including interpersonal health,[13] better physical health,[14] and longer life.[15] This may be because positive emotions produce a preference for the global, while negative emotions produce a preference for the details. Positive emotions, therefore, can play a role in maintaining one's resiliency during negative events, as they are associated with the ability to allow oneself to not focus on the negative details but take a broader and more clear perspective toward the future.[5]

Fredrickson and colleagues note that practicing LKM can help one to decrease negative emotions, as individuals are able to see their thoughts and emotions from a broader perspective, making them more impervious to relapses of depressive episodes.[8] In addition, the unconditional friendliness inherent in LKM can serve as an antidote to self-loathing and self-judgment, which involves rejecting oneself or one's experience, consciously or unconsciously. Rather than rejecting oneself, LKM encourages one to embrace all aspects of one's experience, allowing one to be gentle and kind to himself/herself and, correspondingly, to others.[16]

Further, LKM, through the cultivation of positive emotions in the present, helps support positive emotions in the future. Positive emotions beget positive emotions: Experiencing a positive emotion in the present confers a greater likelihood for the experience of a positive emotion in the future. For example, Fredrickson and colleagues'[8] research suggests that people take deliberate actions to cultivate experiences of positive emotions and benefit both "in terms of self-generated positive emotions, and over time, in terms of increased resources and overall well-being."[8]

Broaden and Build

Another hypothesis, which extends the positive emotion hypothesis, is Fredrickson's broaden-and-build theory.[9] This theory suggests that LKM increases positive emotions, which enables people to build resources and thus report greater health and experience their lives to be more satisfying and fulfilling. Fredrickson and colleagues point out that the increased satisfaction and well-being are not only because participants feel more positive emotions per se but also because their greater positive emotions help them build resources for living successfully.[8] Fredrickson's broaden-and-build theory suggests that these positive emotions enhance health by broadening people's attention and perspective and helping them discover and build important personal resources. As she and colleagues note, these resources can be

> cognitive, like the ability to mindfully attend to the present moment; psychological, like the ability to maintain a sense of mastery over environmental challenges; social, like the ability to give and receive emotional support; or physical, like the ability to ward off the common cold.[8]

The theory suggests that the personal resources that are developed through frequent experiences of positive emotions are significantly related to subsequent increases in well-being. Thus, it is hypothesized that an important mechanism of action through which LKM enhances health is through the cultivation of positive emotions, which subsequently, through the broaden-and-build pathways, lead to greater health. Preliminary research supports this finding that LKM does indeed increase positive emotions.[8] However, it is important to note that the goal of LKM is not simply to enhance positive emotional experiences but, instead, to learn about the nature of one's mind and move toward greater degrees of freedom and toward the cultivation of unconditional kindness toward oneself and all beings.

Interconnectedness

Another mechanism through which LKM may enhance well-being is through the cultivation of a sense of interconnectedness. As we begin to cultivate care and kindness for ourselves, we begin to understand the pain and suffering that come from self-judgment, separation, and criticism. As we learn to offer ourselves kindness and love, we begin to see that just as we want to be healthy, happy, and peaceful, so too do all beings yearn for health, happiness, and peace. An awareness of this shared desire and this common humanity helps one develop a greater sense of interconnectedness, which in turn increases empathetic responding; trust and co-operation, which have mutually reinforcing and resource-building effects, beget trust, care, and cooperation in return.[3]

Future research will benefit by continuing to explore the possible mechanisms of action of how LKM positively affects health and well-being. Below, we briefly discuss additional potential directions for future research.

Directions for Future Research

The results of pioneer research are qualified by their limitations in their numbers and methodology. We suggest the following criteria to enhance future rigorous designs and strengthen the preliminary findings. First, it will be important to continue to demonstrate the effects of LKM across diverse populations, both clinical and nonclinical. In addition to greater diversity and breadth across populations, greater diversity is needed in methodological assessment. Increasing multimethod, multiple measures of the effects of LKM is essential. It will be interesting for future work to move beyond using solely self-report assessment to additionally utilize implicit or behavioral measures, observer reports, and physiological markers.

Future research can also help examine how to best teach LKM. For example, is a group format or individually tailored sessions better? Along these lines, future research could determine how to best help people begin a LKM practice. As Fredrickson and colleagues[8] point out, starting a meditation practice may "involve a period of doing something unfamiliar, difficult, and draining without immediate rewards. Contemplative traditions have articulated five obstacles facing novice meditators, including craving, anger, boredom, restlessness, and doubt."[17] It will be helpful for future research to explicitly discuss these obstacles and help participants move through them, because, as Fredrickson and colleagues note, "if people can endure these first difficult weeks, meditation becomes more effective, and positive emotions begin to accumulate and compound, changing people for the better".[8] The authors support this statement with their findings that the majority of attrition occurred during the initial weeks of the intervention, when participants may not have been "experienced" or "skilled" enough to feel the benefits of the meditation practice yet.[8]

Another important future direction is to examine dose response. The pioneering work of Fredrickson and Carson and colleagues can be used as a model. Future research can include assessment of daily practice to further strengthen the findings that there is a dose response with LKM practice. For example, Fredrickson and colleagues[8] found that "the amount of positive emotions participants gained per hour spent meditating increased over the course of the study, tripling from the first week to the last, suggesting that participants were building a dependable skill for self generating positive emotions."[8] Future research could benefit by continuing this line of research, rigorously monitoring the amount participants practice and the effects of this practice on outcome. In addition, it will be helpful for future research to not only examine quantity of practice but also explore ways of assessing quality of practice. For example, do the specificity of the specific phrases of loving-kindness matter, or the clarity of LKM images, or level of awareness of specific affective states or felt senses in the body? It will be helpful to develop some form of manipulation check to determine if participants are indeed practicing the specific practice and for what percentage of any given meditation practice session. It is out of the scope of this chapter to discuss how to define or measure quality of LKM practice; however, this will be an important topic for future exploration.

Another direction for future research will be differentiation between types of meditation. Now that LKM has shown efficacy in increasing well-being, future work can control for nonspecific effects and expectancies by comparing LKM with other meditative techniques. There are many types of meditation. This is crucial to recognize for theoretical, practical, and research reasons. Yet researchers often implicitly assume that different meditations have equivalent effects. This is an assumption to be empirically tested. Most likely, different techniques have overlapping but by no means equal effects.[18]

Additionally, future research could benefit by including experienced meditators as participants. Researchers should include long-term, experienced meditators as well as beginning meditators. Also, when matching control subjects to long-term meditators in retrospective studies, in addition to age, gender, and education, it would be important to consider matching subjects on the dimension of an alternative attentional practice (e.g., playing a musical instrument).

LKM is a multifaceted process with multiple potentially potent components. These range from nonspecific factors such as belief and expectancy through postural, somatic, attentional, cognitive, and other factors. Research can attempt to differentiate the effects and interactions of various components. In addition to this kind of component analysis, it will be helpful to examine interaction effects. The LKM practice may interact with a variety of relevant psychological, spiritual, and clinical factors. Factors of current interest include other health and self-management strategies and especially psychotherapy.[18]

Another direction is to explore mediating variables. Development of subjective and objective measures to determine the mediating variables that account for the most variance in predicting change is of potential exploratory interest. One important method to do this is to use qualitative as well as quantitative data. The subtlety and depth of meditation experiences do not easily lend themselves to quantification. Further, the interplay between subjective and objective is essential to understanding meditation. Qualitative data provide a means to access the subjective experience of the meditator.

Conclusion

The above pioneering work suggests that LKM appears to have the potential to enhance physiological and psychological well-being on a wide variety of measures. As Fredrickson and colleagues[9] conclude, "LKM appears to be one positive emotion induction that keeps on giving, long after the identifiable 'event' of meditation practice. Positive emotions feel good, and feelings like love, joy, and contentment can be valuable in and of themselves."

And even more importantly, on a societal and global level, cultivating LKM may have significant interpersonal and transpersonal benefits: When people intentionally open their hearts and focus on care for themselves and all beings, they seed not only their own health and well-being, but they have great potential for effecting the well-being of others. However, for research to continue to refine and expand our knowledge of meditation and its effects, it is essential to develop broader paradigms for the field and to bring great creativity, rigor, and heart so that this research may be of benefit.

Notes

1. Walsh, R., & Shapiro, S. L. (2006). The meeting of meditative disciplines and Western psychology: A mutually enriching dialogue. *American Psychologist, 61*, 227–239.

2. Hofmann, S. G., Sawyer, A. T., Witt, A. A., & Oh, D. (2010). The effect of mindfulness-based therapy on anxiety and depression: A meta-analytic review. *Journal of Consulting and Clinical Psychology, 78(2)*, 169–183.

3. Salzberg, S. (1995). *Loving-kindness: The revolutionary art of happiness*. Boston: Shambhala.

4. Kornfield, J. (1993). *A path with heart*. New York: Bantam Books.

5. Fredrickson, B. L., & Cohn, M. A. (2008). Positive emotions. In M. Lewis, J. M. Haviland-Jones, & L. F. Barrett (Eds.), *Handbook of emotions* (3rd ed., pp. 777–796). New York: Guilford Press.

6. Carson, J. W., Keefe, F. J., Lynch, T. R., Carson, K. M., Goli, V., Fras, A. M., & Thorp, S. R. (2005). Loving-kindness meditation for chronic low back pain: Results from a pilot trial. *Journal of Holistic Nursing, 23*(3), 287–304.

7. Rollnick, S., & Miller, W. R. (1995). What is motivational interviewing? *Behavioural and Cognitive Psychotherapy, 23*, 325–334.

8. Fredrickson, B. L., Cohn, M. A., Coffey, K. A., Pek, J., & Finkel, S. M. (2008). Open hearts build lives: Positive emotions, induced through loving-kindness meditation, build consequential personal resources. *Journal of Personality and Social Psychology, 95*(5), 1045–1060.

9. Fredrickson, B. L. (2001). The role of positive emotions in positive psychology. The broaden-and-build theory of positive emotions. *American Psychologist, 56*(3), 218–226.

10. Hutcherson, C. A., Seppala, E. M., & Gross, J. J. (2008). Loving-kindness increases social connectedness. *Emotion, 8*(5), 720–724.

11. Johnson, D. P., Penn, D. L., Fredrickson, B. L., & Meyer, P. S. (2009). Loving-kindness meditation to enhance recovery from negative symptoms of schizophrenia. *Journal of Clinical Psychology, 65*(5), 499–509.

12. Lazar, S. W., Kerr, C. E., Wasserman, R. H., Gray, J. R., Greve, D. N., Treadway, M. T., et al. (2005). Meditation experience is associated with increased cortical thickness. *Neuroreport, 16*, 1893–1897.

13. Waugh, C. E., & Fredrickson, B. L. (2006). Nice to know you: Positive emotions, self–other overlap, and complex understanding in the formation of new relationships. *Journal of Positive Psychology, 1*, 93–106.

14. Doyle, W. J., Gentile, D. A., & Cohen, S. (2006). Emotional style, nasal cytokines, and illness expression after experimental rhinovirus exposure. *Brain, Behavior, and Immunity, 20*, 175–181.

15. Danner, D. D., Snowdon, D. A., & Friesen, W. V. (2001). Positive emotions in early life and longevity: *Findings from the nun study. Journal of Personality and Social Psychology, 80*, 804–813.

16. Wegela, K. (2009). *The courage to be present: Buddhism, psychotherapy, and the awakening of natural wisdom.* Boston: Shambhala.
17. Kabat-Zinn, J. (2005). *Coming to our senses: Healing the world through mindfulness.* New York: Hyperion.
18. Shapiro, S. L., & Walsh, R. (2003). An analysis of recent meditation research and suggestions for future directions. *The Humanistic Psychologist, 31*(2/3), 86–114.

Appendix A. The Metta Sutta

This is what should be done
By one who is skilled in goodness,
And who knows the path of peace:
Let them be able and upright,
Straightforward and gentle in speech.
Humble and not conceited,
Contented and easily satisfied.
Unburdened with duties and frugal in their ways.
Peaceful and calm, and wise and skillful,
Not proud and demanding in nature.
Let them not do the slightest thing
That the wise would later reprove.
Wishing: In gladness and in safety,
May all beings be at ease.
Whatever living beings there may be;
Whether they are weak or strong, omitting none,
The great or the mighty, medium, short or small,
The seen and the unseen,
Those living near and far away,
Those born and to-be-born,
May all beings be at ease!
Let none deceive another,
Or despise any being in any state.
Let none through anger or ill-will
Wish harm upon another.
Even as a mother protects with her life

Her child, her only child,
So with a boundless heart
Should one cherish all living beings:
Radiating kindness over the entire world
Spreading upwards to the skies,
And downwards to the depths;
Outwards and unbounded,
Freed from hatred and ill-will.
Whether standing or walking, seated or lying down
Free from drowsiness,
One should sustain this recollection.
This is said to be the sublime abiding.
By not holding to fixed views,
The pure-hearted one, having clarity of vision,
Being freed from all sense desires,
Is not born again into this world.

Appendix B. Loving-Kindness Meditation Instructions

Loving-kindness meditation (LKM) can be cultivated through formal meditation practice. There are numerous ways to practice LKM; however, all involve intentionally wishing well for oneself and for all beings. Below are instructions for LKM; these are offered as a loose guide. What is most important is to discern what practice feels most authentic and helpful to you. Sharon Salzberg's (2002) book, *Loving-kindness*, is a wonderful guide for further in depth instruction.

Beginning LKM involves first finding a space that is quiet and where you will not be interrupted for a period of time. Begin by setting an intention to cultivate care and kindness to the extent that you are able for yourself and for others. Allow yourself to rest in a seated position and bring your hands together, resting on your heart. Reflect on a time when you felt safe and loved. It could be a time in which a family member, close friend, significant other, or other gifted you with kindness, compassion, and love. Remember the experience of it, recollecting it as vividly as possible. Imagine yourself during this time, recalling as clearly as possible how you looked, the expression of your face, how your body felt. And as you are ready, begin to silently repeat the following phrases: "May I be safe and protected. May I be happy. May I be peaceful. May I be free and at ease." With each phrase, allow it to resonate in the body, notice the felt sense, notice any images. Offer yourself each phrase with care and kindness, slowly repeating them one after the other, building momentum and concentration. If at any time your mind wanders, simply bring it back to the phrases and to the felt sense of the experience.

After some time has passed, and when you feel ready, call to mind a benefactor, someone who has supported, loved, and/or inspired you. This can be anyone living, including someone you have never met, such as H. H. Dalai Lama. Choose someone who easily opens your heart and who readily evokes the phrases of loving-kindness from you. Begin silently repeating the same four phrases, sending them to this person: "May you be safe and protected. May you be happy. May you be peaceful. May you be free and at ease." With each phrase, allow it to resonate in the body, notice the felt sense, notice any images. Offer this other person each phrase with care and kindness, slowly repeating them one after the other, building momentum and concentration. If at any time your mind wanders, simply bring it back to the phrases and to the felt sense of the experience.

When you are ready, follow this person with a neutral person, someone for whom you do not have strong positive or negative feelings. Examples of "neutral" persons include the checkout person at the grocery store or a neighbor or coworker you do not know or have had minimal interactions with. The intention of practicing with the neutral person is to develop loving-kindness even for someone who you do not have strong affection toward.

When you are ready, continue from the neutral person to the "difficult" person. This person is someone who you have difficulty feeling kindness toward. This may be a challenging aspect of the LKM, and it is helpful to go slowly. If at any point it becomes too difficult, it is helpful to go back to sending Loving-kindness to oneself or one's benefactor. It is important to remember that we are practicing LKM for ourselves, not for anyone else. You are learning to open your heart and create a pattern of kindness not out of weakness or to help the other person but to create greater health and well-being in your own life.

When you are ready, shift focus to the final category of the LKM, which includes all sentient beings. As best you can, send the four phrases of loving-kindness to all sentient beings, in all directions. "May all sentient beings be safe and protected. May all sentient beings be happy. May all sentient beings be peaceful. May all sentient beings be free and at ease." With each phrase, allow it to resonate in the body, notice the felt sense, notice any images. Offer these beings each phrase with care and kindness, slowly repeating them one after the other, building momentum and concentration. If at any time your mind wanders, simply bring it back to the phrases and to the felt sense of the experience.

Once you have completed all the categories of the LKM, it is helpful to return to yourself, sending yourself the phrases of loving-kindness one final time, and then resting for a period of silence, simply noticing the resonance of the LKM practice. It is helpful not to judge or evaluate the experience but to simply notice it. As the meditation practice ends, it is helpful to make an intention to bring a piece of this care and kindness into each moment of your life. It can also be helpful to take a moment and thank yourself for taking the time and devoting the energy to cultivating greater health and well-being in your life.

9

Vocation: Finding Joy and Meaning in Our Work[1]

Diane E. Dreher

As more people today seek greater meaning in their work, we're witnessing a resurgence of the Renaissance concept of vocation. Tracing this concept back to its Renaissance roots, this chapter explains how a sense of vocation can enrich our lives both individually and collectively. Current research shows that having a vocation makes us happier, healthier, and more successful, providing a sense of meaning and "flow," while building morale, nurturing community, and promoting excellence.

A major Renaissance meme, a vocation or calling (from the Latin *vocare*, "to call") was a catalyst for creativity, transforming people's lives in Western Europe from the 15th through the 17th centuries. While in the Middle Ages, vocations were limited to priests, monks, and nuns, and work for most people was primarily a means to earn their daily bread, in the Renaissance, the view of work shifted dramatically. Reformation theologians Martin Luther and John Calvin affirmed that *everyone* had a calling, possessing God-given gifts, and was called to use them in loving service to their neighbors.[2] In this cultural climate, Renaissance men and women embraced their vocations, becoming artists, poets, humanists, saints, scientists, political leaders, and committed citizens, their identities informed by a sense of personal destiny.

In a self-fulfilling prophecy of tremendous proportions, the concept of vocation inspired the Renaissance as generations of men and women used their gifts to change the world, making unprecedented contributions to science, religion, philosophy, politics, and the arts. Transcending the class system, Leonardo da Vinci, Desiderius Erasmus, Christopher Marlowe, Antony van Leeuwenhoek, Galileo Galilei, St. Teresa of Avila, and others became artists, writers, scientists, and saints. In one memorable example, a young man from the English countryside whose parents could only sign their names with an X brought his gifts to the London stage as William Shakespeare.

Vocation Today

We're witnessing a growing awareness of vocation today. Positive psychology has begun exploring the construct of vocation. Paralleling the Renaissance concepts of gifts and vocations, research has shown that each of us has our own "signature strengths" from among 24 character strengths and virtues common to humankind.[3] Psychologist Martin Seligman has said that "if you can find a way to use your signature strengths at work often and you also see your work as contributing to the greater good, you have a calling."[4] The literature on organizational leadership has noted this growing trend, seeing "a new interest in the idea of vocation and calling ... emerging as people search for more humane and meaningful ways to understand their work lives."[5]

A sense of vocation or calling can be found in almost any occupation.[6] Seligman tells of a hospital orderly whose job involved delivering patients' food trays, changing bed linens, and cleaning rooms. Yet this man saw his work as vital to people's recovery, performing his duties with special care and hanging new pictures on the walls each week to bring his patients hope.[4] Our attitude determines whether we see our work as a job, a career, or a calling. We can work at a job to earn money to support ourselves and our families; advance ourselves professionally in a career, earning promotions, power, and prestige; or we can live with a sense of calling, finding deeper meaning in our work. Regardless of rank or socioeconomic status, whether their work is paid or unpaid—in art, public service, or volunteer work—people with a sense of calling use their time and talents in meaningful ways. Connecting to a larger purpose, they see their work as contributing to the greater good.

Vocation and Meaning

"A vocation is not so much something one has as a pattern of meaning one lives" according to psychologist Larry Cochran.[7] This "pattern of meaning" also informed Abraham Maslow's concept of self-actualization. "All human beings prefer meaningful work to meaningless work," Maslow observed. "If work is meaningless, then life comes close to being meaningless." Work for self-actualizing people, Maslow believed, "might better be called 'mission,' 'calling,' 'duty,' 'vocation,' in the priest's sense."[8] And, indeed, vocation is often linked to a life of faith. A 1994 study of Christian denominations found that people with a strong faith were more likely to see their work as a calling.[9] Gandhi found inspiration for his work in the Hindu ideal of *ahimsa* or nonviolence; Buddhists aspire to a life of "right livelihood"; and Jews have a long history dedicated to justice and the teaching of *tikkun olam*, the call to repair the world. This vision of work as a calling expands our sense of identity into what positive psychology calls "self-transcendence," deepening our sense of meaning in life.[10]

For those inspired to a life of service, any task, no matter how routine, can become a form of spiritual exercise. Longtime peace activist Gertrude Welch finds in her faith the strength to persevere in the long struggle to build bridges of understanding between citizens and legislators, establish shelters for the homeless, resolve conflicts, and teach peace. Letters, emails, phone calls, visits, and vigils—the proverbial "journey of a thousand miles" proceeds one small step at a time. For years, she has begun each day in prayer, recognizing "that we are called not so much to be successful as to be faithful," faithful to our values, our ideals, no matter how far they seem from the events of the day. To live with this sense of vocation requires a deep sense of purpose and an abiding faith in possibility.

Vocation and Happiness

The sense of vocation combines what positive psychology has seen as two active orientations to happiness: (1) the Aristotelian concept of *eudemonia* or meaning—identifying our strengths and virtues, then living by them, as discussed in the previous section, and (2) *engagement*—or the sense of flow, becoming so involved in our work that we become one with it.[11]

With flow, time passes quickly. Embracing a challenge that actualizes our highest level of skill, we blend with our work as in a dance. Mihaly Csikszentmihalyi found this sense of flow often occurs in the work of dedicated artists, doctors, scientists, writers, teachers, and performers, those for whom work becomes an engaging creative act, calling upon the best of their abilities.[12] These two qualities of happiness are measured by the Vocation Identity Questionnaire (2007), which includes questions such as "I see my work as a way to make a positive difference in the world," "In my daily life I often feel connected to larger patterns of joy and meaning," and "I sometimes get so involved in my work that I lose track of time."[13] People with a sense of vocation are always learning, always in discovery, from the concert pianist learning a new concerto to the scientist beginning a new experiment, therapists and doctors using their skills to support their patients in healing, the choreographer creating a new dance, the teacher who reaches out to help a struggling student, seeing the flash of insight on a young face. As Cochran has recognized, "one cannot rest in a vocation. Rather, one strives unceasingly to realize it."[7] In this continual striving, reaching out to serve our world by reaching deep within themselves, people with a sense of vocation find happiness and fulfillment, feeling vibrantly, joyously alive.

Vocation and Health

With this sense of joy comes greater well-being. A 1997 study found that people with a sense of calling were healthier than those who considered their work only a job or career.[6] A 2005 study found that people who identified their signature strengths and used them were healthier and happier than those who did not.[14] Studies in 2009 and 2010 found that people with greater meaning and engagement in their lives were not only happier but also healthier and more successful, experiencing greater subjective well-being, less depression, anxiety, and substance abuse, as well as greater educational and occupational success.[15, 16]

The connection between health and a sense of calling was recognized decades ago during World War II by Viktor Frankl, as he struggled to survive in Nazi concentration camps. After his book manuscript was confiscated when he entered Auschwitz, he faced dehumanizing, demoralizing conditions and suffered from bouts of typhus, yet the hope of completing his book gave him a sense of purpose. He scribbled down notes on scraps of paper and later said that this hope, this call to finish his book and share it with the world, gave him the strength to survive as many others around him lost hope and died, surrendering to the despair that depleted their weakened immune systems. Again and again, he witnessed examples of our essential human need for meaning, the core of his concept of logotherapy, saw how suicides were prevented when one man remembered that as a scientist he had important work to do and another realized that a beloved child was waiting for him in another country.[17] Frankl's recognition that meaning strengthens our immune systems was confirmed by a 2005 UCLA study in which students who simply reflected on their personal values before a stress test had stronger immune systems, lower cortisol levels, and significant reductions in their psychological responses to stress.[18]

The engagement and meaning offered by a sense of vocation are so conducive to health that a Calling Protocol has been developed for use in clinical practice to help treat people suffering from depression, anxiety, low self-worth, chronic stress, and debilitating illnesses. Following the four steps to vocation described at the end of this chapter, the protocol helps clients discover their gifts, detach from unhealthy behaviors, discern their guiding values, and chart a new direction with hope. The first step, discovering their gifts, brings them greater energy and self-worth, opening their eyes to new possibilities. They have the motivation to detach from unhealthy habits and reconnect with what brings their lives meaning (often their church or synagogue). Drawing upon these vocational resources, they work with their therapist to develop new ways to use their gifts, connect with their values, and chart positive new directions in their lives.[19]

Vocation, Leadership, and Organizational Excellence

A sense of vocation inspires better leadership, promoting excellence not only for ourselves but also for the larger human community. Research has shown that leaders create their own cultural climate, exerting a powerful influence upon the lives around them. With their actions and attitudes, they can promote a repressive culture of fear or a dynamic culture of trust.[20] Today's unprecedented challenges demand a new paradigm of leadership, leaders with vision, courage, and creativity—leaders with a sense of vocation. Such leaders possess intrinsic motivation, which has been linked with higher creativity, the ability to see new possibilities and find new solutions to prevailing problems.[21]

A sense of calling supports leaders not only professionally but also personally. Seeking to integrate their deepest values with their daily activities, more than 800 senior executives, CEOs, and professional MBAs have participated in André Delbecq's Spirituality for Organizational Leadership seminar at Santa Clara University. Delbecq has found that "unless a leader feels that his or her organizational role is a 'calling,' the heavy burdens of leadership become separated from the spiritual journey, a separation that often contributes to burnout and cynicism."[22] Benefiting from Ignatian spirituality and research in the growing field of authentic leadership development, these executive leaders connect with their personal gifts, seek the wisdom of detachment through regular contemplative practice, and begin to discern the deeper meanings in their challenges, developing a profound sense of vocation that transforms their organizations.[22, 23]

A sense of vocation does this by providing focus. As Delbecq and his colleague James J. McGee have explained, a leader's vocation "integrates the hopes and needs of both the individual leader and the organizational members into a common purpose."[22] Inspired by a larger sense of purpose, leaders go on to make a positive difference in their organizations by implementing more just and inclusive decision making, empowering employees to reach their personal potentials and encouraging excellence, innovation, and environmentally sustainable development. Research has shown that such leaders see the larger picture, finding a common vision that inspires those around them with higher morale, greater cooperation, and a stronger sense of commitment and motivation than either tangible rewards or punishment. Becoming creative catalysts for their organizations, such leaders bring out the best in the people around them.[22]

Leaders with vocation recognize the vocations of others, creating an atmosphere of excellence by acknowledging people as individuals and encouraging them to use their gifts instead of forcing them to conform to preconceived Procrustean expectations. In such an atmosphere, creativity flourishes: Instead of shrinking back in fear, people reach out to innovate. Effectiveness is not reduced to efficiency and people are respected and trusted, not treated like replaceable parts. Human warmth, understanding, challenge, excitement, a deep sense of joy, often highlighted by humor and fun—all of this comes with this kind of exemplary leadership.

Leaders with vocation have always inspired us, including the people around them in an overarching vision of purpose and meaning. Great leaders in history—Franklin Roosevelt, Winston Churchill, Mohandas Gandhi—struck this chord in the hearts of their people. But leaders with vocation are not limited to major corporations or the national or international stage. In our hectic, conflicted world, they are quietly building community, humanizing and healing fragmented lives. Dr. David Reed's northern California veterinary hospital reflects his personal commitment to his patients. In his white lab coat and stethoscope, Dr. Reed greets his patients and their owners by name, taking time to listen, to answer their questions, to explain any treatments. His office is efficient, equipped with all the latest veterinary services, but more than efficiency is the tangible feeling of care. Staff members call after each appointment to check on their patients, and Dr. Reed gives out his cell phone number and makes house calls to care for seriously ill animals. His staff members say they feel like an extended family, and over the years Dr. Reed has mentored dozens of high school students as veterinary technicians, modeling compassion, patience, and professionalism. Eight of them have gone on to become veterinarians themselves. With such mentoring, leaders with vocation inspire others to "go and do likewise," transforming more lives in an expanding circle of community.

Cultivating Vocation in Our Lives

The following four-step approach to vocation—discovery, detachment, discernment, and direction—has been used in education, religious retreats, rehabilitation, and psychotherapy. It has brought a greater sense of calling to college undergraduates, retired people, delinquent youth, and people suffering from depression and other psychological disorders. It has helped people find new directions in life after graduation, job layoffs, relationship breakups, and episodes of "creative discontent," a restless feeling that there must be something more to life.[1, 19, 24]

Discovery

The first step in vocational discernment is discovering our gifts. We all begin discovering our gifts in childhood, reaching out to explore our world, discovering what we're good at, what we love to do. Some children are natural scientists, filled with curiosity about the natural world. Others are artistic, musical, or athletic; gifted with a love of animals; with compassion for those around them; with ingenuity solving puzzles; or with leadership in sports or neighborhood games. Some gifts are talents we're born with, like perfect pitch. Others are strengths of character, such as patience or compassion, or skills we develop such as computer programming or public speaking. Each person has a combination of character strengths, skills, and natural abilities—their own personal gifts.

People can begin discovering (or rediscovering) their gifts by:

- *Reflecting on what they loved to do as children*, asking, "What did I enjoy doing? "What did my teachers or other adults say I was good at?" "What did I do well?"

- *Recalling a peak experience*, a time when they felt filled with joy and vitality, strongly and authentically themselves. When people focus on what they were doing and the strengths they demonstrated, they can discover more about their gifts.

- *Asking friends and family.* People can get another perspective on their gifts by asking three people who know them well to list five of their strengths or talents. Reviewing the list, they can then ask which strengths feel most like them—another indication of their gifts.

- *Signature Strengths Survey.* People can take Martin Seligman's on-line survey, VIA-IS, on www.authentichappiness.org. The 24 character strengths are: zest, enthusiasm, and energy; spirituality, sense of purpose and faith; curiosity and interest in the world; leadership; industry, diligence, and perseverance; love of learning; gratitude; fairness, equity, and justice; self-control and self-regulation; forgiveness and mercy; hope, optimism, and future-mindedness; humor and playfulness; kindness and generosity; creativity, ingenuity, and originality; honesty, authenticity, and genuineness; bravery and valor; citizenship, teamwork, and loyalty; judgment, critical thinking, and open-mindedness; perspective or wisdom; capacity to love and be loved; social intelligence; appreciation of beauty and excellence; modesty and humility; caution, prudence, and discretion.[3] To take the survey, people need to sign in, then click on the VIA-IS. Answering the questions takes about 30 minutes. They can then print out the results. Their top five strengths are their signature strengths, their primary strengths of character.

- *Contemplation and prayer.* People can also spend time in prayer, asking for clearer insights about their gifts, and for the next 3 days simply notice what they find. At the end of each day, they can pause to ask themselves what brought them joy, when they felt energized, and what they were doing at the time, all of which gives them new insights about their gifts.

Since research has shown that we become healthier, happier, and more successful by focusing on what we love to do, you'd think that people would naturally spend their time using their gifts, but most people do just the opposite. A 2004 Gallup survey found that the majority of people in the United States, Britain, Canada, France, Japan, and China were spending more time focusing on their weaknesses than on their strengths.[25] Why is this? Perhaps it's cultural, perhaps some inherent survival mechanism that makes us focus on our weaknesses, striving to improve them. On one level this makes sense: We need to develop the necessary skills for success in life. But spending most of our time working on our weaknesses results, at best, in competence, while building our strengths is the pathway to excellence.

Well-meaning friends or family members may discourage people from using their gifts. In the Renaissance, Michelangelo's father felt that art was a waste of time. Demanding that his son become a successful cloth merchant to bring money into the family, he would beat the boy whenever he caught him drawing. Fortunately, Michelangelo persevered. This short-sighted parental behavior did not end in the Renaissance. Too many college students struggle with majors in practical fields chosen by their parents when their hearts call them in other directions. Brazilian novelist Paolo Coelho's parents insisted that he pursue a career in law. When he told them he wanted to become a writer, they had him committed to a mental institution. Years later, after dropping out of law school, he chose his own path, writing *The Alchemist*, a best-selling novel about finding vocation.

Discovering our gifts is energizing and empowering. In 2005, psychologists found that people who used their signature strengths in a new way each day for a week significantly reduced their depression and increased their happiness for up to 6 months later.[14] Getting back in touch with what they love to do, recognizing what they do well, gives people a stronger sense of their own possibilities.

Detachment

Once people discover their gifts, they need to make time to use them. As Henry David Thoreau recognized long before the advent of cell phones and computers, "Our life is frittered away by detail. . . . Simplify, simplify."[26] In our fast-paced multitasking lives, following our vocation requires detachment, clearing away the mindless distractions that keep us from doing what we love. Becoming energized by rediscovering their gifts, people are more motivated to do this. And strong motivation is essential, for detachment is countercultural: We are surrounded by electronic demands and distractions 24/7, leaving little time for contemplation. It's hard to listen to the still small voice within when the voices around us are so relentless and demanding. As an exercise in detachment, people can choose one of the following practices to clear a space for vocation to grow—just one practice, for with detachment, "less is more."

- Schedule a "time out": a weekly Sabbath, or 2-hour block of time each week alone to reflect, walk by the lake, browse in a bookstore or library, or sit in a coffee shop and write in a journal. Dan, a busy Silicon Valley executive, takes a 2-hour Sabbath each Thursday afternoon, returning to his regular routine with creative new ideas, renewed, refreshed, and recharged.

- Eliminate a chronic distraction. People can identify something in their lives that steals their time and drains their energy, such as compulsive shopping, excessive television or Internet use, a chronic complainer, mindless socializing, continual interruptions, a cluttered household, or a cluttered desk. Once they've recognized this distraction, they can take steps to eliminate it: stop when they catch

themselves falling into an unproductive habit (compulsive shopping, television, or Internet use, saying yes when they'd rather say
no, listening to chronic complainers); or set aside time to begin
organizing their households or their desks—one small step at a
time.

- Stop hurrying. Rushing puts our bodies into chronic stress. People
  can follow Thoreau's advice and simplify. Instead of cramming
  their schedules with too many activities, they can decide what's
  most important to them and schedule those activities first, eliminating the nonessential.

- Begin a meditation practice. People can sign up for a meditation
  class or begin spending 10 minutes in silence at the beginning or
  end of each day, then work up to half an hour. They can simply
  close their eyes, breathe deeply, focus on their breath, and observe
  their thoughts and feelings or focus on an inspirational passage, or
  they can follow the suggestions of Shapiro and Sahgal or Zhu (this
  volume).

These detachment practices are just that: practices. The process of meditation involves returning to the breath or passage every time our minds wan-
der. Eliminating a chronic distraction or constant rushing takes practice.
Keeping a Sabbath and saying "no" to others' demands takes practice.
Yet repeated practice builds inner strength.

Discernment

Detachment leads to discernment. Slowing down, taking a regular "time
out," eliminating distractions, and beginning a contemplative practice—
all of these make people less stressed, less reactive, more open to the
wisdom of their hearts.

Finding his own way to discernment, Iñigo Lopez was a young noble-
man in Renaissance Spain with charm, charisma, and courtly manners
who read the books of chivalry and followed their example. While defend-
ing the fortress of Pamplona from a French invasion, he was wounded in
the leg by a cannon ball. Taken to his family castle of Loyola, he suffered
repeated settings of his shattered leg. While lying in bed for the long,

painful months of recovery, he grew restless, wanting to read the books of chivalry he enjoyed, but his family had only religious books. So he read a book of saints' lives, then daydreamed about his life at court—the daring deeds, duels, and adventures. But these memories left him restless and discontent. Then he imagined what it would be like to live like St. Francis of Assisi and felt a deep sense of joy. Discernment, he found, meant listening to his heart, asking which choices brought only fleeting pleasures and discontent, which ones deep and abiding joy. Embracing a new religious vocation, he founded the Jesuit order, becoming St. Ignatius Loyola. His process of Ignatian Discernment is still used by thousands of people today in retreats, counseling, spiritual direction, and leadership development.

Discernment means becoming mindful of our feelings, asking which choices bring us the deep joy St. Ignatius called *consolation*, which he described as being closer to God, experiencing inspiration, clarity, authenticity, gratitude, love, appreciation, grace, generosity, energy, growth, and creativity. It means recognizing which choices lead to *desolation*—the sense of isolation, egocentrism, anxiety, frustration, confusion, self-pity, defensiveness, hopelessness, turmoil, guilt, self-hate, depression, and lack of meaning. Consolation and desolation are the keys to discernment, the two points on our inner compass.

When people find themselves at a crossroads in their lives, consulting their inner compass can help them make important choices. As a graduating senior, Catherine was accepted by seven prestigious law schools. To decide upon which one, she compared their educational programs, locations, and costs, but also exercised discernment, visiting the campuses and listening to her heart to find the program that was right for her.

Direction

The fourth step in our vocational journey is to set our direction, or what the Buddhists call "intention." More than a single goal, direction is a guiding star, a vision of possibility from which our individual goals flow.

While seeking vocation, people embark on what Joseph Campbell described as the mythical hero's journey, with the call to adventure, threshold guardians, road of trials, and return with a treasure. The call to adventure is the call of their gifts to be discovered and used. The journey begins when they detach from the world they know to follow their hearts in a new direction. Threshold guardians are those who would block their way, from active adversaries to well-meaning friends and family wishing to direct or protect them to their own inner threshold guardians of fear and self-doubt. The road of trials represents the challenges along the path, and the treasure is vocation, at once a gift to themselves and the world around them.[27]

After a high school athletic injury introduced him to the world of medicine, Stephen dreamed about becoming a doctor. But bowing to family pressure—a familiar threshold guardian—he began college as a business major, expected to enter the family business. His first-year business classes left him restless and unfulfilled, with mediocre grades and in the state Ignatius called "desolation." Then taking a biology course to fulfill a general education requirement reawakened his passion for science, leading him to discernment. He switched majors to biology, excelling in his premed courses, but when he applied to medical school, he got only rejection letters because of low grades his freshman year—the road of trials. Refusing to give up, Stephen worked in a medical lab after graduation and kept applying to medical schools, this time with glowing letters from the doctors at the lab. He was finally accepted to the University of Southern California medical school, chose a residency in neurosurgery, and has become a doctor who supports his patients not only with outstanding surgical skills but also with deep compassion and heartfelt intention.

Stephen's story illustrates the importance of setting a direction and continuing to move forward when our initial efforts don't work out, using the "hope skills" described in David Feldman's chapter in this volume. Stephen set a goal—applying to medical school—and took steps to achieve that goal (sending out applications, getting recommendations). Disappointed but not discouraged when he reached a roadblock, he chose what hope psychology calls an "alternate pathway"—working in the medical lab. Two years later, with more experience and supportive recommendations, he applied again successfully. The important lessons here are perseverance and flexibility. With strong motivation—what hope psychology calls "agency"—Stephen continued moving in the direction of his dreams, finding alternative plans or "pathways" to get him there, achieving his goal and going on to become an outstanding doctor.[28]

The vocation journey is, of course, not over, for Stephen or for any of us. With every challenge, every change, every season of our lives, we may hear a new call to begin the journey on another level, discovering more about ourselves and our world. Each time we hear the call, we can gain greater perspective by cultivating our vocation: rediscovering our gifts, detaching from distractions, taking time for discernment, and asking, "What is my intention?" "Where am I called in this season of my life?"

Notes

1. Portions of this chapter have been presented elsewhere, initially in Dreher, D. & Plante, T. G. (2007). The calling protocol: Promoting greater health, joy, and purpose in life. In T. G. Plante & C. E. Thoresen (Eds.), *Spirit, science and health: How the spiritual mind fuels wellness* (pp. 129–140). Westport, CT: Greenwood Press; and most extensively in Dreher, D. (2008). *Your personal renaissance: 12 steps to finding your life's true calling.* New York: Da Capo. This book discusses the Renaissance concept of vocation as well as current theory, applications, and research in positive psychology. All of the examples in this chapter are taken from real life, although some names have been changed to ensure personal privacy.

2. See discussion in Hardy, L. (1990). *The fabric of this world.* Grand Rapids, MI: Eerdmans.

3. See Peterson, C., & Seligman, M. E. P. (2004). *Character strengths and virtues: A Handbook and classification.* New York: Oxford University Press.

4. Seligman, M. E. P. (2002). *Authentic happiness* (p. 173). New York: Free Press.

5. Weiss, J. W., Skelley, M. F., Haughey, J. C., & Hall, D. (2004). Calling, new careers and spirituality: A reflective perspective for organizational leaders and professionals. In M. L. Pava & P. Primeaux (Eds.), *Spiritual intelligence at work: Meaning, metaphor, and morals* (pp. 175–201). Quote on p. 180.

6. Wrzesniewski, A., McCauley, C., Rozin, P., & Schwartz, B. (1997). Jobs, careers, and callings: People's relations to their work. *Journal of Research in Personality, 31,* 21–33.

7. Cochran. L. (1990). *The sense of vocation* (pp. 172, 160). Albany: State University of New York Press.

8. Maslow, A. H., with Stephens, D. C., & Heil, G. (1998). *Maslow on management* (pp. 39, 38). New York: John Wiley.

9. Davidson, J. C., & Caddell, D. P. (1994). Religion and the meaning of work. *Journal for the Scientific Study of Religion, 33*, 135–147.

10. Steger, M. F., & Dik, B. J. (2010). Work as meaning: Individual and organizational benefits of engaging in meaningful work. In P. A. Linley, S. Harrington, & N. Garvea (Eds.), *Oxford handbook of positive psychology at work* (pp. 131–142). New York: Oxford University Press.

11. Peterson, C., Park, N., &. Seligman, M. E. P. (2005). Orientations to happiness and life satisfaction: The full life versus the empty life. *Journal of Happiness Studies, 6*, 25–41.

12. Csikszentmihalyi, M. (1990). *Flow: The psychology of optimal experience*. New York: HarperCollins.

13. Dreher, D. E., Holloway, K. A., & Schoenfelder, E. (2007). The vocation identity questionnaire: Measuring the sense of calling. *Research in the Social Scientific Study of Religion, 18*, 99–120.

14. Seligman, M. E. P., Steen, T. A., Park, N., & Peterson, C. (2005). Positive psychology progress: Empirical validation of interventions. *American Psychologist, 60*, 410–421.

15. Steger, M. F., Oishi, S., & Kashdan, T. B. (2009). Meaning in life across the life span: Levels and correlates of meaning in life from emerging adulthood to older adulthood. *Journal of Positive Psychology, 4*, 43–52.

16. Schueller, S. M., & Seligman, M. E. P. (2010). Pursuit of pleasure, engagement, and meaning: Relationship to subjective and objective measures of well-being. *Journal of Positive Psychology, 5*, 253–263.

17. Frankl, V. E. (1966/1946). *Man's search for meaning*. New York: Washington Square.

18. Cresswell, J. D., Welch, W. T., Taylor, S. E., Sherman, D. K., Gruenewald, T. L., & Mann, T. (2005), Affirmation of personal values buffers neuroendocrine and psychological stress responses. *Psychological Science, 16*, 846–851.

19. Dreher, D., & Plante, T. G. (2007). The calling protocol: Promoting greater health, joy, and purpose in life. In T. G. Plante & C. E. Thoresen (Eds.), *Spirit, science and health: How the spiritual mind fuels wellness* (pp. 129–140). Westport, CT: Greenwood Press.

20. Sekerka, L. E., & Fredrickson, B. L. (2010). Working positively toward transformative cooperation. In P. A. Linley, S. Harrington, & N. Garvea (Eds.), *Oxford handbook of positive psychology at work* (pp. 81–94). New York: Oxford University Press.

21. Amabile, T. M. (1996). *Creativity in context*. Boulder, CO: Westview.

22. McGee, J. J., & Delbecq, A. L. (2003) Vocation as a critical factor in a spirituality for executive leadership. In O. F. Williams (Ed.), *Business, religion, and spirituality: A new synthesis* (pp. 94–110). Notre Dame, IN: University of Notre Dame Press.

23. Avolio, B. J., Griffith, J., Wernsing, T. S., & Walumbwa, F. O. (2010). What is authentic leadership development? In P. A. Linley, S. Harrington, & N. Garvea (Eds.), *Oxford handbook of positive psychology at work* (pp. 39–51). New York: Oxford University Press.

24. Dreher, D. E. (2006). Renaissance lessons for today: A course to promote purpose and personal growth in later life. *LLI Review, 1*, 105–112.

25. Hodges, T. D., & Clifton. D. O. (2004). Strengths-based development in practice. In P. A. Linley & S. Joseph. (Eds.), *Positive psychology in practice* (pp. 256–268). Hoboken, NJ: Wiley.

26. Thoreau, H. D. (2004/1854). *Walden* (p. 73). New York.

27. Campbell, J. (1968/1949). *The hero with a thousand Faces*. Princeton, NJ: Princeton University Press.

28. See Snyder, C. R. (1994). *The psychology of hope*. New York: Simon & Schuster.

Section II

Cultivating the Fruit

10

Psychotherapy and Virtue: Positive Psychology and Spiritual Well-Being

Len Sperry and Jonathan J. Sperry

Both moral philosophy and psychology have traditionally emphasized the concepts of virtue and character. Virtue was viewed as good or bad (vices) habits, while character was understood as emerging from a network of virtues (or vices).[1] The relationship between virtue and character is captured in the age-old maxim: Plant an act, reap a habit; plant a habit, reap a virtue; plant a virtue, reap a character; plant a character, reap a destiny. Until the advent of scientific psychology in 1879 when Wundt established the first laboratory in experimental psychology, virtue was a central construct in psychology. Over the years, virtue was defined as the psychological disposition that moves one to accomplish moral good—or, in more contemporary language, as a value in action.[2] Essentially, virtue was increasingly "lost" for more than a century as scientific psychology developed, until its recent "recovery" as the positive psychology movement emerged.

This chapter begins with a discussion of the gradual loss of the virtue tradition and its eventual recovery. Next, it describes current efforts to incorporate virtue and well-being in psychotherapy. For example, research demonstrates that treating conditions such as chronic depression by focusing on virtues, building positive emotions, and increasing the client's sense of meaning and well-being instead of simply reducing symptoms not only leads to symptom reduction but also reduces the likelihood of relapse.

Such a focus is superior to conventional treatment and reduces the need for medication. The chapter emphasizes positive psychotherapy and well-being therapy and provides a clinical case example that illustrates a virtue- and well-being-focused treatment process.

The Loss of the Virtue Tradition: The Quest for a Value-Free Psychology

Over the past century, psychology has been equivocal about virtue and character. Initially, psychology easily incorporated both of these constructs from moral philosophy. However, as psychology began to evolve into a scientific discipline and field of inquiry, it attempted to distinguish and distance itself from its roots in moral philosophy. The most effective strategy for both distinguishing and distancing itself from its roots in moral philosophy was to differentiate the study of personality from the study of character. Gordon Allport insisted that psychology could not become a science unless it banished character from American psychology. His famous dictum, "Character is personality evaluated, and personality is character *devalued*" (italics added),[3] reflected psychology's increasing disdain for the concept of character.

As a result of this shifting focus, psychology succeeded in establishing a scientific and, presumably, a value-free foundation distinct from a philosophical foundation for understanding human behavior and actions. For all practical purposes, the concept of character, once a staple of everyday conversation as well as clinical practice, has been almost entirely replaced with the concept of personality. From the late 1950s through the early 1990s, the profession of psychology endeavored to reformulate psychotherapy into the same scientific, value-free discipline framework as the other natural sciences.

Unfortunately, many psychotherapists have become increasingly dissatisfied with this supposedly value-free, scientific view of psychotherapy as represented by DSM-IV, clinical practice guidelines, and treatment outcome measures. Nevertheless, critiques of psychotherapy's value-free stance are long standing. They include Philip Rieff's provocative analysis in *Freud: the Mind of a Moralist*[4] and Jerome Frank's *Psychotherapy and the Human Predicament*.[5] Frank observes that all psychotherapies share a value system that accords primacy to self-fulfillment and views individuals as the center of their moral universe, that is, the autonomous self. He believes that this value system can easily become a source of misery in itself because of its unrealistic expectations for personal happiness and because it downplays traditional values such as "the redemptive power of suffering, acceptance of one's lot in life, adherence to tradition, self-restraint and moderation."[5]

More recently, Philip Cushman[6] suggests that the goal of attaining and maintaining an "autonomous self" may be misguided. Furthermore, Cushman contends that such a preoccupation with an inner self that is self-soothing, self-loving, and self-sufficient eventually leads to an "empty self." Furthermore, there is mounting concern that traditionally practiced psychotherapy tends to foster individual self-fulfillment over community well-being.[7] In short, the effect of the shift to a value-free psychology has changed the moral calculus from a social ethic to an individual ethic in America.

The Recovery of the Virtue Tradition: The Promise of Positive Psychology

Positive psychology is having a remarkable influence on nearly every aspect of the field of psychology, including its basic premises and interventions. Although Maslow used the term *positive psychology* in 1954 and subsequent psychologists emphasized the promotion of mental health over the treatment of mental illness, Martin Seligman is considered the animator of the modern positive psychology movement. Positive psychology's roots are in humanistic psychology with is focus on happiness and fulfillment. However, earlier influences on positive psychology came primarily from philosophical and religious sources that predated the development of scientific psychology. Chief among these was Aristotle's belief that happiness is constituted by rational activity in accordance with "virtue." In his *Nicomachean Ethics*, Aristotle proposed a classification of virtues that included 11 moral virtues. Four of the so called "cardinal virtues" (prudence, justice, temperance, and courage) were later reaffirmed and appropriated from the Aristotelian tradition to Christianity by Thomas Aquinas. Christianity added three theological virtues (faith, hope, charity), which served as a counterpoint to the seven deadly sins or vices that centered on self-indulgence and narcissism.

The publication of Peterson and Seligman's *Character Strengths and Virtues: A Handbook and Classification*[2] represents a landmark research effort in identifying and classifying positive psychological traits, also called virtues or strengths. This publication identifies six classes of virtue consisting of 24 measurable character strengths. These include: (1) wisdom and knowledge: characterized by creativity, curiosity, open-mindedness, love of learning, perspective, and innovation; (2) courage: characterized by bravery, persistence, integrity, and vitality; (3) humanity: characterized by love, kindness, and social intelligence; (4) justice: characterized by citizenship, fairness, and leadership; (5) temperance: characterized by forgiveness and mercy, humility, prudence, and self-control; and (6) transcendence: characterized by appreciation of beauty and excellence, gratitude, hope, humor, and spirituality.

The Scientific Study of Character

Character has a long and venerable tradition in the study of personality. Although there was a biological tradition in the study of personality that emphasized temperament, the psychological tradition that emphasized character was in vogue for the first two-thirds of the 20th century. Currently, personality is being conceptualized in a broader perspective and has come to be described as the confluence of both character and temperament.[8]

There is an extraordinary line of psychological research that appears to validate the description of character as basic psychological construct. Cloninger and his colleagues have found that individuals with mature personalities or character structures tend to be self-responsible, cooperative, and self-transcendent.[8] In contrast, those with personality or character disorders are noted to have difficulty with self-acceptance, were intolerant and revengeful toward others, and felt self-conscious and unfulfilled. This suggested that the presence or absence of a personality disorder could be defined in terms of the character dimensions of self-directedness, cooperativeness, and self-transcendence.

The basic concept of self-directedness refers to self-determination, which is an individual's ability to control, regulate, and adapt behavior in accord with one's chosen goals and values. Individuals differ in their capacity for self-determination. Individuals with moderate to high levels of self-determination are considered to be mature, effective, and well-organized who exhibit self-esteem, are able to admit faults and accept themselves as they are, feel their lives have meaning and purpose, can delay gratification in order to achieve their goals, and take initiative in overcoming challenges. On the other hand, individuals with lower levels of self-determination have low self-esteem, blame others for their problems, feel uncertain of their identity or purpose, and are often reactive, dependent, and resourceless.

The character factor of cooperativeness was formulated to account for individual differences in identification with and acceptance of other people. This factor is a measure of character that is related to agreeability versus self-centered aggression and hostility. Low levels of cooperativeness contribute substantially to the likelihood of a concomitant personality or character disorder. Cooperative individuals tend to be socially tolerant, empathic, helpful, and compassionate, while uncooperative individuals tend to be socially intolerant, disinterested in other people, unhelpful, and revengeful. Cooperative individuals are likely to show unconditional acceptance of others, empathy with others' feelings, and willingness to help others achieve their goals without selfish domination. It is not surprising that social acceptance, helpfulness, and concern for the rights of others are correlated with positive self-esteem and the capacity for compassion. For instance, such compassion involves the willingness to forgive and be kind to others regardless of their behavior rather than to seek revenge or to enjoy their embarrassment or suffering; it involves feelings of familial love and the absence of hostility.

Self-transcendence is the capacity to perceive and experience reality beyond one's own thoughts, beliefs, and needs. Victor Frankl noted that when encountering adversity, an individual's optimal functioning depends on the ability to find meaning in challenge and suffering and to find a transcendent or spiritual purpose.[9] Self-transcendence is noted in empathic understanding as well as in intense concentration in which an individual may experience a sense of spiritual union with anything or everything. The stable self-forgetfulness of self-transcendent people has been described as the same as experienced transiently by people when they are totally absorbed, intensely concentrated, and fascinated by one thing. Examples of self-transcendent behaviors include finding meaning and

value in past and present life experiences, connecting with others by helping and receiving help, reaching out to a higher entity or purpose, having
an interest in learning, living fully in the present, and being able to adjust
to difficult situations.[10] Obviously, spiritual growth requires an increasing
capacity for self-transcendence.

The Scientific Study of Virtue

While originally the domain of theology, virtue was also a part of the
psychological domain. Erik Erikson discussed virtues as representing
the strengths of the ego over the instinct of the id and the demands of the
superego.[11] In short, for Erikson, ego strength is equivalent to virtue. As
noted earlier, a postmodern critique of contemporary psychology and
psychotherapy makes a compelling case that there can never be a value-
free psychology or psychotherapy and that the psychology would do well
to reconsider its relationship with moral philosophy. In a somewhat related
vein, major figures in the psychology research community are beginning
to retrieve psychology's early interest in character and virtue. This
retrieval effort is being called positive psychology.[2] *Positive psychology*[12]
refers to an emphasis on strengths and the developmental or growth
model rather than on the dark side of psychology with its emphasis on
human foibles and the disease or psychopathology model. In other words,
much of contemporary psychology and psychotherapy has become preoc-
cupied with healing within a disease model of human functioning. Such a
focus on pathology neglects the fulfilled individual and the thriving community. One wonders how it is that the social sciences, particularly psychology, have come to view the human strengths and virtues—altruism,
courage, honesty, duty, joy, health, responsibility and good cheer—as
derivative, defensive, or downright illusions, while weakness and negative
motivations—anxiety, lust, selfishness, paranoia, anger, disorder, and
sadness—are viewed as authentic. The aim of the field of positive psychology "is to begin to catalyze a change in the focus of psychology only with
repairing the worst things in life to also building positive qualities."[2]

Three pillars have been proposed for positive psychology: subjective
well-being, positive character, and positive community. Subjective well-
being includes "contentment, satisfaction, hope, and optimism," while
positive character includes "the capacity for love and vocation, courage,

interpersonal skill, aesthetic sensibility, perseverance, forgiveness, originality, future mindedness, spirituality, high talent and wisdom." Finally, positive community includes "the civic virtues and the institutions that move individuals toward better citizenship: responsibility, nurturance, altruism, civility, moderation, tolerance and work ethic."[2]

Because subjective well-being has clinical significance, it will be emphasized here. Subjective well-being has been defined as an individual's subjective cognitive and affective evaluation of his or her own life situation.[13] Cloninger defined well-being as "a stable condition of coherence of personality that leads to a full range of emotions and no negative emotions regardless of external circumstances."[14] Essential to well-being is coherence, which is defined as the integration of the body, mind, and spirit. He posits that any treatment that ignores any aspect of the body, mind, and spirit is inadequate to facilitate the development of biopsychosocial health and well-being.

Ryff and Singer[15] have linked biological correlates (cardiovascular, neuroendocrine, immune) of psychological well-being to health benefits associated with living a life with meaning and purpose, continued growth, and high-quality relationships. Ryff has developed a psychological well-being measure that measures psychological adjustment. This well-being measure is a cognitive adaptation inventory that measures people's ability to positively evaluate themselves and their ability to find meaning and purpose in life and to have a sense of mastery and self-determination.[15] Ryff distinguishes between hedonic well-being (moods and feelings) and eudaimonic well-being, which is related to having purpose in life, continued personal growth and development, and good relationships with others. She has incorporated theories that measure health and well-being beyond the "absence of illness," based on clinical work, life span development, and mental health, to develop a multifaceted theory of psychological well-being.[15]

From a psychological perspective, virtues are defined "as any psychological process that enables a person to think and act so as to benefit both him- or herself and society."[16] This is similar to the philosopher Roberts's proposition that virtues operate to help a person to live well among people.[16] This dual emphasis on individual and community is notably distinct from the implicit or explicit advocacy of radical individualism characteristic of much of contemporary psychology and psychotherapy. Similar to

Aristotle, those advocating positive psychology emphasize thriving or flourishing as the result of virtuous living.

While some humanistic psychologies have also championed human strengths and self-actualization over the past four decades, only positive psychology has endeavored to achieve a scientific understanding and effective interventions to achieve virtue and human flourishing. A special issue of the *Journal of Social and Clinical Psychology* consists of articles describing the current state of research data and findings on seven virtues: self-control, hope, forgiveness, gratitude, humility, wisdom, and love.

Psychotherapies Reflecting Positive Psychology and Well-Being Models

The recovery of the virtue tradition via positive psychology has influenced the theory, research, and practice of psychotherapy. This section describes two such approaches. They are positive psychotherapy and well-being therapy.

Positive Psychotherapy

Positive psychotherapy (PPT) is a branch of positive psychology designed to build on positive emotions, engagement, or "flow," character strengths, and meaning rather than reducing or ameliorating negative symptoms. It was developed by Seligman and colleagues at the University of Pennsylvania to treat conditions like depression by focusing on virtues, building positive emotions, and increasing the client's sense of meaning instead of simply reducing symptoms such as sadness.[17] Typically, PPT utilizes a combination of 12 exercises that can be practiced individually or in groups. The technique, "using your signature strengths or virtues," is a primary intervention in positive psychotherapy. When tested in a randomized controlled trial, it was found that this technique did lead to positive treatment outcomes.[17]

The effects of PPT have been validated in intervention studies among clinical populations, undergraduate college students, and mental health professionals[17] (clinical psychologists, life coaches, psychiatrists, and educators). Seligman, Rashid, and Parks identified the following empirically supported PPT exercises[17]:

1. *Using Your Strengths:* Take the Values in Action Inventory of Strengths (VIA-IS) questionnaire to assess your top five strengths, and think of ways to use those strengths more in your daily life.

2. *Three Good Things/Blessings:* Each evening, write down three good things that happened and why you think they happened.

3. *Obituary/Biography:* Imagine that you have passed away after living a fruitful and satisfying life. What would you want your obituary to say? Write a 1- to 2-page essay summarizing what you would like to be remembered for the most.

4. *Gratitude Visit:* Think of someone to whom you are very grateful but who you have never properly thanked. Compose a letter to that person describing your gratitude, and read the letter to that person by phone or in person.

5. *Active/Constructive Responding:* An active-constructive response is one where you react in a visibly positive and enthusiastic way to good news from someone else. At least once a day, respond actively and constructively to someone you know.

6. *Savoring:* Once a day, take the time to enjoy something that you usually hurry through (examples: eating a meal, taking a shower, walking to class). When it's over, write down what you did, how you did it differently, and how it felt compared to when you rush through it.

Seligman's positive psychotherapy approach is one of a number of emerging forms of psychotherapy influenced by positive psychology. Another promising approach is well-being therapy.

Well-Being Therapy

Well-being therapy (WBT) is a theoretically and empirically derived treatment approach with promising treatment outcomes data. WBT was developed by Fava[18] specifically as a relapse-preventive strategy in the residual phase of affective disorders and for nonresponders to standard treatment for affective disorders. Subsequently, it was expanded as a treatment intervention for anxiety disorders, including OCD and affective disorders, particularly depression, and as a strengths-based strategy in school counseling and in life coaching. Several studies show its superiority when compared to CBT alone, including a 6-year follow-up of nonmedication treatment for preventing recurrence in depression, which showed that when WBT strategies were included in treatment, results were only 40% relapse rate compared to 90% rate with clinical management.[19] Based on Ryff's model of well-being,[20] WBT is structured, directive, and problem oriented, yet it is client centered in that client's positive appraisals of well-being lead the course of treatment. This contrasts with most other therapy approaches in which the therapist takes considerable responsibility in specifying the destination and goals of treatment and leading the process. WBT is an eight-session therapeutic intervention that emphasizes both self-observation and interactions with the therapist. Interestingly, the therapist's role in WBT is more that of a coach, with the client being largely responsible for leading the change process.[18]

The overall goal of WBT is to enhance the client's sense of well-being. This is accomplished by three a three-fold strategy: First, enhance the client's awareness of positive moments. Second, discuss and change negative thoughts that disrupt episodes of well-being. Third, improve the client's impairments in six well-being dimensions. The therapeutic process in WBT is rather straightforward. It begins with teaching the client to record (in a structured diary) current episodes of well-being and thoughts that sidetrack those experiences. It then involves reinterpreting those thoughts viewed from an observer's standpoint. Then it utilizes reinterpretations to increase a sense of well-being in any of the six well-being dimensions that are impaired. A variety of therapeutic interventions are utilized in WBT. These include cognitive restructuring, distancing, fostering positive thinking, and homework, as well as happiness interventions and spiritual practices. WBT can be provided individually or in small groups. It has been used with adults, older adults, children, and adolescents in clinical and in nonclinical settings.[21] WBT is a directive and structured treatment approach in which the focus of treatment can be specified. As it is currently formulated, in the initial sessions, the focus is on identifying periods of well-being through a structured diary. Clients are taught to rank episodes of well-being on a scale from 0 to 100, where 0 represents the absence of well-being and 100 represents the most intense well-being that could be experienced. The focus on inter-mediate sessions is on discovering how thoughts and behaviors character-istically prevent well-being once this pattern is recognized. These sessions emphasize self-monitoring moments and feelings of well-being. During these sessions, the therapist encourages the client to engage in pleasurable activities each day, and specific strategies for enhancing well-being are discussed. The final sessions focus more directly on impaired dimensions of well-being. The therapist guides the client in recognizing errors in thinking and in generating alternate interpretations.[21]

Clinical Case Example

Brandon is a 37-year-old married man who was diagnosed with human immunodeficiency virus (HIV) 2 years ago. He is seeking psychotherapy for depression secondary to chronic cocaine addiction. He presented with social withdrawal, depressed mood, significant decrease in pleasurable activities, and relational difficulties. Since clinical depression can signifi-cantly exacerbate immunodeficiency, it is critical that such depression be aggressively treated in HIV-positive individuals. Accordingly, 8 months ago, before entering psychotherapy, he was prescribed antidepressants but experienced little improvement. In his first therapy session, he stated that God was punishing him by not allowing him to be happy and giving him a terminal illness. A self-described religious individual, he indicated that he recently stopped attending church because he did not feel that God would want him around fellow churchgoers. In addition, Brandon's wife insisted that he enter therapy because their relationship satisfaction had continued to decrease.

Since spiritual beliefs and practices appeared to be exacerbants or per-petuants and because of insurance coverage limitations, a treatment con-tract was established for eight sessions of virtue-focused psychotherapy that incorporated well-being and positive psychology methods. An inte-grative assessment found that Brandon was low in two of the six virtue classes: transcendence and humanity.[17] In the transcendence class, he ini-tially presented with a lack of hope and a significant decrease in spiritual-ity. In the humanity class, he struggled with expressing love toward his wife as his depression increased. Mutually agreed treatment goals were to increase positive mood states, virtue, and well-being. The expectation was that as well-being was enhanced, an increase in relational harmony was likely.

Therapy was tailored to Brandon's levels of virtue, strengths, and personal sense of well-being. Cognitive and behavioral interventions were utilized to increase positive moods and to enhance his levels of virtue and well-being. Virtue qualities such as persistence, kindness, and self-control were some of his strengths that the therapist emphasized to assist him in achieving the stated treatment goals.

Brandon agreed to journal daily about different episodes of well-being and negative thoughts as well as to engage in two pleasurable activities per day. He also agreed to participate in the following behaviors between sessions: taking a 20-minute walk with his wife at least four times per week, playing his guitar daily, volunteering at a local soup kitchen for 2 hours per week, engaging in daily prayer and meditation, attending 12-step meetings two times per week, and attending Sunday services. It was not surprising that Brandon requested that the therapist pray with him at the end of each session.

Cognitive restructuring addressed his self-defeating beliefs, while the pleasurable activities were behavioral homework assignments designed to promote well-being on a daily basis. He became actively engaged in the treatment process. By the eighth session, Brandon experienced an improved mood, a renewed sense of faith, and increased well-being. His daily average well-being score increased from 15 to 90 (scale of 1–100) over the course of the eight sessions. This increase in well-being was reflected in better relational harmony.

Concluding Note

As psychotherapists move beyond treatment goals of simply reducing symptomatic distress to include increasing virtue and well-being, psychotherapy approaches such as positive psychotherapy and well-being therapy are likely to be more commonly practiced. The recovery of the virtue tradition and the rise of positive psychology reflect what appears to be a paradigm shift in psychotherapy. A discernable shift is underway from the conventional pathology and deficits-based perspective to a strengths-based, virtue, and well-being perspective. As clients in psychotherapy are assisted to move beyond a focus on the autonomous self and pathology to a focus on self-and-community and strengths, the likelihood of higher-level functioning and the enhancement of virtue and well-being increases.

Notes

1. McBrien, R. (1994). *Catholicism, new edition*. San Francisco: HarperSanFrancisco.
2. Peterson, C., & Seligman, M. (2004). *Character strengths and virtues: A handbook and classification* (p. 5). Oxford: Oxford University Press.
3. Allport, G. (1937). *Pattern and growth in personality*. New York: Holt, Rinehart & Winston.
4. Rieff, P. (1966). *Freud: The mind of a moralist*. Chicago: University of Chicago Press.
5. Frank, J. (1978). *Psychotherapy and the human predicament* (pp. 6–7). New York: Shocken.
6. Cushman, P. (1995). *Constructing the self, constructing America: A cultural history of psychotherapy*. Reading, MA: Addison-Wesley.
7. Hillman, J., & Ventura, M. (1992). *We've had a hundred years of psychotherapy and the world's getting worse*. San Francisco: HarperSanFrancisco.
8. Cloninger, R., Svrakic, D., & Prybeck, T. (1993). A psychobiological model of temperament and character. *Archives of General Psychiatry, 50*, 975–990.
9. Frankl, V. (1959). *Man's search for meaning: An introduction to logotherapy*. New York: Simon & Schuster.
10. Reed, P. G. (1991). Self-transcendence and mental health in the oldest-old adults.*Nursing Research, 40*(1), 5–11.
11. Erikson, E. (1963). *Childhood and society*. New York: Norton.
12. Seligman, M., & Csikszentmihalyi, M. (2000). Positive psychology: An introduction. *American Psychologist, 55*, 5–14.
13. Campbell, D. T., Converse, P. E., & Rodgers, W. L. (1976). *The quality of American life*. New York: Russell Sage.

14. Cloninger, C. R. (2004). *Feeling good: The science of well-being* (p. 8). New York: Oxford University Press.
15. Ryff, C., & Singer, B. (1996). Psychological well-being: Meaning, measurement, and implications for psychotherapy research. *Psychotherapy and Psychosomatics, 65,* 14–23.
16. McCullough, M. E., & Snyder, C. R. (2000). Classical source of human strength: Revisiting an old home and building a new one. *Journal of Social and Clinical Psychology. Special Issue: Classical Sources of Human Strength: A Psychological Analysis, 19*(1), 1.
17. Seligman, M., Rashid, T., & Parks, A. (2006). Positive psychotherapy, *American Psychologist, 61,* 774–788.
18. Fava, G. (2003). Well-being therapy: Conceptual and technical issues. *Psychotherapy and Psychosomatics, 68,* 171–179.
19. Fava, G. A., Ruini, C., Rafanelli, C., Finos, L., Conti, S., & Grandi, S. (2004). Six-year outcome of cognitive behavior therapy for prevention of recurrent depression. *American Journal of Psychiatry, 161,* 1872–1876.
20. Ryff, C. (1989). Happiness is everything, or is it? Explorations on the meaning of psychological well-being. *Journal of Personality and Social Psychology, 6,* 1069–1081.
21. Fava, G., & Runi, C. (2003). Development and characteristics of a well-being-enhancing psychotherapeutic strategy: Well-being therapy. *Journal of Behavioral Therapy and Experimental Psychiatry, 34,* 45–63.

11

Ordinary Mind: Meditation-Initiated Integrative Therapy (MIIT)

Caifang Jeremy Zhu

Chan, known as Zen in Japanese, sees enlightenment as very significant because it is the starting point for the subsequent cultivation of attaining and sustaining a liberated-minded body or embodied mind. Similarly, psychoanalysis values insight through free association, analysis, dream interpretation, or other psychoanalytic tools. Traditional cognitive-behavior therapy (CBT) drives the client to realize and correct the faulty schema or belief on which he or she has been operating. Chan, psycho-analysis, and CBT each have similar moments of "insight" that carry much weight for the success of the subsequent practice. The content of the "insight," however, differs greatly from one to the other. So does the treatment of the insight by each of the three practices in question. This chapter proposes and demonstrates that the traditional practice of *ping chang xin* popularly known as Ordinary Mind in Chan Buddhism can be more comprehensive and efficacious when it integrates some practical methods and skills of psychotherapy. It culminates in the develop-ment of a new psychospiritual model called meditation-initiated integra-tive therapy.

Traditional Practice of Ordinary Mind

Historical Context

Let us contextualize the teaching and practice of Ordinary Mind, which is shortened from Ordinary-Mind-Is-the-Way in classical Chan Buddhism. There seems to be a general consensus in Chinese Buddhist studies that Mazu Daoyi 馬祖道一(709–788 C.E.; Jap. Baso) was the Chan master who initiated monastic community practice of Ordinary-Mind-Is-the-Way.[1, 2, 3] In fascicle 28 of *The Jingde Record of Lamp Transmissions* (*Jingde chuandeng lu* 景德传灯录), Mazu said,

> The Tao (Way) does not need to be cultivated so long as it is not defiled. What is defilement? It is anything like thinking life and death, pretentious performance and mental orientation. If one wants to attain Tao straightforwardly, Ordinary Mind is the Way. What is the Ordinary Mind? It is freedom from pretentious performance, from duality of yes and no, taking and giving, discontinuity and permanence, temporal and sacred. The Scripture says, "It is neither the deluded behavior nor the sacred one. It is the Bodhisattava's behavior. Everything from walking, standing, sitting to lying down, from responding and receiving at the moment is the Way."[4]

Mazu's thought of Ordinary-Mind-Is- the-Way was elaborated by Nanquan 南泉 (748–834 C.E.; Jap. Nansen), one of Mazu's eminent disciples. Nanquan's most frequently quoted elaboration on Ordinary Mind is the one when Nanquan had an encounter dialogue with his foremost disciple Zhaozhaou 赵州 (or Chao-Chou, 778–897; Jap. Joshu). It goes as follows:

Zhaozhaou: Nanquan, 'What is the Way?'

Nanquan: 'Ordinary Mind is the Way.'

Zhaozhaou: 'Then may I direct myself toward it or not?'

Nanquan: 'To seek [it] is to deviate [from it].'

Zhaozhaou: 'If I don't seek, how can I know about the Way?'

Nanquan: 'The Way does not belong to knowing or not knowing. To know is to have a concept; to not know is to be ignorant. If you truly realize the Way of no doubt, it is just like the sky: wide open vast emptiness. How can you say 'yes' or 'no' to it?'

At these words, Zhaozhaou had sudden enlightenment. His mind became like the clear moon.[5, 6]

Apparently, the Ordinary Mind Mazu and Nanquan referred to is a nondual, nondiscriminatory state of mind like vast emptiness. It is onto-logical, transpersonal, and spiritual. It is not ordinary but extraordinary. It is certainly not the ordinary mind people function with in a daily life of interaction. The Masters called it *ping chang xin* from a less transper-sonal but more functional perspective in order to make the practice and its psychospiritual state sound accessible to average people.

To avoid the confusion between the Ordinary Mind Chan masters embody and the ordinary mind of average people without any meditation or spiritual practice, it is useful and necessary to distinguish them by using uppercase and lowercase of the first letter of the two words: *Ordinary Mind* versus *ordinary mind*. In Chinese, *xin* 心 signifies heart or mind; *ping chang* 平常 is often translated as *ordinary*, although etymologically *ping* denotes plain and *chang* lasting or everlasting. The set phrase *ping chang xin*, consisting of the three Chinese characters 平常心, can *not* be written ideographically differently as in lower-versus-upper-case in English. Only the context will help interpret the specific meaning of the term. Besides, between Ordinary Mind that is spiritual or transpersonal and ordinary mind that completely operates on sensory motor stimuli, pre-operational, operational, and formal operational thinking,[7] there must be another state in between the two if we make a thorough examination of all teachings on this subject. This intermediate state is characterized by a spon-taneously and effectively functioning mind that engages and is engaged in performing daily tasks not only in a relaxed monastic setting but also in the social and professional life of a working person in modern society. This intermediate state is designated as mindfulness-based ordinary mind.

In comparison with the aforementioned ontological definitions of the Ordinary Mind by Mazu and Nanquan, Zhaozhaou is credited with embodying the phenomenology of Ordinary Mind by rigorously and expediently applying it to daily-life situations in a monastic milieu. It is believed also applicable and adaptable to secular settings, which Chan masters[8] have been advocating in China over the past two decades. In light of contemporary studies of mindfulness and meditation, I would term many of Zhaozhaou's statements as mindfulness-based ordinary mind.

Five of the 21 classical sources Wu Yan-shen[9] collected on *ping chang xin* refer to Chan master Zhaozhaou, who has been venerated not only in China, Japan, and Korea but also in the West as long as Chan/Zen Buddhism is practiced.

Since medieval China, the practice of *ping chang xin* has become part and parcel of the collective Chinese way of thinking, feeling, and behavior. *Ping chang xin* has already become a household term in Chinese literature, media, and the daily lives of people from all walks of life.

The Psychological Characteristics of the Traditional Practice

When Chan Buddhists practice Ordinary Mind in the traditional light, be it meditation on or off the cushion, they equally let go of random thoughts, emotions, and memories that surface from the unconscious to consciousness. This is true, too, of the less diffuse state of *ping chang xin*, mindfulness-based ordinary mind (mbom). Off-cushion meditation such as walking meditation is more likely a mbom practice.

The characteristic of letting-go subjugates *ping chang xin* practices to intentionally ignore the revealed and possibly useful messages that emerge from the unconscious. If such ignoring or detachment is necessary during meditation, then it is psychologically mistaken to ignore the surfaced contents even after the practitioner comes out of the formal sitting or walking meditation. The consistent practice of letting go of even psychotherapeutically very valuable insights in order to just aim at spiritual liberation makes traditional practitioners of Chan/Zen less concerned about their cognitive, emotional, and/or behavioral problems. Likewise, it might lose the opportunity of examining the origin of one's problems or disorders from the development of one's early life, especially in infancy and childhood. John Welwood[10] calls this phenomenon a spiritual bypass. Welwood defines spiritual bypassing as "a wide spread tendency to use spiritual practice to bypass or avoid dealing with certain personal or emotional 'unfinished business'" (p. 11). Put in another way, spiritual bypassing is a "tendency to avoid or prematurely transcend basic human needs, feelings, and developmental tasks" (p. 12).

To avoid possible spiritual bypass and to encompass a wider scope of service area, Chan may need to integrate some methods and skills from psychotherapy to renew the practice of *ping chang xin* with a model I call meditation-initiated integrative therapy (MIIT).

Contemporary Integrative Practice in the West

Chan is basically concerned with the transpersonal attainment that, if realized, would bring psychotherapy to greater satisfaction.[11, 12] This aspect of mutual complementarity between Chan and psychotherapy is not going to be further explored due to limited scope in this chapter. I have given considerable space to elaborate the contribution of Chan practice to psychotherapy in my other article, titled "The Ordinary Mind in Chan/Zen Buddhism and Psychotherapy: What Can One Offer to the Other?" The present study concentrates on how the steep path of Ordinary Mind and mindfulness-based ordinary mind can positively maximize its function at a psychological level that is needed for everyone living and working in a modern or postmodern society.

At the psychotherapeutic level, Chan practitioners may just need to note silently when they experience in formal meditation something unique,[13, 14] much like the "aha" experiences in psychoanalysis. Following the "aha" insight from Chan practice (more often in a formal seated practice, especially for beginners), practitioners will then need to go through some psychological treatment of what emerged in meditation. They even need to do homework accordingly to modify and change some of their behaviors. Before I go into details along this line with my model of meditation-initiated integrative therapy, I would like to review briefly what has been done in the contemporary movement of integrating Buddhist meditation practice with psychotherapy in the West.

Contemporary therapies featuring an integration of meditation or mindfulness practice include but are not limited to mindfulness-based stress reduction (MBSR), mindfulness-based cognitive therapy (MBCT), analytic Zen, dialectical behavioral therapy (DBT), acceptance and commitment therapy (ACT), and the Japanese naukan therapy. Due to limited space, I choose MBSR and MBCT only to show briefly how such integrated practices may contribute to buffering the steep path of Chan.

Mindfulness-Based Stress Reduction

Mindfulness-based stress reduction (MBSR) has been widely used either directly or in a modified way in the healthcare profession since Jon Kabat-Zinn published his *Full Catastrophe Living: Using the Wisdom of Your Body and Mind to Face Stress, Pain and Illness.*[15] Kabat-Zinn emphasizes up front the basic attitudes and commitment as the foundations of successful mindfulness practice. These attitudes include seven factors, namely, non-judging, patience, a beginner's mind, trust, nonstriving, acceptance, and letting go. They "constitute the major pillars of mindfulness practice" (p. 32) that Kabat-Zinn and his colleagues teach in the stress clinic affiliated with the medical center at the University of Massachusetts.

These attitudinal factors are more or less the same as those followed in Chan Buddhist practice. What MBSR and Chan differ on, among other things, is that MBSR is apparently pivoting around breathing as its base camp—both a starting point and finish line that can be in a circular relation. The chief concern of Chan Buddhism, however, gravitates toward the ultimate liberation through the practice of cultivating and sustaining a nondifferentiating mind or Ordinary Mind. Although Kabat-Zinn[15] also mentions "choiceless awareness" that is characterized by "simply being receptive to whatever unfolds in the moment" (p. 71), MBSR touches upon it very cursorily. Even if choiceless awareness seems to be the highest or deepest state or stage of practice in MBSR, it is still watching and witnessing that retains a dualism of watching/watcher and the watched. The complete mingling of the watcher and watched, like a symbolic zero in Chan Buddhism, is completely missing. Instead, MBSR focuses on how the techniques of breathing from the belly (interestingly, this is a Daoist technique) can help develop mindfulness. MBSR aims at a more practical and less abstract side of meditation practice. What seems less profound in MBSR practically buffers the steep road that Chan Buddhists claim to walk.

Mindfulness, as Kabat-Zinn[16] defines, "means paying attention in a particular way: on purpose, in the present moment, and nonjudgmentally" (p. 4). Mindfulness can be used to respond gently and acceptingly rather than to react in a "knee-jerk" manner to negative thoughts, emotions, discomfort, pains, and illness. Healing and therapeutic effects occur this way. It is the nuanced awareness into the breathing, into the thoughts and emotions, and into the body epitomized by what is called "body scan" that is complementing the Chan Buddhist practice of jump-starting and often staying with the transpersonal state or stage for a soteriological purpose. For Chan Buddhists in China, today and in history alike, getting out of the cyclic wheel of birth and death to attain Enlightenment or become a Buddha is the ultimate goal and presumably the primary motivation as well. Mindfulness, for Kabat-Zinn (1994), is better treated as secular, although it could be spiritual from a philosophical perspective of interconnectedness of all that is in the universe.

Mindfulness practice in MBSR boasts a simple but powerful means to possibly improve the quality of "our relationships within the family, our relationship to work and to the larger world and planet" (p. 5).[16] In "parenting as practice" of *Wherever You Go, There You Are*, Kabat-Zinn[16] looked at bringing up his children as a challenging but self-growing experience of practicing mindfulness and even attending a retreat, except that raising kids was not as quiet and simple. For each child, Kabat-Zinn says, it was like an 18-years-long retreat that consists of easy and then hard periods, wonderful and then deeply painful moments. His practice consists in seeing constantly changing needs of his children as

> All perfect opportunities for parents to be fully present rather than to operate in the automatic pilot mode, to relate consciously rather than mechanically, to sense the being in each child and let his or her vibrancy, vitality, and purity call forth our own. (p. 249)[16]

For Kabat-Zinn,[16] parenting as such is an "on-the-job, moment-by-moment training" so that the parent has to "be continually mindful and present" (p. 250) rather than linger with a mechanical view or views based on the parent's perspectives. Kabat-Zinn concludes that the practice of parenting as a meditation retreat that honors his children and family situation as his teachers "has proven its primacy and value time and time again" (p. 249). The fact that Kabat-Zinn and his wife, Myla, published in 1997 their co-authored book *Everyday Blessings: The Inner Work of Mindful Parenting* is a further concrete contribution to benefiting a full range of meditation practitioners, including working moms and dads in a challenging society today.[17] Such attitude and practice can be complementary, especially to contemporary lay practitioners who may or may not be

Buddhists, and to monasticism-based Chan Buddhist practice vis-á-vis the Ordinary Mind.

Mindfulness-Based Cognitive Therapy

Inspired by and modeling on MBSR, Segal, Williams, and Teasdale[18] established a mindfulness-based cognitive therapy for prevention of depression. Their clinical and research experiences together with mindfulness meditation practices make their work bear a lucid, rational, and explainable tone. The lucidity and expressivity of mindfulness-based cognitive therapy (MBCT) provides another model of complementing the steep or subtist approach of traditional Chan practice that is highly intuitive and might fall into the snare of spiritual bypassing.

As its name suggests, MBCT is an integrative practice of mindfulness meditation and cognitive therapy. The definition of mindfulness in MBSR is applied to MBCT. So a brief mention of cognitive therapy is necessary for understanding MBCT.

Beck and Weishaar[19] define cognitive therapy as one "based on a theory of personality which maintains that people respond to life events through a combination of cognitive, affective, motivational, and behavioral responses" (p. 238). The purpose of cognitive therapy is to

> adjust information-processing and initiate positive change of all systems by acting through the cognitive system. In a collaborative process, the therapist and patient examine the patient's beliefs about himself or herself, other people, and the world. The patient's maladaptive conclusions are treated as testable hypotheses. Behavioral experiments and verbal procedures are used to examine alternative interpretations and to generate contradictory evidence that supports more adaptive beliefs and leads to therapeutic change. (p. 238)

Applying mindfulness to cognitive therapy, Segal and colleagues[18] articulate that

> Intentionally (on purpose) changing the focus and style of attention is the "mental gear lever" by which processing can be switched from one cognitive mode to another. And nonjudgmental, present moment focus of mindfulness indicates that it is indeed very closely related to

the being mode of mind. In other words, mindfulness provides both the means to change mental gears when disengaging from dysfunctional, "doing-related" mind states, and an alternative mental gear, or incompatible mode of mind, into which to switch. (p. 77)

It is essential for patients or whoever practices MBCT and MBCR to learn to experientially switch from the "doing mode" of mind to the "being mode" state. The task of mindfulness training in MBCT is to teach individual participants "ways to become more aware of their mode of mind ('mental gear') at any moment, and the skills to disengage, if they choose, from unhelpful modes of mind and to engage more helpful modes" (p. 70).[18] The shift from the "unhelpful modes" to the "helpful modes" mostly refers to the mental gear shift from the doing mode to the being mode.

The being mode and doing mode MBCT describes resemble the Ordinary Mind or mindfulness-based ordinary mind and the untrained ordinary mind, respectively. What makes MBCT as well as MBSR different from the practice of Ordinary Mind is that MBCT and MBSR do not transcend but instead pay close attention to thoughts, emotions, and body sensations and respond skillfully to them. Chan is already very pragmatic as compared with other denominations and schools of Buddhism in that Chan prioritizes the now-and-here experience. In light of psychotherapy, however, Chan still appears lacking in attention to the emotional and interpersonal needs of people working and living in a society. This is much the same way as Chan is lacking in addressing different needs at developmental stages given the fact that Chan Buddhism is a medieval practice evolved from India further back.[20, 21]

The core teaching of the MBCT program boils down to developing the awareness and ability, at times of potential relapse, for the patient to recognize and disengage from mind states characterized by self-perpetuating patterns of ruminative, negative thought. ... This involves moving from a focus on content to a focus on process, away from cognitive therapy's emphasis on changing the content of negative thinking, toward attending to the way all experience is processed. (p. 75)[18]

Specifically, the disengagement from negative mind states involves "distancing" or "decentering." Decentering has been recognized in cognitive therapy, too, but it is usually used "as a means to an end, changing thought content, rather than an end in itself" (p. 38).[18] Decentering, according to Segal and colleagues, is looking at thoughts in a perspective wide enough so that people will be able to see thoughts simply as thoughts rather than as facts. In this way, decentering allows MBCT practitioners to step out of the "automatic pilot" mode of mind and "nip in the bud the escalation of self-sustaining patterns of depressive thought" (p. 53). This fundamental aspect of MBCT protects people against future depression. If such decentering did not take place, patients might be left arguing with themselves about whether their thoughts were true or not, marshaling evidence for or against a negative thought. Consequently, they might simply get caught up in the thought pattern.

Characterized technically by decentering, MBCT emphasizes the importance of changing a patient's relationships to negative thoughts and feelings rather than changing a person's degree of belief in his or her thoughts and attitudes. If people adopt a decentered perspective, detaching from their habitual patterns of thinking, then there is no need to change the content of their thoughts and feelings. It is this change from working on contents of thoughts to the relationship to the thoughts that makes what is implicit in cognitive therapy explicit in MBCT.[18] Persons[22] expressed her reservations, however, on the truthfulness of such a distinction or change from Beck's change of thoughts and beliefs to what MBCT claims as mere change of relationship.

The progressive eight-session MBCT training has a focus for each session. It goes from mindfulness practice by eating raisins to getting out of our habitual, often unconscious tendency of reacting on "automatic pilot," from practicing body scan in a gentle, interested, and friendly way to practicing formal sitting mindfulness meditation. It also trains participants on staying present with difficult things via breathing as well as sitting with thoughts as thoughts rather than as facts.

There is something about the "everydayness" of the practice of MBCT as well as MBSR that is relevant to the Chan motto "Ordinary Mind is the Way." When mindfulness practice comes to everyday practice, any daily activity such as brushing your teeth, washing up, putting on your shoes, eating a meal, and doing your job can be a target of practice. What needs to be done is to just bring your mindfulness to each activity, either by taking a conscious breath, which is popularly practiced in insight meditation, or just by reflecting back, which is prevalent in Chan. This level of mindfulness is easy and doable in relation to the nondual transpersonal state, and the outcome is the functioning mindfulness-based ordinary mind but not the nondifferentiating Ordinary Mind.

Meditation-Initiated Integrative Therapy (MIIT)

MIIT that I have developed over the past few years differs from MBSR and MBCT in three major ways. First, MBSR and MBCT seem to crush their training into an invariable mindfulness practice. MIIT develops a three-stage model for beginning, intermediate, and advanced practitioners. Second, MIIT allows individual clients or group participants to recall after formal meditation and process with my assistance what came up from their unconscious to consciousness. Third, MIIT invites practitioners to bring their particular problem or issue into the process of mediation practice. That problem or issue becomes the object of meditation, and insights are likely to come up at certain point from the unconscious. This involves the same mechanism as does the practice of investigating a koan in the traditional practice of Chan/Zen that hopefully will result in a breakthrough—enlightenment. Such effects may come immediately or may take several sessions or a much longer time. The meditation session itself, however, can be a relaxing and therapeutic practice, regulating thoughts and emotions as well as interconnection between mind, body, and spirit.

Mechanism

MIIT is a psychospiritual practice. On the one hand, it follows the mind–body regulation practice that meditation produces in order to achieve well-being characterized by harmony, serenity, and, at advanced stages, liberation. On the other hand, it operates on the emergence of unconscious contents as clues or insights for postmeditation therapeutic treatment in the framework of psychoanalysis and cognitive behavior therapy.

Procedures of Applying the Model

MIIT normally operates according to the following procedure:

During meditation proper:

1. seated meditation with instructions given to beginners
2. unconscious contents emerging in the realm of consciousness
3. seeing clues and insights to problems
   In postmeditation session:
4. exposure/catharsis verbally or nonverbally (e.g., expressive arts)
5. analysis, association, and treatment
6. training on maladaptive thoughts and behaviors with homework
7. growth and enhanced meditation

MIIT at the beginning level normally asks participants to meditate 10 to 15 minutes. At intermediate and advanced stages, the meditation time will increase incrementally to 25 and 30 minutes, respectively, for workshops more often than for individual clients. Regardless of stage, no specific posture is required. The basic instructions include

- assuming a comfortable and relaxed posture to sit in a noninterfering setting that is neither too bright nor completely dark
- observing just inhaling or exhaling of one's breath
- just patiently bringing the attention back to observing inhaling or exhaling if attentiveness is lost
- paying peripheral attention to what is going on in thoughts, emotion, and body.

Coming out of the meditation session, participants are given a piece of blank paper and oil pastels to express linguistically or artistically what they each have experienced in the silent meditation. No logic, order, or grammar is needed for their expressions. Among the list of expressed items, I then invite the client or a chosen volunteer in a group to pick three items she or he thinks more significant and wants to explore. Therapeutic counseling proceeds from there.

In another design used more frequently at postbeginning levels, participants are asked to watch their mental process or mentally concentrate on a targeted issue. In watching the mental process, random thoughts, emotions, and images pop up from the unconscious. In concentrating on the targeted issue with which one is having difficulties in life, she might be able to see sparking clues or ideas leading to a solution of the problem being investigated.

My clients are either individuals or attendants of small-group workshops or salons. In the case of individual clients, a 1-hour session might not begin with instructed meditation right away. If it appears useful and is accepted, it will be introduced at an appropriate time of the session. In group counseling, the first three steps during the meditation proper can be executed as in an individual session, but Step 5 will not be guaranteed for all of the group members. The operation of individual counseling in a group may begin with a volunteer. If more volunteers request the personal service than can be handled in the limited session, then the surplus clients will have to wait for another session of the whole workshop, or they will simply have to accept the fact that they are not selected.

The results presented in the present study project refer mostly to Steps 4 and 5 of the MIIT model. They are postmeditation procedures of counseling and therapy to which traditional Chan practice finds no equivalents. MIIT assumes that without the follow-up psychological counseling, Chan practice itself is perhaps merely aiming at the spiritual dimension of life. To create the wholeness of personality, unfinished psychological issues must be brought to light and worked through psychoanalytically and reinforced behaviorally. The following cases serve this purpose in general.

Case One

H is from the United Kingdom and speaks good Chinese (*pu tong hua* or Mandarin). While she was formally sitting in meditation, a scene occurred in her mind that she verbally described this way: "An Eagle is flying up in the sky. I see it fly freely. It flies higher and higher and I (my problems as well) am on the ground getting farther and farther from it."

"How did you feel then?" I asked H.

"I felt inspired, light and free with my stress left on the ground."

"Where did your stress come from?"

"From too much work."

"Did you want and promise too much or did they assign you too much?"

(With moments of thinking) "I promised too much."

"Are you then going to re-consider how much to take?"

(We had eye contact and she smiled) "Yes, I will reconsider it."

Case Two

Y is a schoolteacher, a middle-aged Chinese woman. During a group meditation, she keeps recalling the part of life she lived as a kid with her maternal grandma. In the postmeditation session of counseling, I asked Y what kind of feeling she had while the scenarios of her childhood life emerged in consciousness. She said it was guilt because he felt she fell short of repaying her grandma, who brought her up due to her parents' divorce. I invited Y to meditate on this feeling with her grandma. The group atmosphere then was genuine and supportive of Y's emotional investigation. Shortly I felt galvanized as if a mild current of electricity ran through my body. At this point, I found Y was sobbing, and she reached for facial tissues. I let this silent process linger on a couple of minutes so that Y would be able to achieve a better effect of externalizing her repressed emotions. Then I asked, "Would you like to communicate what is on your mind with your grandma, perhaps just what you have gone through? Or you may want to do this later at home." I did not pursue her immediate communication with her deceased grandma because it was a group process where someone would feel reluctant to go very deep. Also, group counseling usually does not have enough time for each individual to go through a complete round.

In Case One, meditation serves as means to induce unconscious content to surface into the realm of consciousness. She admired flying like an eagle because she had been overworked. Then the method of cognitive approach with a Socratic dialogue is used for counseling. Without the counseling part, the client might not be able to realize where her stress comes from and how to work on reducing it and enhancing self-care.

Psychological counseling and therapy see a client's tears as a breakthrough. Only when the client is feeling extremely authentic and vulnerable can she or he touch upon the deep-set emotional complex. In Case Two, when tears come to her eyes, it suggests a time for possible transformation is around the corner. Traditional practice of Ordinary Mind or mbom in Chan Buddhism often appears either somewhat indifferent to emotional processes or does not explicate how to handle them. Instead, traditional Buddhist teachings emphasize calming and detaching without squarely facing emotional issues in the first place. Therefore, psychological issues are suppressed and supposed to be transcended. A good chance to unravel the emotional knot is missed and the transcendence may prove to be a spiritual bypass. The supposedly transcended issue or problem may well come back unconsciously in the waking life as well as dreams.

Conclusion

Meditation-initiated integrative therapy is a renewed model of practice of *ping chang xin* (Ordinary Mind and mbom). It consists of primary, intermediate, and advanced stages. This chapter is essentially introducing the primary level of MIIT. As a psychospiritual practice, MIIT always contains a dimension of spiritual attainment that brings about greater satisfaction than psychotherapies. The more advanced stage MIIT is at, the deeper spiritual attainment (e.g., oneness, nondualism, enlightenment) the practice realizes. MIIT adopts some methods and techniques from psychotherapies such as psychoanalysis and CBT in order to make the traditional Chan practice of *ping chang xin* more applicable at the psychological level to people today who work and socialize in a modern or postmodern society. Such integrated methods and techniques are demonstrated in the postmeditation session either in the individual counseling or group setting. Individual clients or group participants get a chance to deal with their personal, interpersonal, or work-related issues or problems, old or current, with the assistance of the counselor.

Notes

1. Poceski, M. (2007). *Ordinary mind as the Way*. New York, NY: Oxford University Press.
2. Wu, Y. 吳怡. (1989). *The mind of Chinese ch'an: The Chan school masters*. San Francisco: Great Learning Publishing Company.
3. Yinshun. 印順. (1978). Zhongguo chanzong shi 中国禅宗史 (A History of Chinese Chan Buddhism). Shanghai: China Bookstore.
4. Chinese Buddhist Electronic Text Association (CBETA). (2009a). *Jingde chuandeng lu. vol. 28* 《景德傳燈錄》第二十八卷 *(The jingde record of the lamp transmission, vol. 28.)* T51n2076, 440a 04–08. Retrieved on May 9, 2009, from http://www.cbeta.org/result/normal/T51/2076_028.htm.
5. CBETA. (2009b). *Jingde chuandeng lu. Vol. 10* 《景德傳燈錄》第十卷 *(The jingde record of the lamp transmission, vol. 10)*. T51n2076: 276c14–19. Retrieved on May 9, 2009, from http://www.cbeta.org/result/normal/T51/2076_010.htm.
6. Green, J. (Trans.). (1998). *The recorded sayings of Zen master Joshu*. Boston: Shambhala.
7. Piaget, J. (1950). *Psychology of intelligence*. D. E. Berlyne (Trans.). London: Rutledge and Kegan Paul.
8. Jinghui 净慧. (2005). *Zhongguo fojiao yu shenghuo Chan* 中国佛教与生活禅 (Chinese Buddhism and Everyday Chan). Beijing: Culture and Religion Press.
9. Wu, Y-S. 吴言生 Pingchangxin shi dao" ji ping. "平常心是道" 集評 (Collected sources of the-Ordinary-Mind-Is-the-Way). Retrieved on February 22, 2012, at http://www.fjdh.com/wumin/
10. Welwood, J. (2002). *Toward a psychology of awakening*. Boston: Shambala.
11. Engler, J. (2003). Being somebody and being nobody: A reexamination of the understanding of self in psychoanalysis and Buddhism. In J. Safran (Ed.), *Psychoanalysis and Buddhism: An unfolding dialogue*. Boston: Wisdom Publication.
12. Epstein, M. (1995). *Thoughts without a thinker: Psychotherapy from a Buddhist perspective*. New York: Basic Books.

13. Sīlānanda, U. (2002). *The four foundations of mindfulness*. Boston: Wisdom Publications.

14. Thich, N. H. (2001). *Anger: Wisdom for cooling flames*. New York: Riverhead Books.

15. Kabat-Zinn, J. (1990). *Full catastrophe living*. New York: Delta Publishing Group.

16. Kabat-Zinn, J. (1994). *Wherever you go, there you are: Mindfulness meditation in everyday life*. New York: Hyperion.

17. Kabat-Zinn, J., & Myla, (1997). *Everyday Blessings: The Inner Work of Mindful Parenting. New York, NY: Hyperion Books*.

18. Segal, Z. V., Williams, J. M. G., & Teasdale, J. D. (2002). *Mindfulness-based cognitive therapy for depression: A new approach to preventing relapse*. New York: Guilford Press.

19. Beck, A. T., & Weishaar, M. E. (2005). Cognitive therapy. In R. J. Corsini & D. Wedding (Eds.), *Current psychotherapies, seventh edition, pp. 263–294*. Belmont, CA: Brooks/Cole.

20. Engler, J. (1986). Therapeutic aims in psychotherapy and meditation. In K. Wilber, J. Engler, & D. P. Brown (Eds.), *Transformations of consciousness: Conventional and contemplative perspectives on development, pp. 219–283*. Boston: Shambhala.

21. Zhu, C. 朱彩方 (2010). *The Ordinary Mind in Chan/Zen Buddhism and its psychological significance*. Ann Arbor, MI: UMI Dissertation Publishing.

22. Persons, J. B. (2008). *The case formulation approach to cognitive-behavior therapy*. New York: Guilford Press.

12

Life Contingencies and the Psychosocial Fruits of Faith in Late Adulthood

Michele Dillon and Paul Wink

The first decade of the 21st century was intellectually demanding for observers of religion who had to make sense of some contrasting developments. On the one hand, several best-selling books denigrating all things religious made their already well-known authors household names across the United States. These books variously framed religious belief as poisonous,[1] delusional,[2] vacuous,[3] and terroristic.[4] The consistent message conveyed by their authors is that religious beliefs (e.g., the Christian belief in salvation, the Buddhist belief in reincarnation)[i] are insidious superstitions anathema to the principles of common-sense rationality and science. On the other hand, in intellectual circles in Western Europe and North America, the possibility of religion as a cultural resource for the contemporary age received much attention from scholars previously indisposed toward the emancipatory relevance of religion. Most notably, Jurgen Habermas, the foremost social theorist of our times, argued that "a contrite modernity," one characterized by excessive economic inequality and global consumerism, might find use for religious resources in helping human society deal with "a miscarried life, social pathologies, the failures of individual life projects, and the deformation of misarranged existential

---

[i]Hitchens (2007, pp. 195–215), for example, is as critical of Eastern as of traditional Western religions.

relationships."[5] His religious turn gives acknowledgment to the age-old presumption that faith and/or religious rituals are a way of coping with the ontological insecurities and awkward practical dilemmas of life and death; thus, Habermas noted, "faith in a 'higher' or cosmic power" helps individuals "to cope with uncontrolled contingencies."[6] At the same time, while the pews in most Western European countries have almost emptied, social surveys indicate that many Europeans[7] and most Americans[8] continue to profess a belief, if not in a personal God, then in some kind of a transcendent or sacred force. To use modern terminology, we seem to possess a spirituality gene or, in Jungian terms, the individual's psychic life seems to be organized around a God/Transcendent Being archetype.

Religion in Context

This chapter uses the contradiction posited by these contrasting views of religion either as delusional and poisonous or as a promissory positive force in meeting individual needs, as the springboard for an evidence-based analysis of the place of religious and spiritual engagement in psychosocial functioning. Of course, the fact that religion has a positive or, for that matter, a negative effect on life has no bearing on the ontological argument concerning God's existence. We draw on our research using longitudinal data from a representative community sample of close to 200 men and women who were born in the San Francisco Bay Area in the 1920s and who were studied from childhood until late adulthood (ages 69–77).[9] Although Berkeley and Oakland, the two California communities in which our participants grew up, are seen today as bastions of multiculturalism and liberalism, in the period before World War II, these two communities were virtually all white, Republican, and predominantly Protestant. When interviewed in late adulthood (1997–2000), 45% reported weekly church attendance and 81% said that religion was important or very important currently in their lives—numbers that correspond closely to national rates of religious belief and participation. Most (83%) were still living in California, 71% were living with their spouse or partner, and the median household income was $55,000. For the purpose of this chapter, we draw mostly on the research findings from the in-depth interviews and questionnaire survey conducted in late adulthood, and we contextualize those patterns in terms of their longitudinal antecedents.

The generalizability of our study's findings is limited by the age and generational specificity and by the relative geographical and racial homogeneity of the participants. Nevertheless, while we do not expect to put to rest the lack of consensus among cultural commentators and scholars today about the role of religion, our study's in-depth and longitudinal examination of the participants' lives yields findings that can help provide a balanced view of religion's influence on everyday life. In particular, our study allowed us to use the same group of participants to trace the relationship between religion and a wide range of psychosocial characteristics ranging from life satisfaction, depression, and physical health to social attitudes and openness to experience. In contrast to other research that typically reports on the link between religion and a very specific aspect of functioning, our study can be compared to a variegate and bountiful garden that bears many fruit and, therefore, allows the opportunity to assess whether factors that are conducive to growth in one area might be inhibiting or stifling to growth in another.

A second advantage of our study is that its participants' lives spanned the major social changes of the 20th century. Their childhood coincided with the Great Depression, they were adolescents in the 1940s, an era shadowed by the country's mobilization for World War II, they established families and careers during the 1950s at the height of the postwar suburban boom, they encountered midlife during the cultural turmoil and religious transformation of the 1960s and 1970s, they witnessed the conservative resurgence of the Reagan 1980s, and at the turn of the 21st century were living in a high-tech, multicultural society whose hallmarks are global trade, Internet communication, and a host of geopolitical and militaristic tensions. In terms of mainstream American religious beliefs and practices, this means the men and women in our study entered adulthood at a time when it made little sense to decouple religiousness from spirituality, but from middle age onward, they were exposed to and participated in a religious landscape in which an increasing number of individuals (close to 20% in recent U.S. surveys) identify themselves as spiritual but not religious.[10]

The increased decoupling of spiritual engagement from denominational affiliation and church-centered religious practices is captured in our data and allowed us to explore the similarities and differences in the life trajectories and psychosocial correlates and outcomes of church-centered religiousness and a non–church-centered, spiritual seeking. Importantly, in distinguishing between religiousness and spiritual seeking, we rated our interviewees not simply in terms of their self-described religiosity or spirituality (as is typical in large-scale surveys) but also in terms of the nature of their beliefs (e.g., belief in a personal God, scripture, church-sanctioned prayers; compared to belief in a cosmic power, non–Western spiritual tenets), and the frequency of their disciplined participation in specific religious (e.g., church attendance) or spiritual (e.g., focused meditation) practices. Our theoretical assumption was that spirituality, for example, cannot simply be a passing feeling or a self-identifying label but must be evidenced by a discipline of practice intended to forge connection with a sacred or transcendent force.

Lived Religion

Unlike many of today's youngsters who are growing up in families whose parents have no religious affiliation and/or do not emphasize formal religious socialization, the vast majority of our study participants grew up in households in which religion mattered at least to some degree. As children, most went on a fairly frequent basis to church and/or Sunday school (87%), and in adolescence, religion played a salient role in the lives of a majority of them (55%). This early religious grounding had lifelong effects on participants' subsequent religious and spiritual habits. We found, for example, that adolescent church participation was a significant long-term predictor of both religiousness and spirituality in late adulthood (age late 60s/mid-70s), and further, among those who were neither religious or spiritual in late life, several commented that the basic moral rules they had learned through church and Sunday school still informed how they thought about various ethical issues.

The long-term impact of childhood religious socialization on late-life religious and spiritual engagement does not mean that our study participants maintained a consistent pattern of active religious engagement across their life course. Quite the contrary. Although some in the study maintained a solidly high level of religiousness throughout their lives, the more typical pattern was for individuals' engagement to ebb and flow across time. In particular, many of the interviewees showed a decline in religiousness during middle age. With their children already independent and leaving home, many of our interviewees experienced midlife as a time of new personal freedom, and some drifted away from church in favor of other activities and hobbies. Most of these, however, returned to church in the postretirement years. Others, mostly women who were intellectually curious as adolescents, began at midlife (age 40s, 1970s) to explore the new spiritual opportunities opened up by the 1960s' cultural transformation, and by late adulthood had developed a moderately high level of commitment to Eastern and other non–church-centered spiritual practices. In late adulthood, one-fifth (20%) of the study participants scored moderately high on spiritual seeking, 43% scored moderately high on religiousness, and more than a third (37%) were neither religious nor spiritual. In keeping with the well-established gendered patterns of religious engagement, women were more likely than men at all stages of life (from childhood and adolescence through early, middle, and late adulthood) to be more religious and more involved in church. Women and men did not differ in their levels of spiritual seeking in early or middle adulthood, but because of a higher rate of spiritual growth from middle adulthood onward, women were significantly more spiritual than men in late-middle and late adulthood.

In late adulthood, the study participants' living circumstances were impressively good and conducive to positive everyday functioning. Most of them were economically well off, and a remarkable 90% said that they were not financially constricted from doing any of the activities they wanted to do. Very few of the participants had remained single (4%); most were still married (70%), some were divorced (9%), and quite a few were widowed (17%). Among those who were married, a majority (55%) said they were exceptionally happy and that their marriage fulfilled most of their expectations, and a further third (33%) described their marriage as a good one. Most of the study participants reported feeling close to their children, and it was also apparent that they enjoyed their grandchildren's company and took pride in their activities and accomplishments. Individuals' socioeconomic status was unrelated to their level of religious or spiritual commitment. High scorers on religiousness, however, were more likely than others to report being highly satisfied with marriage. And perhaps reflecting their life-long openness to experience, spiritual seekers were more than twice as likely as others in the study to have been divorced.

The study participants as a whole were remarkably healthy. Almost all described their health as good or moderately good (89%) and their energy level as good (93%). Based on detailed health narratives that they provided, it was evident that a solid 25% of our participants were in excellent health with virtually no physical complaints. An additional 41% had relatively minor ailments; these included such chronic problems as arthritis or blood pressure that were kept under control due to regular medication. Notwithstanding, the generally upbeat subjective health evaluations made by the participants themselves, however, one-third (34%) had one or more serious chronic or life-threatening illnesses. The most common illnesses among our participants were diabetes, some form of cancer, and cardiovascular and related problems. The participants' psychological health was also good. Almost all were well satisfied with their lives in late adulthood; 87% rated their life satisfaction as very or moderately high, and very few indicated any sign of depression (14% of the interviewees were classified as depressed).

Not surprisingly, given the constellation of positive economic and social circumstances shaping our study participants' lives in late adulthood, most of them were leading a fairly purposeful and active older adulthood. Large majorities read newspapers, magazines, and books, and many (between a fifth and a half) frequently engaged in physical exercise such as walking, tennis, swimming or golf; traveled, informally visited with relatives, friends, and neighbors, participated in community service, engaged in a range of personal hobbies, took adult education classes, and went to concerts, plays, and museums. Notwithstanding the high level of functioning among the study participants as a whole, nonetheless, individuals who were either religious or spiritual had a significantly higher level of involvement in various everyday activities. In particular, highly religious individuals tended to gravitate to social activities and community service, whereas spiritual seekers tended to be involved in creative, and self-enhancing, and knowledge-building activities. Overall, individuals high in religiousness or spiritual seeking tended to be involved in more daily activities and to participate in them more frequently than those study participants for whom religion or spirituality were of little or no relevance. Although these differences were important and statistically significant, the relatively low magnitude of the difference between the religious/spiritual and the nonreligious individuals indicated that there were many nonreligious and nonspiritual older-age individuals who were living actively engaged, purposeful lives.

The fact that religiousness and spiritual seeking were associated with purposeful engagement in late adulthood does not mean that this can be attributed directly to religious or spiritual beliefs and practices. It is quite possible, for example, that engagement in everyday activities is a function of good physical and psychological health, and, should highly religious and spiritual individuals be more healthy and less depressed than others, this could account for our findings. Supporting this conjecture, we did find that, indeed, involvement in everyday activities was related positively to good physical health and negatively to depression. Nevertheless, controlling for health and depression did not diminish the positive associations between involvement in purposeful activities and religiousness and spiritual seeking, thus suggesting that the leisure activities of highly religious and spiritual older adults cannot be easily explained by nonreligious factors such as their physical and psychological health.

Religion, Spirituality, and Health

Focusing more specifically on the relation between religiousness, spirituality, and the health of our study participants, we found very little evidence supporting a direct or linear relationship between either religiousness or spiritual seeking and physical health. Individuals who scored high either on religiousness or on spiritual seeking did not experience fewer chronic physical illnesses and did not report better physical health or less incapacity due to physical health than their nonreligious and nonspiritual peers. There was also no evidence of a long-term association between religion and physical health; our various indicators of physical health in late adulthood were unrelated to religiousness and spiritual seeking in early or middle adulthood, and additionally in the case of religiousness, to adolescence. Further, we also found no long-term relation between either religiousness or spiritual seeking and mortality. Our findings on religion, physical health, and mortality thus differ from the trends documented by some other researchers showing a positive relation between various aspects of religion and physical health and mortality.[11]

We wondered what might explain the absence of a significant connection between religion and health in our data, and we believe that the answer largely lies in the socio-demographic composition of our sample. Though illness often has a genetic basis, it is also the case that good health is associated with social factors such as income, educational background, and good habits, all of which tend to enhance a person's health. As we have pointed out, our study participants were socially and economically advantaged; hence, they were well primed to be protected from the risk of illness and, because of the greater access to good healthcare associated with high socioeconomic status, to have a greater chance of recovery from any illness they might have experienced. Additionally, our study participants' denominational backgrounds were unlikely to directly enhance their health as a result of particular lifestyle habits. Most were either mainline Protestant or Catholic, traditions that do not impose strict lifestyle rules that might foster good health, as would derive, for example, for Mormons from a ban on alcohol or caffeine. Conjointly, therefore, the socioeconomic and denominational characteristics of our study participants would not lead one to expect a strong association between religious engagement, health, and mortality.

Given the study participants' high levels of energy and morale and their extensive involvement in hobbies and social activities, it is not surprising that the evidence supporting a direct relationship between religiousness and psychological health was mixed. On the one hand, individuals who scored high on religiousness were more satisfied than others with their lives, but, on the other hand, they were not less likely than their nonreligious counterparts to be depressed. In other words, we found only partial support for the claim that religiousness acts as a general buffer against negative affect among older-age individuals.

A critically important way in which religiousness abetted the positive aging of our study participants, however, was its cushioning role during adversity. The assumption that religion props people up in times of trouble has long enjoyed much currency among pastors, scholars, and ordinary people. Our data provided much support for trust in this assumption. We found a consistent pattern of evidence showing that the study participants who were in poor physical health—our proxy for personal adversity—and who were not religious were the most depressed or unhappy and the least satisfied with their lives. In contrast, the study participants who were in good physical health, irrespective of whether they were religious, were especially well satisfied with their lives and in good psychological health (i.e., scoring low on depression). Clearly, these high-functioning, healthy people did not need religion to prop them up. Quite remarkably, however, the study participants who were in poor physical health and who were religious were as well satisfied with their lives and as happy or as positive in outlook as their nonreligious peers who enjoyed good physical health. In short, among those who were physically ill, religiousness acted as a defense against pessimism and feeling down. Religion's protective impact was such that these individuals were able to maintain the same optimistic outlook as those in the study who were not burdened by illness. Our findings thus clearly affirm the positive impact that religion has in the lives of older-age individuals, preventing them from submitting to the despair that frequently accompanies a new illness or the debilitating presence of a chronic disease.

The protective effect of religiousness on psychological health was present after we took account of whether the study participants had relatives and friends with whom they were in close contact and who provided them with ongoing social and emotional support, and it was also independent of gender. Thus, although the religious individuals in our study tended to have closer emotional ties with family and friends than did the nonreligious, this in itself did not explain why they were buffered against depression and a decline in life satisfaction. Consequently, there is something about being religious, independent of friends and social support, that props people up during times of adversity. This finding fits with other research indicating that it is not social support alone that accounts for the positive way in which religion buffers people against depression.[12] Religiousness itself, rather, independent of an individual's social support network, is a safeguard against feeling down.

Moreover, the buffering effect of religiousness in late adulthood (age 70s; 1997–2000) was predicted longitudinally from religiousness in middle adulthood (age 40s; 1970). This held true even after we took account of variation in the physical health and psychological well-being of our study participants in middle adulthood. This result has important implications for the ongoing inquiry into the mechanisms explaining why religiousness cushions against stress and adversity. It makes it unlikely that the buffering effect of religiousness on psychological health in late adulthood is a function of the experience of adversity itself. Both the length of the buffering effect—close to 30 years—and its presence even after controlling for physical health and well-being in middle adult-hood make it unlikely that that the person either drifted toward religious-ness in response to encountering adversity or that religiousness was simply a proxy for good mental health. Our data thus argue against the notion that the protective effect of religiousness emerges because resilient older adults tend to gravitate toward religion in response to hardship. Our findings also make it highly unlikely that the protective effect of religious-ness can be explained by the fact that severely depressed individuals do not have enough energy to go to church and, therefore, religiousness acts as a proxy for good mental health. If this were the case, then, once again, we would not have expected a person's religiousness in his or her 40s to have a cushioning effect against depression resulting from poor physical health some 30 years later.

The impressively long-term buffering effect of religiousness on psychological health is likely due to the fact that our study participants tended to maintain a remarkably stable pattern of religious engagement across adulthood, notwithstanding some significant ebb and flow in this pattern among the study participants as a whole. In this regard, our results indicating the stability of religious commitment across adulthood support the findings from short-term longitudinal studies showing that the stressors associated with aging such as disability and poor physical health do not have a significant detrimental effect on religious involvement,[13] and nor, as we also found, do they push nonreligious individuals toward church.

It is obviously difficult to tease out what exactly about religiousness accounts for its cushioning effect. The remarks of our study participants suggest that religiously engaged individuals use their religious involve-ment in order to inject meaning into their adversity and, importantly too, to provide them with the patience necessary to deal with pain. They are cushioned in times of trouble by their feelings of closeness to God and the sense that he is protecting them, and by the belief that illness or other adversity is part of God's plan for them. Prayer, whether at home or in church, solidifies these feelings and assurances and in turn buffers psycho-logical health. At the same time, it ensures that the individual is more likely to maintain his or her religious commitment rather than decrease or increase in religiousness in response to illness.

Unlike religiousness, which was particularly effective in buffering physically ill individuals against the loss of life satisfaction and depression, spiritual seeking did not have such effects. We found no evidence among our study participants that spiritual seeking had any relation to psychological health in late adulthood. Thus, spiritual seekers did not report higher—or, for that matter, lower—levels of life satisfaction or lower levels of depression than their peers who were not spiritual seekers. Further, unlike for religiousness, there was no evidence to suggest that spiritual seeking had a buffering effect on psychological health—either life satisfaction or depression—in response to physical illness. Because highly spiritual individuals have a personality profile that shows openness to experience and personal growth, they may, therefore, be more tolerant of both positive and negative feelings in response to life events and experiences. Thus, they may respond to the decline in physical health by seeing it as an opportunity to achieve personal growth and to further integrate both the good and the bad that life throws in their path.

Interestingly, however, spiritual-seeking women (but not men) who were in poor physical health maintained the same sense of personal mastery and control over their lives as their healthy spiritual peers, and highly religious women who were in poor physical health had a greater sense of control than women who were not religious/spiritual and in poor physical health. In contrast, women who were neither religious nor spiritual and who were in poor physical health had a significantly lower sense of control than all of the other women in our study.

If we consider *in toto* our findings on sense of control, depression, and life satisfaction, it is evident that religiousness has a broader buffering effect than spiritual seeking against adversity stemming from poor physical health. Thus, highly religious women not only preserve their sense of control, but they also tend to maintain high levels of life satisfaction and to ward off feelings of depression in the face of poor health. Church-centered religiousness seems to provide women experiencing adversity with a contentment that, in turn, may enhance their sense of mastery and control. Highly religious women, therefore, are able to adjust to illness and personal adversity in a relatively seamless manner that does not threaten their sense of self. Spiritual seekers, on the other hand, accommodate illness and adversity into their self-definition, but in a way that demands different psychological work, an openness to learning from, rather than the seamless incorporation of, adversity. In this sense, spiritual seeking appears to be more closely tied to eudaimonic well-being derived from personal growth rather than to hedonic well-being associated with high levels of life satisfaction.

Fear of Death

What can we say about the impact of religious and spiritual engagement on fear of death, the individual's confrontation with the ultimate and universal contingency? Many Americans, including our study participants, exhibit a disjuncture between religious belief and practice that has been postulated to increase fear of death. Thus, while 79% of our participants believed in an afterlife, far fewer went to church or a regular basis (45%). Further complicating the relation between religion and fear of death in late adulthood, older adults tend to fear death less than younger-age adults. Indeed, in late adulthood, only 23% of our study participants indicated unequivocally that they were afraid of death, though twice as many said they were afraid of the process of dying or of a painful death. Not unexpectedly, both religiousness and spiritual seeking were positively related to belief in an afterlife. There was, however, no linear relation between our study participants' fear of death and either their church-centered religiousness, spiritual seeking, or belief in an afterlife. In other words, the fact that an individual was rated as high on religiousness or as high on spiritual seeking, or the fact that he or she independently expressed a strong belief in an afterlife were, in and of themselves, irrelevant to whether the person was afraid of death (and this was true of both men and women). Instead, we found that individuals who were moderately religious were afraid of death the most, and those who were either highly religious or not religious at all were the least afraid. There was no parallel relationship evident between spiritual seeking and fear of death. Further, individuals who were highly religious and who believed in an afterlife feared death the least, whereas those for whom there was a disjuncture between belief and practice (those who scored low on religiousness but who believed in an afterlife) feared death the most. The study participants who were not religious at all—that is, who did not go to church and who did not believe in an afterlife—feared death less than those who were low on religiousness but who believed in an afterlife. In short, consistency between an individual's beliefs and practices, irrespective of whether it is on sacred or secular premises, appears to pay off, at least when it comes to thoughts of the Grim

Reaper. In other words, our findings suggest that it is naïve to think of religion as a magic bullet against death anxiety or that religious beliefs and practices have evolved primarily as an adaptive way of dealing with life's finality. As argued by Erik Erikson, what protects in old age against ego despair is the sense of having lived a meaningful life.[14]

As with several other aspects of psychosocial functioning, the patterns regarding religiousness and fear of death in late adulthood also held using the person's religiousness in middle adulthood (an interval of 25 years). Thus, individuals who were high or low in religiousness in their 40s tended to be less afraid of death in their late 60s and mid-70s than those who were moderately religious in their 40s. Knowing a person's level of religiousness in middle adulthood was thus as good a predictor of fear of death in late adulthood as was his or her level of religiousness in late adulthood. The fact that spiritual seeking and fear of death were not related either positively or negatively may stem from the fact that belief in an afterlife, whether understood in traditional (e.g., heaven) or less conventional terms (e.g., reincarnation), is not as central to the worldview of spiritual seekers as it is to a church-centered religious theology (especially Christianity). It may also be true, moreover, that just as spiritual seekers are open to the negative affect associated with personal illness and adversity, they may be similarly open to the imminence of death.

Religion and Sociopolitical Attitudes

Much of the recent criticism of religion is based on the argument that not only is religion an illusion but that it leads to intolerance, hatred, and war and, therefore, is positively bad for humankind. In the scientific study of religion, this criticism manifests in the debate concerning the link between religiousness and authoritarianism. In line with several recent studies, we found a positive association between religiousness and conformity to institutional authority, the affirmation of traditional social values, and lackluster support for the rights of women and gays. Spiritual seekers, by contrast, demonstrated an anti-authoritarian disposition and, in keeping with their general openness to experience, showed significantly high levels of tolerance. This was the one area of everyday functioning in which religious and spiritual individuals sharply diverged, a difference that both reflects and amplifies the assumption that church-oriented individuals are more likely than spiritual seekers to yield to the authority of established institutions and practices rather than to the more autonomous authority of the self. Clearly, as conservers of tradition, religious individuals are unlikely, on average, to be in the vanguard of social and political change, but this does not mean that they necessarily are "evil" or have a poisonous impact on society.[1] Social change is always a complex process, and the airing of oppositional views should not simply be seen as obstructionist or regressive, but as part and parcel of the promise and vibrancy of democratic participation. Moreover, the social conservatism associated with church participation should be balanced against the well-documented evidence of the significant role played by religious ideas, leaders, and church-based groups in advancing social reform, whether with regard to civil rights, immigration reform, or global human rights. Further, in support of Jurgen Habermas's[5] contention that religious resources can be fruitful in remedying the social pathologies of modernity, we found that our religious and spiritual participants were characterized by altruism and a generative concern for others evident not only as a personality characteristic but also reflected in concrete participation in a variety of local communal (e.g., helping the homeless) and global (e.g., environmental sustainability) projects.

Conclusion

The research results we have highlighted here point to a complex and varied role for religion and spirituality in individual lives. Unlike critics who frame religion as a sweepingly negative force, our research shows that in the context of the lives of highly functioning older-age Americans, religion tends to provide a positive charge. At the same time, our findings add nuance to presumptions that religion exerts an overwhelmingly positive impact on psychosocial functioning. It certainly helps individuals cope with the contingencies of life,[6] but it does so in tempered ways. Although our findings suggested that older adults do not need religion to maintain a high level of life satisfaction, being religious does help during times of adversity. As we showed, the study participants who were not religious and who were in poor physical health were significantly more vulnerable to depression and loss of life satisfaction and personal mastery than their peers who, though in poor physical health, were religious. By the same token, while we found clear support for the idea that individuals who were highly religious and had a firm belief in an afterlife were not afraid of death, the same was true of those study participants who did not espouse a belief in an afterlife nor attend church.

Our data also showed that religiousness and spiritual seeking had varying effects in the lives of the study participants in late adulthood. Whereas religiousness acted as a buffer against loss of life satisfaction and against depression, spiritual seekers were not similarly buffered during times of adversity. Spiritual seeking did, however, cushion women in poor health against losing their sense of personal mastery and control (as did religiousness, too). Although spiritual seeking does not provide the same protective canopy as religiousness and does not function to increase or to preserve individual happiness during stressful times, life satisfaction and happiness in and of themselves are not the only criteria by which to judge positive aging. The ability to accept and integrate stress and unpleasant emotional concerns (e.g., fear of death) is also adaptive for some older-age individuals and seems especially so for spiritual seekers. Our findings also support the premise that religious individuals are more socially conservative than spiritual seekers, but as we noted, there is nothing inherently bad or unnatural in conservatism. Contemporary society would be better understood and public dialogue better served if conservatism and liberalism, religiousness and spirituality, transcendence and immanence, belief and disbelief were acknowledged as complementary or dialectical motions rather than anathema forces.

Notes

1. Hitchens, C. (2007). *God is not Great: How religion poisons everything*. New York: Twelve/Hatchette Book Group.

2. Dawkins, R. (2006). *The God delusion*. Boston: Houghton Mifflin.

3. Dennett, D. (2007). *Breaking the spell: Religion as a natural phenomenon*. New York: Penguin.

4. Harris, S. (2010). *The end of faith: Religion, terror, and the future of reason*. New York: Norton.

5. Habermas, J. (2006). In Virgil Nemoianu. The church and the secular establishment: A philosophical dialog between Joseph Ratzinger and Jurgen Habermas. *Logos, 9*, 17–42.

6. Habermas, J. (2008). Notes on a post-secular society. *New Perspectives Quarterly, 25*, 4.

7. Houtman, D., & Aupers, S. (2007). The spiritual turn and the decline of tradition: The spread of post–Christian spirituality in 14 Western countries, 1981–2000. *Journal for the Scientific Study of Religion, 46*, 305–320.

8. Pew Forum on Religion and Public Life. (2008). *The U.S. religious landscape survey.* Washington, DC: Pew Research Center.

9. Dillon, M., & Wink, P. (2007). *In the course of a lifetime: Tracing religious belief, practice, and change.* Berkeley: University of California Press.

10. *General Social Survey.* (2008). University of Chicago: National Opinion Research Center.

11. Koenig, H., McCullough, M., & Larson, D. (2001). *Handbook of religion and health.* New York: Oxford University Press.

12. Musick, M. A., Koenig, H. G., Hays, J. C., & Cohen, H. (1998). Religious activity and depression among community-dwelling elderly persons with cancer: The moderating effect of race. *Journals of Gerontology Series B: Psychological Sciences and Social Sciences, 53B*, S218–27.

13. George, L. K., Ellison, C. G., & Larson, D. B. (2002). Explaining the relationship between religious involvement and health. *Psychological Inquiry, 13*, 190–200.

14. Erikson, E. (1963). *Childhood and society* (2nd ed.). New York: Norton.

Section III

Harvesting the Fruit

13

Temperance and Addiction

Michelle J. Pearce and Amy Wachholtz

Self-Control and Spiritually Integrated Treatments for Addiction

The notion that temperance, defined as moderation in action, thought, or feeling, is an important aspect of religion is not new; it has been the subject of many philosophical, theological, and psychological musings and is found in most religions' sacred writings. The effect of religion on social behavior and conformity, as well as health and well-being, has also been well-documented.[1] However, the idea that religion works at the level of the individual to develop temperance, or self-control, leading to positive physical, emotional, and behavioral outcomes, is a new and intriguing topic in the study of religion and psychology.[2] This chapter will specifically explore this mediation model with regard to recovery from addiction.

The relationship between self-control and addiction is historically a socially and politically provocative subject. Throughout the last century, blame has been assigned first to the addictive substance, then to the substance consumer's lack of willpower, and, more recently, to the complex way the consumer's brain metabolizes the substance, as well as to complex social, psychological, and environmental factors. Despite these changes in popular and medical opinion, self-control is still inherent in the current *Diagnostic and Statistical Manual of Mental Disorders* definition of addiction, whose criteria includes the continued use of a substance despite the knowledge of problems caused by it.

Self-control has been defined as "the internal resources available to inhibit, override, or alter responses that may arise as a result of physiological processes, habit, learning, or the press of the situation."[3] In other words, those with high self-control are more able to break bad habits, resist temptation, and exert self-discipline.[4] Adherents of most, if not all, religions are expected to regulate their behavior according to their sacred teachings, requiring discipline, restraint of impulses, and striving to meet a set of standards.

In Christianity and Judaism, self-control is one of the virtues emphasized in the Old Testament (e.g., "He who is slow to anger is better than the mighty, and he who rules his spirit than he who takes a city"; Proverbs 16:32), and is described in the New Testament as one of the Fruits of the Spirit (Galatians 5:23). In Buddhism, self-control is necessary to fulfill the third and fifth precepts and is emphasized in the Eightfold Path. There are many verses in the Dhammapada, the Buddhist scriptures, promoting self-control (e.g., "Self-control is as necessary to the inner life as skill in shaping wood, metal, or water is required for good industry"; Dhammapada 80). The practice of Islam also emphasizes self-control: "Abu Huraira reported God's Messenger as saying, 'The strong man is not the good wrestler; the strong man is only he who controls himself when he is angry'" (Bukhari and Muslim Hadith). Hinduism, too, encourages self-denial and temperance (e.g., "When a man has discrimination and his mind is controlled, his senses, like the well-broken horses of a charioteer, lightly obey the rein; Katha Upanishad 1.3.3–6), and Jainism calls adherents to "conquer" themselves (Uttaradhyayana Sutra 9.34–36).

There are a number of treatments for substance abuse that incorporate religious and spiritual themes as a means to enhance individuals' ability to withstand triggers and achieve abstinence. To further understand the role of religion/spirituality (R/S) in recovery from addiction, in this chapter we explore the relationship between R/S, self-control, chemical addiction, and recovery. Specifically, we explore the concept that the primary pathway through which spiritually integrated treatments influence recovery from addiction is through the development and strengthening of self-control. Given the extensive literature on addictions, we have narrowed the focus of this chapter to chemical-related addictions (i.e., alcohol and illicit drugs). However, we believe much of the theory discussed applies to other types of addictions, as well (e.g., gambling, food, sex).

Religious and Spiritually Integrated Treatments for Addiction

There are a number of spiritually integrated treatment approaches for addiction. The efficacy of some of these treatments has been well established in the literature, while others are in the early stages of empirical investigation and primarily rely on anecdotal information for validity. Spiritually based treatments are well accepted by many patients seeking treatment for substance abuse.[5] Moreover, many of these spiritually integrated treatments appear to be effective for the treatment of substance abuse, but few head-to-head studies of effectiveness exist.[6] We will review the clinical research on the most popular spiritually based treatments to identify those that have been deemed most effective and those that require further study before conclusions are drawn.

Salvation Army

The Salvation Army offers faith-based residential and outpatient substance abuse treatment. Residential treatment is usually 30 to 90 days. Psychotherapy services largely consist of cognitive behavioral therapy with an integrated spiritual component that is offered in both group and individual treatment settings.[7] Voluntary spiritual activities are offered outside of therapy, as well. On average, the program completion rate is 67.4%; this rate increases if individuals are involved in additional spiritual activities outside of therapy (93.1%),[8] suggesting there is something unique about participating in spiritual activities that enhances the likelihood of successful program completion.

Spiritual Self-Schema Therapy

Spiritual Self-Schema therapy is an eight-session manualized treatment that integrates cognitive behavioral therapy with Buddhist, nontheistic principles and practices. Its goal is to move participants from "addict self" to "true self" by changing how they interact with the world around them and by developing spiritual qualities. Upon completion of the program, individuals reported more spiritual qualities and a greater influence of spirituality on their behavior; objective assessments also revealed a significant decrease in drug use. There was a strong correlation between daily spiritual experiences and decrease in drug use.[9]

Alcoholics Anonymous/12-Step Programs

Alcoholics Anonymous (AA) is probably the most widely studied spirituality-integrated program for addressing alcohol abuse.[10] AA is an open, peer-led support group that encourages its members to abstain from alcohol use. The formation of AA was based on Christian teachings, but it is not currently tied to any particular religious tradition. The founders of AA believed recovery involves a spiritual transformation and requires admission of one's powerlessness over addition and submission to a higher power. Many other 12-step programs have been developed based on the AA model (e.g., Narcotics Anonymous, Overeaters Anonymous). Progress in AA is assessed by completion of the 12 steps of recovery that are clearly stated at the beginning of each meeting. Small token rewards and peer recognition are given for meeting abstinence goals. Other research has shown that increases in spirituality over the course of AA participation partially mediate this treatment effect.[11]

Mindfulness Practices

Mindfulness is an amalgamation of Buddhist-based spiritual practices that is designed to help patients distance themselves from cravings and enhance awareness of automatic behaviors that perpetuate addiction. Research is mixed on these outcomes, with some studies showing significantly better outcomes than treatment as usual and other studies showing minimal differences.[12]

Transcendental Meditation

Transcendental Meditation (TM) is based on a Hindu form of meditation founded by Maharishi Mahesh Yogi. Patients who use this technique are encouraged to meditate daily. Under TM philosophy, as practitioners shift their focus away from harmful substances, they experience decreased psychological distress and better coping that reduce cravings for substances of abuse. Continued active participation appears to be effective in treating substance abuse. After 18 months of active participation, 65% of participants were abstinent from substances of abuse, compared to 25% of treatment-as-usual participants.[13]

Teen Challenge

Despite its name, Teen Challenge is a program for both adolescents and adults. It is a residential, "Bible-based" treatment program that does not include psychotherapy or pharmacological treatment as part of its substance abuse treatment. The typical duration of a residential stay is between 12 and 18 months. While few studies have empirically assessed Teen Challenge, program officials report that at a 2-year follow-up, 51% of adult graduates and 71% of adolescent graduates reported no relapses.[14]

In summary, the quality and quantity of empirical studies varies widely across the different types of spiritually integrated approaches for treating substance abuse. Although more empirically rigorous studies are needed, there does appear to be sufficient evidence to suggest that for some patients, spirituality is a critical component in their recovery from substance abuse and addiction.

Self-Control as Mediator in the Relationship Between R/S and Addiction

We will now review the various bodies of research that provide theoretical and empirical evidence to support the hypothesis that self-control mediates the relationship between R/S and recovery from addictions. We will identify potential mediators that may affect the relationship between addiction and religion and spirituality, although we will not be able to statistically test this model, as this is a conceptual chapter. We hope that the theoretical evidence presented for this hypothesis will provide useful information for future empirical research.

R/S and Addiction

Religion and spirituality have been examined in a number of ways in the addiction literature, including as a predictor of attitudes about and frequency of substance use, a protective or risk factor, a part of the course of addiction, a mechanism of recovery, and as an outcome of recovery.[15] Many religions condemn the excessive use of alcohol and drugs resulting in intoxication (e.g., Judaism, some Christian denominations), some prohibit any use (e.g., Islam, fundamental Christian sects, Mormonism), and a few, such as Native American, Polynesian, and other indigenous religions, actually encourage the use of psychoactive substances to induce a state of transcendence; however, these groups generally frown on excessive use or abuse of these substances outside of religious practices.

Most of the empirical studies conducted in the United States have reported less substance use and abuse among the more religious.[16] A recent analysis of data from three major national surveys revealed that adults and adolescents who attended religious services weekly or more were much less likely to drink or use illegal drugs.[17] Notably, both the age of the individual during religious participation and the level of internalization of the self-control message during that religious participation appear to be critical in the development of substance abuse. Specifically, when individuals rated their childhood religiosity as important to them, they were significantly more likely to have internalized messages of self-control and have a decreased risk for lifetime abuse of alcohol.[18] Other research has also found that maintenance of recovery from addictions is related to greater use of spiritual practices.[19] As reviewed earlier in this chapter, some recent research has found a positive relationship between involvement in spiritually based treatments and recovery and maintenance of sobriety.

Self-Control and Addiction

Research on the constructs of self-control, self-regulation, and conscientiousness has revealed that those high in these traits tend to have more positive outcomes in many areas of life, including health, health behaviors,[20] academic achievement, and relationships,[4] and buffer against the negative effects of stress and trauma.[21] Those who are low in these traits are more likely to abuse alcohol and drugs and engage in risky behaviors.[20]

Interestingly, results from a positive psychology character strengths survey suggest that self-regulation, which is often grouped with temperance, is one of the least prevalent character traits endorsed by individuals in the United States.[22]

Individuals with high self-control are more likely to have a healthy emotional response when they make mistakes; they are less likely to feel shame and more likely to feel appropriately guilty for their actions.[4] They are also more likely to take responsibility for their mistakes and work toward making amends, while those low in self-control are more likely to become defensive, deny their responsibility, and blame others.

Research on delayed gratification also provides some evidence of the positive influence of self-control on later success. Mischel and colleagues[23] conducted a number of studies with children who had to choose between receiving an immediate small reward or a delayed large reward (i.e., delayed gratification). Ten-year follow-up data revealed that the children that who exerted self-control by demonstrating delayed gratification had higher scores on measures of academics and social functioning. A recent 35-year longitudinal study revealed that temperance in children and adolescents is predictive of better psychological and social functioning in middle age.[24]

Finally, the relationship between self-control and addiction is explained well by Baumeister and colleagues' theory:[20] Self-control can be likened to a muscle.[25] If an individual is in a situation where his or her self-control is constantly taxed, his or her self-control will eventually reach exhaustion. In this state of depleted self-control, the individual is more likely to make impulsive decisions based on wants and desires. However, if self-control is exercised regularly, like a muscle with strength training, it will grow stronger, and over time, the individual will find it is easier to control his or her behavior and be less impulsive.[25] This explains why an individual who has been abstinent for many years can suddenly relapse during times of significant stress. It may also explain why an individual who is exposed to multiple drug-associated cues in his or her environment and social network may be more likely to relapse after a brief period of abstinence.

Relationship between Religion and Self-Control

McCullough and Willoughby's[2] comprehensive review of the relationship between religion, self-regulation, and self-control provides strong theoretical evidence for their proposal that religion indirectly controls behavior by facilitating self-control and self-regulation. In their meta-analysis, they found a consistent relationship between religiousness and intrinsic religious motivation and higher scores on measures of self-control and personality traits reflecting self-control (e.g., agreeableness, conscientiousness). Evidence was also cited that children raised in religious families are more likely to have higher levels of self-control than are children raised in nonreligious families. Childhood religiosity and internalizing messages of self-control from religious sources may increase self-control and/or delay experimentation with substances[18] until after the critical brain plasticity period of adolescence. Childhood religiosity may also provide alternative avenues of positive reinforcement to modulate the impact of chemical substances on the dopamine channels in the brain that increase impulsivity.[26]

It may be that the relationship between religion and self-control is predicated upon the practice of one's religious beliefs rather than on holding the beliefs alone. In other words, the discipline of engaging in R/S acts may produce more of the fruit of self-control. Indeed, there appears to be a relationship between the engagement in R/S practices, such as prayer and meditation, and the development of self-control and self-regulation.[2] Brain scans of experienced meditators while in a meditative or prayerful state have found increased activity in the prefrontal cortex and/or the anterior cingulate, areas associated with executive functioning, reasoning, judgment, response inhibition, and attention.[27] There is also some evidence that engagement in prayer helps to regulate negative emotions for those who are religious.[28]

Self-Control as Mediator of the R/S–Addiction Relationship

Two out of three studies examining self-control as a mediator of the relationship between religion and addiction provide some preliminary support for this hypothesis. Walker and colleagues[29] found that among middle and high school students, the inverse relationship between self-rated importance of religion and the use of addictive substances, including alcohol, marijuana, and cigarettes, was mediated by self-control. Similarly, among a nationally representative sample of the same age group, Desmond and colleagues[30] found that self-control partially mediated the inverse relationship between religiousness and alcohol and marijuana use. In contrast, Wills and colleagues[31] found that self-control did not mediate the relationship between religiousness and substance use among African American adolescents. Of note, all of these studies were cross-sectional designs; longitudinal and experimental designs are needed to determine causality— that is, whether religiousness results in less substance use because of higher self-control.

In summary, the research reviewed above provides theoretical and empirical support for each arm of a mediation model: (1) R/S is associated with less addiction; (2) R/S is associated with greater self-control and self-regulation; (3) self-control and impulse regulation are associated with less addiction; and (4) there is some limited evidence that self-control may mediate the inverse relationship between religiousness and addiction, at least among middle and high school students.

How R/S-Based Treatments for Addiction Increase Self-Control

Among those in recovery from addictions, individuals who rate themselves higher in religiousness or spirituality tend to be more optimistic about their chances for recovery and report lower anxiety, greater stress resilience, and increased levels of social support.[32] Researchers and clinicians have noted that religiousness can be a resource for helping individuals overcome addiction and substance abuse and, as reviewed above, have integrated R/S into a number of different treatment approaches for addiction.

Alcoholics Anonymous (AA) is probably the most widely studied and empirically validated spirituality-integrated program for addressing alcohol abuse.[10] Although AA and other spiritually based treatments have shown empirical validity, researchers are calling for more complete and comprehensive models to explain why these treatments appear to be effective.[33] The question still remains: What does spirituality add that makes treatment successful and desirable to patients? As we proposed earlier in the chapter, we believe one possible answer to this question is that R/S-based treatments increase individuals' ability to exert self-control and to experience alternative and compelling avenues of reward, leading to successful treatment outcomes.

There are at least five ways in which spiritually integrated treatments may increase self-control. First, acknowledging the presence of a watchful higher power heightens patients' perception of being monitored, both during and outside of treatment. Across a wide variety of impulse-control behaviors (e.g., substance abuse, binge eating, nail biting), monitoring by oneself or others has been shown to decrease the impulsive behavior.[34] The knowledge that there is an ever-present, supportive power that is watching all one's movements at all times may decrease the likelihood of relapse and increase motivation for abstaining.[25] Even if patients perceive that their higher power is condemning and punishing, this too may increase motivation for abstinence.

Second, participation in religious groups outside of treatment will likely expose an individual to more stringent standards and expectations about substance use and provide accountability and social support for avoiding these substances. Further, the more frequently an individual is exposed to religious social support for drug abstinence, the more likely he or she is to be successful at maintaining abstinence.[35] The expectation for certain behaviors and being part of a group of people who all abstained from certain actions would not only provide positive social support for maintaining abstinence but also reduce exposure to drug cues that can trigger relapse.

Third, spirituality-integrated treatments may increase the inherent value of rewards for abstinence via methods not immediately available to secular treatment programs. The prospect of experiencing these rewards would then likely create a great desire to exert self-control and abstain from substance use. At the basest level, religious experiences (e.g., mystical experiences) may provide a pleasing substitute for the chemically induced high experienced during a period of substance abuse.[36, 37] However, beyond a simple substitution, spiritually integrated treatments may also open alternative reward avenues by facilitating meaning making,[38] changing self-identity,[9] feeling recognized as part of a larger social fabric that includes being cared for by a higher power, and receiving praise and encouragement for internalizing self-control behaviors. In essence, spirituality-integrated addiction treatments may tip the subjective balance of rewards toward exerting self-control and maintaining abstinence rather than using substances.

Fourth, from a neurological standpoint, religious practices may increase impulse control by effectively adding a "pause" button, providing a moment for thoughtful decision making between impulse and behavior. Many religiously integrated treatments include prayer or meditation, and research has found that these religious methods are positively correlated with decreased substance abuse.[39] Meditation, under a number of circumstances, affects brain areas known to decrease impulsive behavior and increase self-awareness of cravings.[40] Further evidence shows that practicing these meditation techniques creates measurable changes in the brain and that these changes increase in a dose–response manner with practice.[41] Specifically, meditation activates brain areas associated with monitoring, including the dorsolateral prefrontal cortex, and focusing attention on one's current activity, such as the superior frontal sulcus.[41] In summary, R/S-integrated addiction treatments that include some form of meditation or meditative prayer may positively impact the areas of the brain associated with self-control, resulting in better treatment outcomes.

Finally, religiously based treatment is somewhat paradoxical because individuals often feel an increase in control over their addiction by giving up control to a higher power, as espoused by the 12-step Anonymous models. Even under the rubric where the individual "gives up control" psychologically, we are aware ultimately, it is the individual, not the higher power, who makes the decisions regarding where to go and what to do. This paradox may be explained by the self-control model developed by Baumeister and colleagues, described previously in this chapter.[25] As individuals make decisions to resist cravings and avoid triggers for substance abuse, they are using their self-control muscle. According to the theory, after a period of intense use of self-control, the self-control muscle becomes exhausted. By "giving up" control to a higher power for a period of time, individuals can rest and regain their strength to continue to resist temptation. Therefore, what appears to be a paradox is instead an example of drawing upon additional religious resources to help resist temptation for relapse. In this sense, self-control is developed with and supported by the assistance of the higher power.

Conclusion

This chapter reviewed the empirical literature on how spiritually inte-grated treatments for addiction and substance abuse may positively impact individuals' ability to engage in recovery and maintain abstinence through the development of self-control. Although we are not able to formally test this mediation model, the literature reviewed does provide some evidence that R/S beliefs and practices increase self-control and that increased self-control is associated with less addiction, greater recovery rates, and main-tenance of sobriety. As such, it seems likely that one of the ways the effective-ness of spiritually integrated treatments for addiction can be explained is by the development and encouragement of participants' self-control.

Although the idea that the practice of R/S teachings produces self-control and, as such, results in better recovery outcomes is a new line of thought in psychology, it is not a new concept. Rather, it is as old as reli-gions themselves. For example, the title of this book refers to a passage in the Bible that states that those who choose to follow the Holy Spirit's direction, instead of their fleshly appetites, will produce the fruit of self-control, among other positive emotions and behaviors. Inherent in this pas-sage is also the notion that followers need the aid of the Spirit to "live according to the Spirit" (Galatians 5:16). In other words, although it takes a decision of the will to pursue behavior that is deemed righteous, self-control is not a predicate but rather a consequence of faith, at least in Christianity. We are not saying that individuals who struggle with addition and the exertion of self-control are not religious or spiritual enough. Rather, we see R/S as a component of addiction treatment that likely facilitates the development of self-control, which then leads to better treatment outcomes.

This concept has implications for both clinical practice and empirical research. In terms of clinical implications, it is important to note that R/S-integrated treatments may influence the development of patients' self-control differently depending on the patients' particular belief system, as well as the belief system on which the treatment is based. For example, Buddhism teaches that individuals are driven by innate desires and aver-sions. Through meditative practices, Buddhists learn how to develop a greater awareness of these innate impulses, allowing them to disengage from the impulses and exert self-control by making conscious choices.

This is similar to the teachings in Hinduism. The Bhagavad Gita, the Hindu sacred writings, states, "It is true that the mind is restless and difficult to control. But it can be conquered, Arjuna, through regular practice and detachment. Those who lack self-control will find it difficult to progress in meditation; but those who are self-controlled, striving earnestly through the right means, will attain the goal" (6.35–36).

In other words, both Buddhism and Hinduism teach that it is the self that can be trained to resist and overcome cravings and harmful behaviors, such as those related to addiction. R/S treatments for addiction that are based on the tenets of Buddhism, such as the Spiritual Self-Schema therapy and mindfulness meditation, likely help patients to develop self-control through the process just described. In contrast, treatments that were founded upon Christianity, such as AA[*] and Teen Challenge, likely develop self-control in a different manner. Christianity is based on the teaching that mankind is inherently sinful and is in need of a Savior, Jesus Christ, to be redeemed from sin. Christian-based addiction treatments likely develop self-control through the paradoxical surrendering of control to God. In this model, the credit, so to speak, for resisting cravings and recovery is given to God rather than to the self, as arguably it is in Buddhism and Hinduism.

In summary, patients seeking an R/S-integrated treatment may feel most comfortable with an intervention that is in line with or can be modified to fit their belief system. Personality characteristics may also be correlated with different methods of developing self-control. Therefore, overall, R/S treatments for addiction may aid in the development of self-control, but the mechanism by which self-control is developed may differ across treatments. Understanding these conceptual differences, not just in terms of type of intervention and specific belief system but also in terms of mechanisms of action for effective change, may help providers to better match treatments, resulting in better recovery outcomes.

In terms of research implications, this is an area that clearly needs more well-developed empirical studies to test meditation effects, the potential benefits of treatment matching based on patient R/S background, psychosocial factors positively influenced by R/S integrated treatment,

---

[*]We acknowledge that although AA was founded upon tenants of the Christian faith, it is currently not formally associated with any particular faith tradition.

and identifying situations where it can be contra-indicated. While early longitudinal research in the laboratory setting has indicated that it is possible to teach participants how to increase their level of self-control over domains unrelated to addiction (e.g., exercises to improve posture,[42] studies have not yet tested whether this can also be done for behaviors related to addiction. In addition, exploring whether R/S-integrated treatments alter individuals' physiological response to the presence of relapse triggers (e.g., needles, powder, and alcohol bottles) would allow researchers to take advantage of cutting-edge research identifying the link between physiological response to triggers and likelihood of relapse. This would allow those interested in R/S-integrated treatments to incorporate "pure" and "applied" research to improve treatment for those struggling with addiction.

As clinical psychologists who adhere to the scientist-practitioner model of practice, both authors strongly support the integration of research and clinical practice. If through research we are able to empirically identify the benefits, challenges, and contra-indications of integrating R/S into addiction treatment, we can provide patients with the most powerful, cost-effective, and patient-acceptable treatments to help individuals with addiction regain control of their lives.

Notes

1. Durkheim, E. (1965). *The elementary forms of religious life* (J.W. Swain, Trans). New York: Free Press.
2. McCullough, M. E., & Willoughby, B. L. B. (2009). Religion, self-regulation, and self-control: Associations, explanations, and implications. *Psychological Bulletin, 135,* 69–93.
3. Schmeichel, B. J., & Baumeister, R. F. (2004). Self-regulatory strength. In R. F. Baumeister & K. D. Vohs (Eds.), *Handbook of self-regulation: Research, theory, and applications* (pp. 84–98). New York: Guilford Press.
4. Tangney, F. P., Baumeister, R. F., & Boone, A. L. (2004). High self-control predicts good adjustment, less pathology, better grades, and interpersonal success. *Journal of Personality, 72,* 271–322.

5. Arnold, R. M., Avants, K., Margolin, A., & Marcotte, D. (2002). Patient attitudes concerning the inclusion of spirituality into addiction treatment. *Journal of Substance Abuse Treatment, 23*, 319–326.

6. Neff, J. A., Shorkey, C. T., & Windsor, L. C. (2006). Contrasting faith-based and traditional substance abuse treatment programs. *Journal of Substance Abuse Treatment, 30*(1), 49–61. doi: 10.1016/j.jsat.2005.10.001

7. Kadden, R. M. (1994). Cognitive-behavioral approaches to alcoholism treatment. *Alcohol Health and Research World, 18*, 279–279.

8. Wolf-Branigin, M., & Duke, J. (2007). Spiritual involvement as a predictor to completing a Salvation Army substance abuse treatment program. *Research on Social Work Practice, 17*(2), 239.

9. Avants, S. K., Beitel, M., & Margolin, A. (2005). Making the shift from "addict self" to "spiritual self": results from a Stage I study of Spiritual Self-Schema (3-S) therapy for the treatment of addiction and HIV risk behavior. *Mental Health, Religion & Culture, 8*(3), 167–177.

10. Tonigan, J. S. (2007). Spirituality and Alcoholics Anonymous. *Southern Medical Journal, 110*(4), 437–440.

11. Kelly, J. F., Stout, R. L., Magill, M., Tonigan, J. S., & Pagano, M. E. (2011). Spirituality in recovery: A lagged mediational analysis of Alcoholics Anonymous' principal theoretical mechanism of behavior change. *Alcoholism: Clinical and Experimental Research, 35*(3), 454–463.

12. Zgierska, A., Rabago, D., Chawla, N., Kushner, K., Koehler, R., & Marlatt, A. (2009). Mindfulness meditation for substance use disorders: A systematic review. *Substance Abuse, 30*(4), 266–294.

13. Gelderloos, P., Walton, K. G., Orme-Johnson, D. W., & Alexander, C. N. (1991). Effectiveness of the Transcendental Meditation program in preventing and treating substance misuse: A review. *Substance Use & Misuse, 26*(3), 293–325.

14. Owen, P., Gerrard, M. D., & Owen, G. (2007). *Following up with graduates of Minnesota Teen Challenge: Results of telephone surveys with persons completing treatment in 2001 through 2005*. St. Paul, MN: Wilder Research.

15. Miller, W. R. (1998). Researching the spiritual dimensions of alcohol and other drug problems. *Addiction, 93*(7), 979–990.

16. Koenig, H. G. (2005). *Faith and mental health: Religious resources for healing.* Philadelphia: Templeton Foundation Press.

17. CASA: The National Center on Addiction and Substance Abuse at Columbia University. (2001, November). *So help me God: Substance abuse, religion, and spirituality.*: Bodman Foundation an John Templeton Foundation. New York, NY: Author.

18. Wachholtz, A., Fortuna, L., Porche, M., & Torres-Stone, R. (2010). *Lifetime alcohol abuse prevalence: Role of childhood and adult religion.* Paper presented at the Society of Behavioral Medicine. Retrieved from http://www.springerlink.com/content/nr2127186336 2252/fulltext.pdf.

19. Koski-Jannes, A., & Turner, N. (1999). Factors influencing recovery from different addictions. *Addiction Research, 7*(6), 469–492.

20. Baumeister, R. F., & Vohs, K. D. (2004). Self regulation. In C. Peterson & M.E.P. Seligman (Eds.), *Character strengths and virtues: A handbook and classification* (pp. 499–516). Washington, DC/ New York: American Psychological Association/Oxford Press.

21. Park, N., & Peterson, C. (2009). Character strengths: Research and practice. *Journal of College and Character, 10*(4), n.p.

22. Park, N., Peterson, C., & Seligman, M. E. P. (2006). Character strengths in fifty-four nations and the fifty US states. *Journal of Positive Psychology, 1*(3), 118–129.

23. Mischel, W., Shoda, Y., & Rodriquez, M. L. (1989). Delay of gratification in children. *Science, 244,* 933–938.

24. Pulkkinen, L., & Pitkanen, T. (2010). Temperance and the strengths of personality: Evidence from a 35-year longitudinal study. In R. Schwarzer & P. Frensch (Eds.),*Personality, human development, and culture: International perspective on psychological science* (Vol. 2, pp. 127–140). New York: Psychology Press.

25. Baumeister, R. F., & Exline, J. J. (2000). Self-control, morality, and human strength. *Journal of Social and Clincial Psychology, 19,* 29–42.

26. Balera, R. D., & Volkow, N. D. (2006). Drug addiction: The neuro-biology of disrupted self-control. *Trends in Molecular Medicine,* *12*(12), 559–566.

27. Aftanas, L., & Golosheykin, S. (2005). Impact of regular mediation practice on EEG activity at rest and during evoked negative emotions. *International Journal of Neuroscience, 115,* 893–909.

28. Koole, S. L. (2007). *Raising spirits: An experimental analysis of the affect regulation functions of prayer.* Unpublished manuscript. Vrije Universiteit, Amsterdam.

29. Walker, C., Ainett, M. G., Wills, T. A., & Mendoza, D. (2007). Religiosity and substance use: Test of an indirect-effect model in early and middle adolescence. *Psychology of Addictive Behaviors, 21,* 84–96.

30. Desmond, S. A., Ulmer, J. T., & Bader, C. D. *Religion, prosocial learning, self control, and delinquency.* Manuscript under editorial review.

31. Wills, T. A., Gibbons, F. X., Gerrard, M., Murry, V. M., & Brody, G. H. (2003). Family communication and religiosity related to substance use and sexual behavior in early adolescence: A test for pathways through self-control and prototype perceptions. *Psychology of Addictive Behaviors, 17,* 312–323.

32. Pardini, D. A., Plante, T. G., Sherman, A., & Stump, J. E. (2000). Religious faith and spirituality in substance abuse recovery: Determining the mental health benefits. *Journal of Substance Abuse Treatment, 19*(4), 347–354. doi: 10.1016/S0740-5472(00)00125-2

33. Longshore, D., Anglin, M. D., & Conner, B. T. (2009). Are religiosity and spirituality useful constructs in drug treatment research? *Journal of Behavioral Health Services & Research, 36*(2), 177–188.

34. Aboujaoude, E., & Koran, L. M. (Eds.). (2010). *Impulse control disorders.* Cambridge, UK: Cambridge University Press.

35. Richard, A. J., Bell, D. C., & Carlson, J. W. (2000). Individual religiosity, moral community, and drug user treatment. *Journal for the Scientific Study of Religion, 39*(2), 240–246.

36. Newberg, A., & Newberg, S. (2005). Neuropsychology of relgious and spritiual experience. In R. Paloutzian & C. Park (Eds.),

Handbook of the psychology of religion and spirituality (pp. 199–215). New York: Guildford Press.

37. Roberts, T. B. (2006). Chemical input, religious output-entheogens: A pharmatheology sampler. In P. McNamara (Ed.), *Where God and science meet: The psychology of religious experience* (Vol. 3, pp. 235–267). Westport, CT: Praeger.

38. Avants, S. K., & Margolin, A. (1995). Self and addiction: The role of imagery in self-regulation. *Journal of Alternative and Complementary Medicine, 1,* 339–345.

39. Bowen, S., Witkiewitz, K., Dillworth, T. M., Chawla, N., Simpson, T. L., Ostafin, B. D., et al. (2006). Mindfulness meditation and substance use in an incarcerated population. *Psychology of Addictive Behaviors, 20*(3), 343.

40. Seybold, K. (2007). Physiological mechanisms involved in religiosity/ spirituality and health. *Journal of Behavioral Medicine, 30*(4), 303–309.

41. Davidson, R. J., & Lutz, A. (2008). Buddha's brain: Neuroplasticity and meditation [In the Spotlight]. *Signal Processing Magazine, IEEE, 25*(1), 174–176.

42. Muraven, M., Baumeister, R. F., & Tice, D. M. (1999). Longitudinal improvement of self-regulation through practice: Building self-control strength through repeated exercise. *Journal of Social Psychology, 139,* 446–457.

14

Educational and Health Disparities: How Faith-Based Organizations Can Address Inequities among Latinos/as

John E. Pérez and Leyla M. Pérez-Gualdrón

There are more than 48 million Latinos/as in the United States. By the year 2050, the U.S. Census Bureau projects that the Latino/a population will grow to 132.8 million people, 30.3% of the total U.S. population.[1] A substantial number of Latinos/as suffer from educational and health disparities—inequities in terms of educational opportunities, disease burden, and access to healthcare. In this chapter, we focus on Latinos/as, although educational and health disparities exist among many other people of color. Latinos/as themselves represent a heterogeneous group, with different countries of origin, different cultural traditions, and exposure to different risk factors for educational and health disparities. Nonetheless, Latinos/as in the United States often share common language, religious beliefs, cultural values, and immigration experiences that impact their educational attainment and health status. Recognizing both the diversity and shared background among Latinos/as, the focus of this chapter is to examine how faith-based organizations can be used to reduce educational and health disparities among Latinos/as.

We propose harvesting the fruits of the spirit—social justice based on religious and cultural values—to address educational and health disparities among Latinos/as. We begin by exploring educational disparities among Latino/a youth, which is a critical period that impacts economic and health outcomes during adulthood. We review research linking religious beliefs and practices with greater educational attainment. In addition, we examine how religious schools, particularly Catholic schools, have intended to promote educational attainment among Latinos/as and other youth of color. Subsequently, we examine health disparities among Latino/a adults. We review research linking religious beliefs and practices with positive health outcomes. Moreover, we examine some examples of how faith-based organizations have been used to promote health among Latino/a adults. Finally, we discuss how faith-based organizations can play a greater role in reducing educational and health disparities among Latinos/as.

We argue that reducing educational and health disparities is a social justice issue linked, in part, to economic disadvantage among Latinos/as. According to a Pew Research Center analysis, the median wealth of white households is 18 times higher than Latino/a households, the largest wealth gap since the government began publishing such data about 25 years ago.[2] Such economic disparity may contribute to both educational and health disparities among Latinos/as. Furthermore, these disparities suggest the need to explore culturally informed ways to promote educational opportunities and health among low-income, underserved Latino/a populations.

Latinos/as and Educational Disparities: Why Religious Beliefs and Religious Schools Matter

Latinos/as less than 18 years of age represent the second largest ethnic group of students after whites enrolled in the American educational system. However, Latinos/as as a group exhibit among the lowest educational attainment and among the highest dropout rates when compared with other ethnic groups. For example, the U.S. Department of Education and the National Center for Education Statistics indicated that, in 2007, the *status dropout* (people without a high school diploma or its equivalent, including those who may have never been enrolled in school) of Latinos/as between the ages of 16 and 26 years was 21.4%.[3] This rate is significantly higher than the 5.3% observed in their non–Hispanic white counterparts and 8.4% observed in their black counterparts of unspecified ethnicity. These educational disparities have been associated with sociopolitical factors such as high levels of poverty, lack of access to educational resources, cultural incongruence between schools and Latino/a populations, and institutional racism. Specifically, under-resourced schools in urban areas tend to be highly segregated, serving predominantly students of color, including Latinos/as.[4]

In order to better understand and address educational inequities for Latinos/as, it is important to recognize cultural strengths that may promote their success in the face of deficient educational opportunities. For example, religious beliefs and practices, as well as faith-based organizations (e.g., religiously affiliated schools), may be important places to address such educational disparities when considering sociopolitical factors. Further, because of the relevance of religion in Latino/a families,[5] it is important to consider the role that religious beliefs and practices may have in promoting educational success in youth. In addition, some religiously affiliated schools (e.g., inner-city Catholic schools) historically aimed to promote greater educational access for low-income students of color, including Latinos/as.

Latino/a Youth Religious Beliefs, Practices, and Educational Outcomes

Although the role of religion in Latino/a educational outcomes has not been widely researched, there is a growing number of scholars studying this association.[6] Religious beliefs and practices appear to be particularly relevant for Latino/a youth. According to a report by the Department of Health and Human Services, 55% of Latino/a youth in the United States participate in weekly religious activities (e.g., worship service attendance, praying, reading of the scripture).[7] In addition, faith-based organizations offer a unique venue for youth to increase their connections with adults and peers as well as promote civic engagement. Researchers have suggested that these relationships and behaviors benefit Latino/a mental health and educational engagement[6] and may be promising venues to promote social justice and equity for Latinos/as. For example, in a qualitative study with three Puerto Rican inner-city boys, researchers found that religious involvement and community participation was one of four factors that these youth attributed to their academic success. Specifically, the youth reported that ties to their religious communities gave them access to information, mentoring, and social support, which were key to their academic success.[8] Some authors have argued that Latino/a students and other students of color may disengage from or disidentify with educational institutions in the face of inequities and negative societal mirroring;[9] however, sources of cultural strength and promotion, such as the ones offered through religious community supports, may be key to counter the potential effects of negative environments.

Furthermore, research evidence suggests that religious beliefs and practices may play an important role in the education of Latinos/as. For example, scholars analyzing data from the National Longitudinal Study of Adolescent Health (a national survey conducted during 1994 and 1996) found a positive association between the students' reported importance of religion (i.e., religion centrality) and their grades in mathematics and sciences. Specifically, higher levels of religion centrality were associated with higher grades in math and science for 1,236 Latino/a students interviewed in this survey.[6] In the same survey, researchers also found that church attendance was associated with students feeling more connected at school. Students who attended weekly church services reported feeling more connected with their peers and teachers at their schools than students who did not attend church regularly. In addition, students who attended services at church had significantly lower rates of suspension than their peers who did not attend church services. Furthermore, scholars analyzing the Adolescent Health Survey, a large-scale national survey, found that the importance of faith for Latinos/as was associated with high quality of relationships with peers and teachers at their school.[6] This association was stronger among adolescents from low socioeconomic backgrounds compared to their Latino/a peers from higher socioeconomic backgrounds. The authors argued that this finding highlights the importance of personal faith and faith-based organizations as resources and social capital for Latinos/as living in low-income neighborhoods.

In sum, Latino/a youth's religion centrality and practices have been associated with positive experiences at school as well as positive academic outcomes. Taking into consideration sociopolitical issues associated with the education of low-income Latino/a students (e.g., access to resources, institutional discrimination), it is important to further consider the role of religious involvement as internal and external resources that help students cope with educational inequities.

Religious Commitment and Academic Outcomes

In a meta-analysis of 15 published research studies of black and Latino/a students, researchers found that religious commitment was consistently associated with high academic achievement (e.g., high grades, high tests scores, academic attainment). Religious commitment was defined as the students' self-perception of religion centrality and importance in their life, as well as attendance at church services or membership in youth religion organizations.[10]

In another study, a positive association between religious commitment and diverse measures of educational success was found in a longitudinal national sample of Latino/a adolescents and black students.[11] Religious commitment was defined as the student self-report of being religious, participating in church activities, and participating in youth religious groups. Academic achievement was measured as performance on standardized tests, not being held back a grade due to academic failure, and completion of core course requirements by 12th grade. Specifically, researchers found that students who reported higher levels of religious commitment had higher levels of academic achievement than their non–religiously committed counterparts. This association was significant after controlling for the effects of socioeconomic status, gender, and type of school attended (e.g., private vs. public) in the students' academic outcomes.

The reviewed research suggests that the religious beliefs and practices of Latino/a students are promising strengths to be considered in the face of educational disparities. However, greater understanding of how religion works in the context of Latino/a culture and educational inequities is warranted to develop interventions that promote their academic and personal well-being.

Religiously Affiliated Schools and Academic Outcomes

Religiously affiliated schools (e.g., Catholic schools) originated as private schools in response to the immigration movements of the early 1900s in an attempt to preserve religious education, spirituality, ethnic identity, and class mobility for immigrant groups (e.g., Italian, Polish, Irish).[12] With time, and changes in population immigration patterns, religiously

affiliated schools continued to be an important institution for new generations of ethnic minority students, particularly Latinos/as and other youth
of color. However, this may not be tied to spiritual or ethnic identity reasons, but largely to access to education in the context of failing public
school systems.[12] According to the 2010 National Private Schools
Universe Survey, religiously affiliated schools have 98% or above graduation rates. In addition, according to the same survey, 84.9% of students
who graduated from Catholic schools enrolled in 4-year colleges.[13]
Although these national statistics are not specific to Latino/a students, it
is important to consider them, as many Latinos/as attend religiously affiliated schools. Although there are schools affiliated with many religious traditions (e.g., Christian, Jewish, Muslim), most of the research available for
this review focuses on Catholic schools because of their greater enrollment
of Latino/a students.

According to a recent study to assess the educational experiences of
inner-city, low-income youth, researchers found that many immigrant
and second-generation Latino/a and black families sent their children to
Catholic private schools as an alternative to a perceived failing public educational system.[12] In their large-scale retrospective study of young adults
(between 18 and 32 years of age) from inner-city New York, attending
Catholic schools was associated with higher educational achievement
(i.e., number of school years completed). However, tuition cost was a significant barrier to attending Catholic schools for many Latino/a youth.
Nonetheless, attending Catholic schools for at least 1 year predicted
greater educational attainment.

When exploring the reasons for the academic success associated with
enrollment in religious schools, researchers observed that the young adult
Latinos/as attributed their educational success to their awareness of their
education's financial cost and the sacrifices their parents made to offer
them a better education.[12] Some of the young Latino/a adults in this study
also commented that school discipline practices and high academic expectations helped them succeed. In addition, some Latino/a students in this
sample commented that small class sizes and being part of a caring community were linked to their success in their religiously affiliated schools;
this finding is consistent with the collectivistic orientation of Latino/a culture. These results only highlight educational practices in religious

schools; however, they do not address the educational impact of religious beliefs in religiously affiliated schools.

The positive association between attending religiously affiliated schools and the academic achievement of Latino/a students has been observed in other studies. For example, in the previously cited meta-analysis, attending religious schools (e.g., Catholic, Evangelical) had a positive impact in the academic achievement of Latino/a and black students.[10] One explanation of these positive outcomes reportedly includes the absence of academic tracking in religiously affiliated schools.[10] In addition, researchers have reported increased parental involvement in the religious schools, which may also play a role in Latinos/as educational success in religiously affiliated schools.[10] Other reported factors associated with academic success in religious schools were high expectations and encouragement for students' academic goals. In this meta-analysis, the positive impact of religious schools on Latino/a students was seen among older students in middle school and high school rather than younger children in elementary school; however, this finding can also be related to a cumulative effect of years enrolled in religiously affiliated schools.[10]

Future Directions: Cultural and Social Justice Orientation in Faith-Based Interventions

The research reviewed in this chapter provides support for using religious beliefs and faith-based institutions to address the educational inequities that impact Latino/a students. In addition, we recommend integrating cultural and sociopolitical factors that are also linked to Latinos/as religious and educational experiences. Although the majority of the Latinos/as in the United States are from Catholic backgrounds, scholars have suggested that there is a high level of hybridity and variability of religious/spiritual practices among different Latino/a groups. For example, some Latino/a groups have incorporated Catholic practices with Native and Afrocentric beliefs and practices, which should be considered in any intervention intended to address the religious beliefs/practices and educational outcomes of Latino/a students.[14] Thus, educators and community leaders working in faith-based schools may strengthen interventions for Latino/a education by acknowledging and evaluating the diversity of the students' religious beliefs and practices.

In addition to integrating religious cultural factors in educational interventions, sociopolitical factors may be addressed by drawing upon Latin American psychology and theology of liberation. Thus, interventions that promote the students' religious beliefs and practices may also incorporate a critical consciousness about societal inequities and motivation for social justice.[15] Moreover, interventions that focus on the promotion of history of Latino/a cultures, circumstances, religion, and in-group strengths may be particularly empowering for Latinos/as. Under these principles, religious interventions that focus on education and social justice should emphasize the role of Latino/a students as agents of social justice and change rather than using deficit perspectives. Deficit perspectives (e.g., consideration of inner-city Latinos/as as "at-risk" youth) emphasize the need to *rescue* or change Latino/a students' cultural practices to *help* them succeed in their education. The liberation perspective of the Jesuit scholar Martín-Baró offers an example of using religion and psychology to embrace Latino/a critical consciousness and avoid the internalization of societal oppressive/deficit-oriented views.[15]

Liberation views of religion and cultural practices may be relevant for religiously affiliated schools that serve students of different racial backgrounds. For example, scholars in multicultural education have suggested that educational curricula and practices that focus on white Anglo-Saxon ideologies are detrimental for both students of color and for students of white racial backgrounds. Specifically, a curriculum that ignores or dismisses diverse cultures, histories, perspectives, religious practices, and sociopolitical circumstances may perpetuate negative cycles of ethnocentrism and racism that impact students, schools, and societies at large.[16] Therefore, the incorporation of multicultural and liberation-oriented curricula may strengthen the role that religiously affiliated schools already have in addressing educational disparities among students of different racial and cultural backgrounds.

The reviewed research indicates that religious beliefs and faith-based institutions are associated with positive educational outcomes in Latino/a communities. In addition, we presented recommendations to further integrate cultural and sociopolitical factors into faith-based interventions to enhance Latinos'/as' educational experiences. As mentioned above, both educational and health disparities likely stem, in part, from economic disadvantage among Latinos/as. In turn, lower educational attainment and poorer health outcomes may reciprocally contribute to lower socioeconomic status. Furthermore, lower levels of education may directly influence health by limiting knowledge about health screening and other preventive health behaviors. In the next section, we focus health disparities among Latino/a adults. We review the literature linking religious beliefs and practices to health and well-being. Subsequently, we describe some examples of health interventions delivered to Latino/a communities via religious organizations. We conclude this section with recommendations on how to bolster the effectiveness of faith-based health interventions.

Latinos/as and Health Disparities: Why Faith-Based Organizations?

Latinos/as face numerous health disparities. For example, Latinas experience late or no neonatal care more often than do white women (12.2% vs. 5.3%).[17] Latinas also have the highest incidence of cervical cancers.[17] Although the incidence is lower for many other cancers compared to non–Latino/a whites, Latinos/as are less likely to survive most cancers.[18] Among other barriers, the higher mortality rate appears to be associated with lower rates of screening for breast, cervical, and colorectal cancers.[18] The death rate due to HIV/AIDS is 2.5 to 3 times higher for Latinos/as compared to non–Latino/a whites.[17] The HIV/AIDS death rate is highest among Puerto Ricans—13 times that of non–Latino/a whites.[17] In addition, the death rate due to diabetes is 1.5 times higher for Latinos/as compared to non–Latino/a whites.[17] This is not a comprehensive list of health disparities; however, it illustrates the need to address the greater disease burden among Latinos/as in the United States. Various factors may contribute to health disparities, including language and cultural barriers, lack of access to preventive care, lack of health insurance, and poor environmental conditions.[17, 18]

Faith-based organizations represent a promising avenue to address health disparities among Latinos/as. Latino/a adults in the United States are deeply religious—90% report membership in a religious group.[5] The majority of Latinos/as are Roman Catholic (68%); the next largest group is Evangelical or Protestant Christian (19%).[5] Faith-based organizations can provide access to low-income, underserved populations that experience health disparities. In addition, faith-based organizations have established social networks, which are critical for promoting health and well-being among their members. Faith-based organizations also have the infrastructure to independently support and sustain health promotion interventions once they are established.

Religious institutions play a prominent role in Latino/a communities, shaping numerous behaviors from political decisions to daily family life.[5] Religious institutions also shape health beliefs and behaviors of Latinos/as. A growing body of research suggests that religious beliefs and practices are associated with better physical health and emotional well-being among Latinos/as. For example, religious coping—the use of religious beliefs and practices to cope with stressful life events and chronic illness—has been associated with greater well-being among Latinos/as with arthritis, cancer, and HIV/AIDS.[19–21] In a study among older adults in Mexico, importance of religion and religious practice was associated with preventive healthcare use.[22] Specifically, importance of religion was associated with greater use of blood pressure and cholesterol screenings; attending religious services and participating in religious activities were associated with greater use of blood pressure and diabetes screening. Attending religious services also was associated with reduced risk for mortality. In an epidemiologic study of 3,050 older Mexican Americans, those who attended church services once per week showed a 32% reduced risk of mortality compared to those who never attended church services.[23]

Many Latinos/as have a holistic view of health. That is, health is viewed as a combination of physical, mental, and spiritual well-being.[20] These dimensions interact reciprocally with each other. For example, both mental health and spiritual health can influence physical health. This holistic view of health suggests that faith-based health interventions can be effective in reaching Latinos/as. However, some authors have suggested that another belief—fatalism—may be a barrier to Latinos/as receiving adequate health screening and care.[24] Fatalism is a general belief that life's outcomes are beyond one's control. Thus, one's health outcomes may be attributed to luck, fate, or a higher power. This is particularly salient among religious Latinos/as, who may passively defer their health to God's will. Despite the suggestion by some authors that fatalism is a normative cultural belief among Latinos/as, recent research suggests that fatalism is not a widespread barrier to health services among Latinos/as.[24] In fact, several studies have shown that the many religious Latinos/as in the United States have a more active, collaborative relationship with God when it comes to managing their health.[19, 20, 25] That is, many Latinos/as believe that God can intervene to impact one's health; however, they also believe that they are responsible for taking care of their own health. This collaborative relationship with God suggests that churches are ideal institutions to promote screening and healthy behaviors among Latino/a members.

In summary, a growing body of research suggests that various religious beliefs and practices are associated with positive health outcomes among Latinos/as. Because of space limitations, we highlight a few illustrative health promotion programs that have focused on addressing health disparities among Latinos/as in cancer, cardiovascular disease, diabetes, and mental health.

Church-Based Cancer Prevention

A handful of studies have focused on church-based interventions to promote cancer education and cancer screening among low-income Latinos/as, with an emphasis on breast cancer health among Latinas. A few of these programs will be highlighted to illustrate how churches have been used to reach low-income, underserved Latino/a communities.

In Los Angeles County, researchers assessed the effectiveness of telephone counseling to promote the use of mammography screening among female members of churches.[26] Thirty churches were matched on key variables (i.e., race/ethnicity, membership size, and religious denomination) and randomized to either receive one telephone counseling session annually or to a control condition that received no counseling. Eight of these churches were predominantly Latino/a. Telephone counseling included education about breast cancer prevalence rates and information about each participant's risk factors. Counselors tailored their sessions to address individual barriers to screening and encouraged participants to talk to their physicians for screening information and referrals. After 1 year, telephone counseling was associated with greater *maintenance* of mammography among women who had received at least one mammogram during the 12 months prior to the intervention. However, the intervention did not increase mammography rates among women who had not received at least one mammogram during the previous 12 months.

In another study in Los Angeles, researchers used diverse outreach efforts to increase mammography utilization among low-income, Latina women in Los Angeles.[27] The primary outreach effort was a Catholic, church-based intervention that included a breast health day and subsidized access to a mobile mammography service. Educational activities included presentations and distribution of printed information sheets. In addition, health educators offered classes on breast cancer risk and screening in several community settings. The intervention increased mammography screening from 12% to 27% in the targeted community.

In Phoenix, Arizona, researchers implemented a church-based cancer prevention program for low-income, low-acculturated Latina women.[28] Compañeros en la Salud (Partners in Health) was a culturally tailored intervention that focused on health education and cancer screening. Bilingual/bicultural lay health workers who were members of the churches recruited participants, taught cancer-prevention classes, and facilitated cancer-screening activities (e.g., clinical breast exam, pap smear, and mammography). Four hundred forty-seven Latina women from 14 churches completed the study. Higher frequency of attendance at program sessions predicted greater cancer prevention knowledge after 1 year. However, program attendance did not predict cancer-screening behaviors.

Faith- and Community-Based Cardiovascular Disease and Diabetes Prevention

A Kansas City-based community coalition was developed to mobilize neighborhoods and faith organizations to address health disparities among African Americans and Latinos/as.[29] This community coalition focused on reducing risk for both cardiovascular disease and diabetes. The five objectives of the project included: increasing fruit and vegetable consumption, increasing physical activity, increasing the number of people who have a primary care provider, decreasing hemoglobin A1c levels among people with diabetes, and increasing neighborhood engagement. Using a community-based participatory research program, the coalition used microgrants (i.e., allocation of small grants) and distribution of informational resources to promote community changes. From 2001 to 2007, partners in neighborhood and faith organizations implemented 306 community changes (e.g., created walking groups, created a place for physical activity, offered health workshops, and provided nutrition classes). The microgrant strategy, which allowed neighborhood and faith organizations to choose and implement what health interventions to pursue, produced significantly more community based behavior changes than the resource (i.e., informational) distribution strategy. This program demonstrated that neighborhood and faith organizations can successfully implement community changes that focus on risk for health disparities. Data showing changes in population-level health outcomes are needed to determine whether the reviewed health interventions lead to sustained behavioral changes and reduced risk for cancer, cardiovascular disease, and diabetes.

Faith-Based Mental Health Promotion

Although religious beliefs and practices are associated with positive mental health,[19-21] there are few documented faith-based interventions that promote mental health. That is not to say that faith-based organizations fail to address the mental health needs of their members. On the contrary, pastoral counseling has long been a part of religious services provided by faith-based organizations. Priests, ministers, and other religious leaders often provide emotional and spiritual support to members of their congregation. Moreover, faith-based organizations may provide mental health services from licensed lay and religious professionals who are members of their faith communities. However, psychological services are typically provided on an individual or family basis.

A multidisciplinary, multifaith, and research-focused program—the Clergy Outreach and Professional Engagement (C.O.P.E.) model—was developed to facilitate consultation and collaboration between clergy and mental health providers.[30] The goal of this program was to reduce the burden of care for both professional groups by sharing direct care expertise with each other. In this model, mental health professionals were taught how religion and spirituality can contribute to emotional well-being. In addition, mental health professionals were taught how clergy can provide referrals for high-risk congregants who demonstrate clinical symptoms as well as provide support for adherence to treatment for congregants with mental disorders. Reciprocally, clergy were taught the circumstances under which they should provide referrals to clinicians, such as when bereavement leads to major depressive disorder. Moreover, clergy were taught how religious involvement can help congregants with mental disorders improve and prevent relapse. The authors described the program as *religious inclusive* rather than faith based. The C.O.P.E. program is currently administered in a community that primarily serves Latinos/as and African Americans in New York City. The authors provided case examples to illustrate how the C.O.P.E. program works. Outcome data are needed to determine if this program indeed promotes the mental health of Latinos/as and other people of color.

Future Directions: Faith-Placed versus Faith-Based Health Interventions

Despite their promise in addressing health disparities, few scientific-based interventions have used faith-based organizations to promote health among underserved Latino/a populations. Moreover, all of the church-based programs mentioned above have used a "faith-placed" approach. That is, researchers have used religious organizations (e.g., churches) to reach low-income, underserved Latino/a populations to address health disparities. Findings suggest that collaborating with religious organizations can improve the feasibility and acceptability of health promotion interventions in Latino/a communities. However, the interventions themselves have been secular (i.e., nonreligious) and the few behavioral changes have been documented.

Given the association between religious beliefs, religious practices, and health outcomes,[19-23] we expect that faith-based health interventions that incorporate people's religious beliefs and values would more effectively produce behavioral change than health interventions that are merely faith placed. Studies conducted among African American populations suggest that incorporation of religious themes into health interventions may enhance their relevance, improve program participation, and, ultimately, boost intervention efficacy.[31] However, similar studies on Latino/a populations have not been conducted.

Future health promotion interventions with Latinos/as should examine whether integrating religious beliefs and values improves the efficacy of the interventions. Researchers and public health advocates can work with religious leaders to incorporate religious themes into health messages. These messages can be incorporated into educational materials that promote healthy behaviors and preventive screening for cancer, cardiovascular disease, diabetes, and other health problems. Priests and ministers can use Biblical scriptures to promote healthy behaviors and screening activities. For example, the metaphor of one's body as the temple of God can be used to promote healthy behaviors, such as good nutrition, exercise, and abstinence from drugs. Such integration of religious beliefs and values into health promotion activities has the potential to create more powerful interventions by tapping into Latinos/as' core belief systems. Investigators should use community-based participatory research to collaborate with religious leaders to examine the feasibility, acceptability, and effectiveness of religiously framed health promotion interventions. Thus, faith-based (rather than merely faith-placed) interventions have significant potential to reduce health disparities among Latinos/as.

Conclusion

Religious beliefs and practices are associated with higher educational attainment and positive health outcomes among Latinos/as. Moreover, faith-based organizations have been used to promote educational and health opportunities for low-income, underserved Latino/a communities. However, faith-based organizations have the potential to have a much greater impact on reducing Latino/a educational and health disparities. With respect to educational disparities, religiously affiliated schools offer a venue to increase educational access for Latino/a students. However, more integration of Latino/a cultural and race-related experiences is needed to better understand and address the educational experiences of Latino/a youth in religiously affiliated educational systems. Educational institutions that build upon the strengths of their students can have a powerful impact in Latino/a students. Further, the inclusion of socio-political factors and social justice orientation in the practice of religious/educational interventions and religiously affiliated schools may be of particular benefit for their Latino/a students. In regard to health disparities, greater collaboration between public health advocates, researchers, and religious leaders in the community is needed to harness the powerful social networks of faith-based organizations. In addition, integration of religious beliefs and values may increase the acceptability and effectiveness of church-based health promotion interventions. In sum, because of the cultural relevancy of religious beliefs and practices in the lives of Latinos/as in the United States, faith-based institutions are unique venues that have the opportunity to improve the educational opportunities and health of Latinos/as.

Notes

1. U.S. Census Bureau. (2008). *An older and more diverse nation by midcentury.* Retrieved from http://www.census.gov/newsroom/releases/archives/population/cb08-123.html.
2. Taylor, P. Fry, R., & Kochhar, R. (2011). *Wealth gaps rise to record highs between Whites, Blacks, Hispanics.* Retrieved from http://www.pewsocialtrends.org/2011/07/26/wealth-gaps-rise-to-record-highs-between-whites-blacks-hispanics/.
3. U.S. Department of Education & National Center for Education Statistics. (2009). *High school dropout and completion in the United States: 2007* (Compendium report NCES 2009-064). Retrieved from http://nces.ed.gov/pubs2009/2009064.pdf.
4. Fine, M., Burns, A., Payne, Y., & Torre, M. E. (2004). Civic lessons: The color of class betrayal. *Teachers College Records, 106,* 2193–2223.
5. Pew Hispanic Center, Pew Forum on Religion and Public Life. (2007). *Changing faiths: Latinos and the transformation of American religion.* Retrieved from http://pewhispanic.org/reports/report.php?ReportID=75.
6. Sikkink, D., & Hernandez, E. I. (2003). *Religion matters: Predicting school success among Latino youth.* Notre Dame, IN: Institute for Latino Studies, University of Notre Dame.

7. Lippman, L. (2000). *Indicators of child, family, and community connections.* U.S. Department of Health and Human Services. Retrieved from: http://aspe.hhs.gov/hsp/connections-charts04/ch5.htm.

8. Garret, T., Antrop-Gonzalez, R., & Velez, W. (2010). Examining the success factors of high-achieving Puerto Rican male high-school students. *Roeper Review, 32*, 106–115. doi: 10.1080/027831910 03587892

9. Suárez-Orozco, C., & Suárez-Orozco, M. (2001) *Children of immigration.* Cambridge, MA: Harvard University Press.

10. Jeyness, W. H. (2002). A meta-analysis of the effects of attending schools and religiosity on Black and Hispanic academic achievement. *Education and Urban Society, 35*, 27–49. doi:10.1177/00131 2402237213

11. Jeyness, W. H. (1999). The effects of religious commitment on the academic achievement of Black and Hispanic children. *Urban Education, 34*, 458–479.

12. Louie, V., & Holdaway, J. (2009). Catholic schools and immigrant students: A new generation. *Teachers College Record, 111*, 783–816.

13. Broughman, S. P., Swaim, N. L., & Hryczaniuk, C. A. (2011). *Characteristics of private schools in the United States: Results from the 2009–10 Private School Universe Survey.* National Center for Education Statistics, U.S. Department of Education. Retrieved from nces.ed.gov/pubs2009/2009313.pdf.

14. King, P. E., Clardy, C. E., & Sánchez Ramos, J. (2010). Religious and spiritual development in diverse adolescents. In D. P. Swanson, M. C. Edwards, & M. B. Spencer (Eds.), *Adolescence: Development during a global era* (pp. 415–446). Burlington, MA: Academic Press.

15. Martín-Baró, I. (1986/1994). Toward a liberation psychology. In A. Aron & S. Corne (Eds.), *Writings for a liberation psychology: Ignacio Martín-Baró* (pp. 17–32). Cambridge, MA: Harvard University Press.

16. Banks, J. A. (2007). Approaches to multicultural curriculum reform. In J. A. Banks & C. A. M. Banks (Eds.), *Multicultural education: Issues and perspectives* (6th ed., pp. 247–267). Hoboken, NJ: John Wiley & Sons.

17. Centers for Disease Control and Prevention, Office of Minority Health and Health Disparities (2010). *Highlights in minority health and health disparities.* Retrieved from http://www.cdc.gov/omhd/Highlights/2010/HSeptOct10.html.

18. American Cancer Society. (2008). *Cancer facts and figures for Hispanics/Latinos 2006–2008.* Atlanta, GA: Author.

19. Abraído-Lanza, A. F., Vásquez, E., & Echeverría, S. E. (2004). En las manos de Dios [in God's hands]: Religious and other forms of coping among Latinos with arthritis. *Journal of Consulting and Clinical Psychology, 72,* 91–102. doi: 10.1037/0022-006X.72.1.91

20. Jurkowski, J. M., Kurlanska, C., & Ramos, B. M. (2010). Latino women's spiritual beliefs related to health. *American Journal of Health Promotion, 25,* 19–25. doi: 10.4278/ajhp.080923-QUAL-211

21. Simoni, J. M., & Ortiz, M. Z. (2003). Mediational models of spirituality and depressive symptomatology among HIV-positive Puerto Rican women. *Cultural Diversity and Ethnic Minority Psychology, 9,* 3–15. doi: 10.1037/1099-9809.9.1.3

22. Benjamins, M. R. (2007). Predictors of preventive health care use among middle-aged and older adults in Mexico: The role of religion. *Journal of Cross-Cultural Gerontology, 22,* 221–234. doi: 10.1007/s10823-007-9036-4

23. Hill, T. D., Angel, J. L., Ellison, C. G., & Angel, R. J. (2005). Religious attendance and mortality: An 8-year follow-up of older Mexican Americans. *Journal of Gerontology: Social Sciences, 60B,* S102–S109.

24. Abraído-Lanza, A. F., Viladrich, A., Flórez, K. R., Céspedes, A., Aguirre, A. N., & De La Cruz, A. A. (2007). Commentary: Fatalismo reconsidered: A cautionary note for health-related research and practice with Latino populations. *Ethnicity and Disease, 17,* 153–158.

25. Flórez, K. R., Aguirre, A. N., Viladrich, A., Céspedes, A., De La Cruz, A. A., Abraído-Lanza, A. F. (2009). Fatalism or destiny? A qualitative study and interpretative framework on Dominican women's breast cancer beliefs. *Journal of Immigrant and Minority Health, 11,* 291–301. doi: 10.1007/s10903-008-9118-6

26. Duan, N., Fox, S. A., Derose, K. P., & Carson, S. (2000). Maintaining mammography adherence through telephone counseling in a church-based trial. *American Journal of Public Health, 90*, 1468–1471.

27. Fox, S. A., Stein, J. A., Gonzalez, R. E., Farrenkopf, M., & Dellinger, A. (1998). A trial to increase mammography utilization among Los Angeles Hispanic women. *Journal of Health Care for the Poor and Underserved, 9*, 309–321.

28. Lopez, V. A., & Castro, F. G. (2006). Participation and program outcomes in a church-based cancer prevention program for Hispanic women. *Journal of Community Health, 31*, 343–362. doi: 10.1007/s10900-006-9016-6

29. Collie-Akers, V., Schultz, J. A., Carson, V., Fawcett, S. B., & Ronan, M. (2009). REACH 2010: Kansas City, Missouri: Evaluating mobilization strategies with neighborhood and faith organizations to reduce risk for health disparities. *Health Promotion Practice, 10*, 118S–127S. doi: 10.1177/1524839908331271

30. Milstein, G., Manierre, A., Susman, V. L., & Bruce, M. L. (2008). Implementation of a program to improve the continuity of mental health care through Clergy Outreach and Professional Engagement (C.O.P.E.). *Professional Psychology: Research and Practice, 39*, 218–228. doi: 10.1037/0735-7028.39.2.218

31. Campbell, M. K., Hudson, M. A., Resnicow, K., Blakeney, N., Paxton, A., & Baskin, M. (2007). Church-based health promotion interventions: Evidence and lessons learned. *Annual Review of Public Health, 28*, 213–234. doi: 10.1146/annurev.publhealth.28.021406.144016

15

Reaping Fruits of Spirituality through Psycho-Spiritual Integrative Therapy during Cancer Recovery

Kathleen Wall, Diana Corwin, and Cheryl Koopman

Historically, people have turned to spirituality in times of crisis, such as when facing a serious illness such as cancer. Research suggests that although the cancer experience has the potential to become a traumatizing event, many people find that it serves as a time for self-reflection, growth, and increased spirituality.[1, 2, 3, 4, 5, 6, 7, 8] This evidence suggests that extremely significant events, such as cancer, can shatter individuals' assumptions about themselves and the world.

This creates an opportunity to restructure these assumptions in a healthier way and lead to positive life changes.[1, 9, 10] Tedeschi and Calhoun used the phrase *posttraumatic growth* (PTG) to capture the various positive life changes that can be activated by such a significant event.[9] Studies show that cancer is a sufficiently important event to lead to PTG.[1, 2, 3, 4, 5]

Very few psychotherapy treatments have been developed that are aimed specifically at helping people achieve spiritual and psychological growth after a crisis such as a cancer diagnosis. Psycho-spiritual integrative therapy (PSIT) aims to enhance this growth by combining modern, evidence-based psychotherapy techniques with spiritual practices. PSIT is designed to help participants develop specific skills and acquire tools to cope with major life stressors, including cancer. Participants have noted that PSIT has helped them cope not only with cancer but also with other stressful events they have experienced.

The psychological and spiritual practices in PSIT support participants in progressing toward the actualization of their life purpose or aspiration while improving their quality of life and reducing their stress. These spiritual practices enable participants to focus their attention on their spiritual connections rather than on ruminative thoughts about their cancer. PSIT is nonsectarian and relies on a personal sense of the sacred; it is therefore suitable for people from any faith or spiritual tradition. Furthermore, PSIT is also appropriate for individuals who may not identify with any explicit spiritual tradition but who are interested in experiencing a greater sense of awe in contemplating the connectedness of humanity, nature, and/or the complexity and vastness of the universe.

This chapter describes psycho-spiritual integrative therapy and includes both an overview of the therapeutic process and the theoretical foundation for PSIT. A case study focusing on "Clara" is used to illustrate the richness of the PSIT process (her name was changed to protect her identity). This case illustrates how a participant defines her personal sense of the sacred and clarifies her highest life purpose, which for many participants is spiritual in nature and provides meaning and guidance in conducting their lives.[10, 11]

Clara, a breast cancer survivor, reported that through a PSIT group, she developed a clearer vision of her spiritual life purpose and could actualize it with more facility. She gained abilities to acknowledge, genuinely accept, and transform personal patterns that helped and hindered achievement of her life purpose. Learning to experience the Divine more readily and consistently led to collaboration with her sense of the sacred in service of making greater transformations that facilitated living a creative and harmonious life. Meditation became a practice that she integrated into her daily life even while waiting in the doctor's office. The meditative state of mindful acceptance of the present moment helped her to face conflicts with greater equanimity, improving her relationships. The PSIT process helped her change her relationship to herself to others and to the Divine. She felt the PSIT experience gave her skillful means to face life challenges even beyond those of cancer survivorship.

The case study of Clara—presented in more depth later in this chapter—illustrates how individuals can identify and develop an active acceptance of the cognitive, emotional, and physical attributes that facilitate or hinder the achievement of their life purpose. It also illustrates how individuals can use the psychological tools and spiritual practices taught in PSIT to overcome barriers and to capitalize on personal strengths. Use of personal strengths has been shown to increase health and happiness in positive psychology studies (see Dreher, this volume). PSIT participants are trained to observe themselves mindfully and without judgment and to identify the aspects of the self that help and hinder their actualization of their life purpose. Drawing upon their personally defined spirituality, they seek personal transformation and progress toward fulfilling their life purpose.

The theoretical foundation for PSIT recognizes that spirituality is an important resource for coping with cancer, particularly for women and minorities.[12, 13, 14] Many studies suggest that spiritually based practices, such as those included in PSIT, can significantly improve physical, psychological, and spiritual well-being.[12, 13, 15, 16] PSIT includes training in spiritual meditations, exploring a personalized sense of the sacred, and developing a greater sense of collaborative spiritual coping in aligning one's sense of personal agency with that of the sacred.[17] Furthermore, PSIT integrates these activities with psychological skills training in cognitive and affective restructuring and regulation.

These skills can be utilized throughout the lifespan to cope with challenges and to maintain the psychological and spiritual benefits associated with PSIT treatment. Each session is designed to teach participants specific tools that will enable them to achieve their goals. Although the scientific research on PSIT is preliminary, it suggests that cancer survivors who participated in PSIT experienced reduced mood disturbance, improved quality of life and posttraumatic growth, and increased spirituality.[18] Findings from qualitative studies also elucidate the experiences of participants who reap the fruits of spirituality in their cancer recovery.[19, 20, 21]

The PSIT process is composed of several psychological and spiritual growth exercises to help participants identify their life purpose and take steps toward achieving it.[22] These exercises are repeatedly practiced, both in session and at home, to help participants refine their skills and gain greater insight into themselves. Participants utilize the skills that they have learned in previous sessions to serve as the foundation for further growth and exploration.

Several types of meditations are woven into each PSIT session, both to reap the documented salutatory physical and mental health effects and to facilitate psychological changes. Mindfulness-based stress reduction (MBSR), which is utilized throughout the PSIT process, includes Hatha yoga postures and meditations aimed at developing nonjudgmental acceptance of the present moment.[23] MBSR also facilitates compassionate acceptance of self and others through loving-kindness meditation (see Shapiro & Sahgal, this volume). This acceptance state is called *witness* in PSIT. The witness is a metacognitive process; from the witness perspective, beliefs are seen as transitory and nondefining of the self, which allows participants to nonjudgmentally accept thoughts, emotions, and sensations.[23, 24]

Acceptance has been found to facilitate changes in behavior and attitudes that allow individuals to actualize their life purpose.[25, 26, 27, 28, 29] The MBSR techniques included in PSIT have consistently been found to reduce psychological symptoms such as stress, anxiety, depression, anger, and confusion and physical symptoms such as fatigue, sleep disturbances, and pain, and improved overall quality of life in cancer patients.[30, 31]

PSIT incorporates passage meditation (PM), which facilitates the acceptance process by encouraging participants to utilize spiritual and compassionate acceptance to transform their helping and hindering personal patterns. This process activates spiritual resources and active coping.[17, 32, 33] This inspirational meditation builds concentrated attention and the mental capacity to translate these ideas into practice and to quickly recall them in daily life.[34] Compared with secular meditation, spiritually oriented meditation has been found to have some additional psychological benefits.[33] Passage meditation has been found to promote stress reduction and improve health,[17, 35] though it has not been specifically studied in a cancer population outside of the context of PSIT.

In passage meditation, participants select a passage from a poem, prayer, song lyrics, or hymn to represent their personal experience of the sacred. They meditate on that passage to encourage a collaborative relationship with their sense of the sacred in an act of spiritual active acceptance or spiritual surrender.[36] This relationship allows participants to transform the helping and hindering personal patterns, allowing them to more fully engage in the fulfillment of their aspiration or highest life purpose.

Psycho-Spiritual Integrative Therapy Process

In the beginning of the PSIT process, participants clarify their highest aspiration or deepest purpose in life. The aspiration is beyond work–life vocation (see Dreher, this volume). Aspiration is that "something really worth living for," the greatest purpose for which we live here on Earth. This aspiration is utilized throughout PSIT. Through inspirational spiritual readings and guided meditation, participants clarify their aspirations. Participants engage in an iterative process of discerning and identifying their true life purpose, including setting goals for the immediate future that they view as stepping stones to achieving their greatest life aspirations. Participants keep a written journal about their aspiration using words and images throughout the PSIT process.

Exercises that invite self-reflection promote acknowledgment and genuine acceptance of personal patterns that facilitate or hinder the fulfillment of one's aspiration. Participants identify the personal patterns that help and hinder the fulfillment of their aspiration and choose one of each to work with throughout the PSIT process. Mindfulness meditations are utilized to develop the nonjudgmental observer state—the *witness*—to enable participants to nonreactively accept their helping and hindering patterns.

Participants physically move from *witness* to the *helper* positions, then back to *witness*, and finally into the *hinderer* stance. When they move into their helper or hinderer stance, they actively assume the posture, movements, emotions, thoughts, images, and motivations of this stance, then write and draw in their journal about these experiences. Moving back to the witness stance facilitates nonjudgmental acceptance of these personal patterns.

Further compassionate acceptance is achieved by an active dialogue between the witness with the helper and the hinderer, clarifying the motivations behind each of these patterns. This is practiced in a dynamic movement with the witness facing the helper and hinderer; the participant, as witness, asks each aspect, "What are your wants or motivations? What are you here for in my life?" As the witness, they actively listen and sense the answers, then discover the motivations behind these patterns, which the participants further describe in their journals.

To actualize their life purpose and aspiration, participants must transform the helping and hindering personal patterns using the spiritual resources activated by passage meditation. Participants stand in the witness position and meditate using the passage selected for passage meditation, evoking an experience of lived spiritually. They then surrender the motivations of the helper and hinderer to their personally defined sense of the Divine. This surrender is enacted by physically taking one step back from the position they assumed for the witness enactment. Through this process of surrendering the motivations of the helping and hindering personal patterns, participants transform these patterns. This transformation is often profound, pervasive, and persistent. After completing this process, participants reflect on their experiences and write and draw in their journal about their insights into this transformation. At the end of the PSIT process, participants summarize the changes, if any, of their life aspiration, the transformation of their helping and hindering personal patterns, and the steps they plan to take to achieve their aspiration. Using a variety of tools, the PSIT process is intended to help participants to cope with the many challenges of cancer survivorship and to live a meaningful life infused with the positive emotions and sense of well-being evoked through continuous use of these tools (for more about positive emotions, see Shapiro & Sahagal, this volume).

The case study depicting Clara, a PSIT participant, will illustrate the PSIT process in its entirety. Materials for this case illustration were drawn from her journal entries and several studies on a PSIT group for cancer survivors.[18, 19, 20, 21] Clara was in her mid-50s and was diagnosed with breast cancer 2 years before she participated in a PSIT group. Clara reported on the study measures an increase in spirituality (52.5%) and quality of life (43.5%) during the 8-week PSIT group process.[21] Clara was raised in a very religious Christian home but rejected most of the doctrine after her mother's death—when Clara was 13—because of the rancor in the congregation that she attended. After participating in PSIT, she describes herself a "pantheist," defining that as " . . . nature is the product of the Creator, . . . I think you can . . . celebrate the spirituality in that way as part . . . , of the living world." She describes her spiritual experience and beliefs, " . . . with meditation and yoga and . . . writing, I feel like . . . I'm a little bit more part of the creator, a little bit more One with the Creator." She describes a sense of the eminence or experiencing the Divine within, as well as a belief in a transcended creator.

Clara had previous experience with Hatha yoga meditation and found that PSIT helped her integrate meditation into her daily life more readily, including meditating when she met with her doctor. Meditation helped her become less emotionally reactive, especially as she developed the witness and a nonjudgmental awareness of her experiences. She used the witness to transform patterns that helped and hindered the facilitation of her aspiration. She also described how this ability was especially helpful in dealing with conflicts with people, such as her relatives and friends. She related an incident with a friend with whom she had a differing opinion; her friend became very angry, while Clara exhibited nonjudgmental acceptance about their disagreement. Beyond the interpersonal benefits of meditation, Clara noted how the practices boosted her connection with her spirituality, citing a Biblical scripture, "In the silence you shall know God." Her personal sense of the sacred was infused throughout the whole PSIT process. Like many participants, Clara found it difficult to let go of her many thoughts during the MBSR meditations. She wrote a poem about this process.

> *Meditation*
> *Breathing deeply*
> *The thoughts come unbidden*
> *Noisy intruders on a quiet place*
>
> *Conversations write themselves*
> *In white chalk*
> *On the black slate board*
> *Of my childhood*
> *She said*
> *I should have said*
>
> *Then I erase them*
> *Leaving a smear*
> *Of white chalk dust*
>
> *Ideas like flowersfloating in rushing watercircling*
> *   the rock midstreamwhere I stand*
>
> *On a narrow wooden bridge*
> *I drop those thoughts over the rail*

Watching them like pooh sticks
Race under and on the river

Scuffing some easily with my shoe
Into the water they drift away

But here's a big one,
Fear carved into a heavy wooden block,
To hoist and heave over the rail

Splash

It settles into the rocks
The water tugging at it
Turning and nudging it
Slowly downstream

In the first few PSIT sessions, Clara, like many participants, began to bring into focus her aspiration based on initial inklings about important values in her life, such as "development of character," "connection with community," "creating safe environments for the communication of disagreements," and "spreading love." She concluded that her aspiration or highest life purpose was "communication of my heart's wisdom through music and writing."

After clarifying her aspiration, Clara listed and chose to work with a helper pattern and one hinderer pattern that facilitated or frustrated the actualization of her aspiration. She then engaged the helping and hindering patterns by moving from the witness stance into the stances of each pattern. She observed her sensations, emotions, thoughts, images, and motivations during this process and wrote about them in her journal to allow for further reflection.

The stance of helper, which was strength and determination, began for her as the Hatha yoga Warrior pose. She reported "a position of strength and determination, a good stance for conflicts, open arms was with direction and purpose, full of mindful movement, energy at its core, strength and courage." Clara felt that this position was physically tiring to maintain. Clara's first hinderer was "an inner critic." The hinderer's movements included "frowning and tapping her foot," with an "annoyed expression." Her feelings were "sadness," "fighting back tears," "the heavy burden of a sensitive soul," "poverty of spirit," and "stifling creativity." Clara was able to fully experience her helper and hinderer and to clearly acknowledge these as personal patterns that facilitated and frustrated the fulfillment of her aspiration.

After enacting the stance of the helper and hinderer and becoming familiar with the witness's calm, nonjudgmental stance, Clara began a journey to accept and transform these patterns. Clara asked each stance to describe its role in her life and to explain its purpose for being there. Clara's hinderer, the inner critic, declared, "I just want perfection. You need to do great things and I am here to help you." The witness then stated, "But don't you see that your constant corrections keep me from doing anything?" The inner critic replied, "I don't care. As long as everything is perfect I am happy. I can't stand to see first drafts. . . . I want you to be esteemed. I want other people to think that you are . . . great."

Clara's helper was strength and determination—enacted and depicted in the form of the Hatha yoga Warrior posture—then stated: "I want you to have . . . strength, encourage you to follow your life's path, to make good judgments. I am about energy. I help you see what is important and what you should let fall away. I am the self that told you to take the uphill path when it would have been easier to follow the river. And see, it was hard and you've had to skip the river walk, but you reached the summit. I am that inner voice that tells you what is important. . . . Know that I am not about violence, but about strength and groundedness. I am a difficult position to hold and you are right to let me flow, to let me change directions." Clara's helper stance and images began to transform from the rigid and demanding Warrior stance into a free-flowing, moving stance, which she later depicted as sea kelp [floating] in the ocean.

Enlisting spiritual resources, Clara began the process of utilizing passage meditation to actively accept and transform the helping and hindering personal patterns. Clara chose this passage from Joseph Campbell: "We must be willing to get rid of the life we've planned so as to have the life that is waiting for us." Clara wrote in her journal, "At first I found that my quote seemed too negative. Particularly the first phrase, 'we must be willing to get rid of the life we've planned.' 'Get rid' did not feel life-affirming enough but then I focused on the willing word [;] it is not necessary to get rid of plans. The necessity is a willingness to let go of our plans for ourselves, for our children. Maybe they will happen and maybe they will not. If we let life happen, 'the life that is waiting for us' is the life that was meant to happen. It is important to be open to possibilities, as they come into lives. Some of these possibilities we can joyously embrace, and sometimes what comes into our lives is more negative. Death or illness, sometimes we cannot influence our lives and the people in the way that we want. Embracing the negative is more difficult but it's important to remember that all things in our lives develop our souls."

As Clara engaged in the spiritual surrender exercise, she experienced the transformation of her helper, the Hatha yoga Warrior pose, into freeflowing sea kelp. She wrote, "The sea kelp image[is] a living being that grows toward the light provides an important cornerstone of the environment, produces oxygen for the sea animals, floats in the water for things to hide in[.] It is perfect in its construction deeply rooted in the ocean floor but flexible with the effects of the waves. It has floatees to hold it aloft. It can withstand the bitter cold of the Pacific, providing nutrients for myriad little animals. It sways with the waves and the storms of life, surviving or not, sometimes losing a bit to float away into the deep sea. Even its lost parts provide nutrients for the ocean as they decay."

The image of the rigid warrior stance of the helper had transformed from rigid strength into an image of sea kelp, strong yet flexible enough to withstand the cold ocean and strong storms, yet nurturing sea life. This transformation allowed Clara to identify values of "community" and "building character;" she determined that these values would be realized through the actualization of her life purpose. The transformation of the hinderer allowed Clara to recognize the importance of planning a schedule that allowed her to develop her artistic talents and to care for herself. The process of spiritual active acceptance or surrender of the motivations of the helper and hinderer transformed them both from rigid stances into flexible facilitators of the actualization of her aspiration.

Clara felt her spirituality was more readily available at the completion of the PSIT group as she concluded, "The activities in [PSIT] . . . have given me tools to access the Divine more readily. I have done [hatha] yoga for years and found that sort of meditation to be helpful but these techniques bring the Divine and surrender more into consciousness [.] Before I would experience surrender at haphazard times when the sun and the moon and the stars would align but now I feel that I can surrender almost anytime I choose to."

Clara beautifully expressed what many PSIT participants report in our research with cancer survivors. Qualitative analysis of a preliminary PSIT study combining thematic and grounded theory approaches found that the PSIT group intervention supports coping efforts and promotes self-acceptance, life purpose and meaning, spirituality, and a reassessment of values and priorities.[19, 20] The results of a quantitative study using a pre-test–posttest design indicated that women with primary breast cancer who participated in PSIT showed improved quality of life, mood, and increased spiritual well-being, especially in regard to the peace and meaning aspects of spirituality.[18] These preliminary studies of PSIT suggest that cancer participants and survivors may experience a variety of benefits from participating in the PSIT process. Further research on the efficacy of this intervention is warranted. Spiritual practices are receiving considerable attention for their potential to improve the lives of persons diagnosed with cancer.[10, 30, 31, 37] Psycho-spiritual integrative therapy provides an innovative treatment for integrating these approaches.

Notes

1. Cordova, M., & Andrykowski, A. (2003). Responses to cancer diagnosis and treatment: Posttraumatic stress and posttraumatic growth. *Seminars in Clinical Neuropsychiatry, 8,* 286–296.

2. Cordova, M., Cunningham, L., Carlson, C., & Andrykowski, M. (2001). Posttraumatic growth following breast cancer: A controlled comparison study. *Health Psychology, 20,* 176–185.

3. Coward, D. (2003). Facilitation of self-transcendence in a breast cancer support group: II. *Oncology Nursing Forum, 30,* 291–300.

4. Lee, V., Cohen, R., Edgar, L., Laizner, A., & Gagnon, A. (2006). Meaning-making intervention during breast or colorectal cancer treatment improves self-esteem, optimism, and self-efficacy. *Social Science and Medicine, 62,* 3133–3145.

5. Taylor, E. (2000). Transformation of tragedy among women surviving breast cancer. *Oncology Nursing Forum, 27,* 781–788.

6. Tomich, P., & Helgeson, V. (2004). Is finding something good in the bad always good? Benefit finding among women with breast cancer. *Health Psychology, 23,* 16–23.

7. Thornton, A. A. (2002). Perceiving benefits in the cancer experience. *Journal of Clinical Psychology in Medical Settings, 9,* 153–165.

8. Yanez, B., Stanton, A., Kwan, L., Edmondson, D., Park, C. & Ganz, P. (2009). Facets of spirituality as predictors of adjustment to cancer: Relative contributions of having faith and finding meaning. *Journal of Consulting and Clinical Psychology, 77,* 730–741.

9. Tedeschi, R., & Calhoun, L. (1995). *Trauma and transformation: Growing in the aftermath of suffering.* Thousand Oaks, CA: Sage.

10. Park, C. L., Edmondson, D., Fenster, J. R., & Blank, T. O. (2008). Meaning making and psychological adjustment following cancer: The mediating roles of growth, life meaning, and restored just-world beliefs. *Journal of Consulting and Clinical Psychology, 76*(5), 863–875.

11. Park, C. L. (2007). Religiousness/spirituality and health: A meaning systems perspective. *Journal of Behavioral Medicine, 30,* 319–328.

12. Koenig, H. G. (2008). *Religion, spirituality and public health: Research, applications, and recommendations.* Washington, DC: Subcommittee on Research and Science Education of the U.S. House of Representatives.

13. Balboni, T. A., Vanderwerker, L. C., Block, S. D., Paulk, M. E., Lathan, C. S., Peteet, J. R., Prigerson, H. G. (2007). Religiousness and spiritual support among advanced cancer participants and associations with end-of-life treatment preferences and quality of life. *Journal of Clinical Oncology, 25*(5), 555–560.

14. Moadel, A., Morgan, C., Fatone, A., Grennan, J., Carter, J., Laruffa, G., . . . Dutcher, J. (1999). Seeking meaning and hope: Self-reported spiritual and existential needs among an ethnically-diverse cancer participant population. *Psycho-Oncology, 8*(5), 378–385.

15. Oman, D., Hedberg, J., & Thoresen, C. E. (2006). Passage meditation reduces perceived stress in health professionals: A randomized, controlled trial. *Journal of Consulting and Clinical Psychology, 74*(4), 714–719.

16. Targ, E. F., & Levine, E. G. (2002). The efficacy of a mind-body-spirit group for women with breast cancer: A randomized controlled trial. *General Hospital Psychiatry, 24*(4), 238–248.

17. Pargament, K. I. (1997). *The psychology of religion and coping: Theory, research, practice.* New York: Guilford Press.

18. Garlick, M. A., Wall, K., Corwin, D., Koopman, C. (2011). Psycho-spiritual integrative therapy for women with primary breast cancer. *Journal of Clinical Psychology in Medical Settings, 18*, 78–90.

19. McDonald, C., Wall, K., Corwin, D., Koopman, C. (2011). Psycho-spiritual integrative therapy: Impacts on coping in women with breast cancer. *Manuscript in Preparation.*

20. Rosequist, L., Wall, K., Corwin, D., Achterberg, J., & Koopman, C. (2011). The experience of surrender in women with breast cancer undergoing PSIT. *Manuscript in preparation.*

21. Rettger, J. (2011). *A multiple case study exploration of women coping with primary breast cancer participating in a psycho-spiritual integrative therapy group.* Unpublished dissertation research. Palo Alto, California: Institute of Transpersonal Psychology.

22. Wall, K. (2009). *Psycho-spiritual integrative therapy group facilitators manual.* Palo Alto, CA: Institute of Transpersonal Psychology.

23. Kabat-Zinn, J. (1990). *Full catastrophe living.* New York: Delacorte Press.

24. Deikman, A. J. (1982). *The observing self: Mysticism and psychotherapy.* Boston: Beacon.

25. Hayes, S. C. (2004). Acceptance and commitment therapy, relational frame theory, and the third wave of behavioral and cognitive therapies. *Behavior Therapy, 35*(4), 639–665.

26. Walser, R. D., & Westrup, D. (2007). *Acceptance and commitment therapy for the treatment of post-traumatic stress disorder and trauma related problems: A practitioner's guide to using mindfulness and acceptance strategies.* Oakland, CA: New Harbinger Publications.

27. Astin, J. A., Anton-Culver, H., Schwartz, C. E., Shapiro, D. H., McQuade, J., Breuer, A. M., et al. (1999). Sense of control and adjustment to breast cancer: The importance of balancing control coping styles. *Behavioral Medicine, 25*(2), 101–109.

28. Astin, J. A., Shapiro, S. L., Schwartz, C. E., & Shapiro, D. H. (2001). The courage to change and the serenity to accept. Further comments on fighting spirit and breast cancer. *Advances in Mind-Body Medicine, 17*, 142–146.

29. Hayes, S. C., Follette, V. M., & Linehan M. M. (Eds.). (2004). *Mindfulness and acceptance: Expanding the cognitive-behavioral tradition.* New York: Guilford Press.

30. Carlson, L. E., Speca, M., Patel, K. D., & Goodey, E. (2004). Mindfulness-based stress reduction in relation to quality of life, mood, symptoms of stress and levels of cortisol, dehydroepiandrosterone sulfate (DHEAS) and melatonin in breast and prostate cancer outpatients. *Psychoneuroendocrinology, 29*(4), 448–474.

31. Speca, M., Carlson, L. E., Goodey, E., & Angen, M. (2000). A randomized, wait-list controlled clinical trial: The effect of a mindfulness meditation-based stress reduction program on mood and symptoms of stress in cancer outpatients. *Psychosomatic Medicine, 62*(5), 613–622.

32. Cole, B., & Pargament, K. (1999). Re-creating your life: A spiritual/ psychotherapeutic intervention people diagnosed http://www .gggrgrggrgrg.ffffff.html with cancer. *Psycho-Oncology, 8*(5), 395–407.

33. Wachholtz, A. B., & Pargament, K. I. (2005). Is spirituality a critical ingredient of meditation? Comparing the effects of spiritual meditation, secular meditation, and relaxation on spiritual, psychological, cardiac, and pain outcomes. *Journal of Behavioral Medicine, 28,* 369–384.

34. Flinders, T., Oman, D., & Flinders, C. L. (2007). The eight-point program of passage meditation: Health effects of a comprehensive program. In T. G. Plante & C. E. Thoresen (Eds.), *Spirit, science, and health: How the spiritual mind fuels physical wellness* (pp. 72–93). Westport, CT: Praeger Publishers.

35. Oman, D., Shapiro, S. L., Thoresen, C. E., Plante, T. G., & Flinders, T. (2008). Meditation lowers stress and supports forgiveness among college students: A randomized controlled trial. *Journal of American College Health, 56*(5), 569–578.

36. Cole, B., & Pargament, K. (1999). Spiritual surrender: A paradoxical path to control. In W. R. Miller (Ed.), *Integrating spirituality into treatment.* Washington, DC: American Psychological Association Press.

37. Grossman, P., Niemann, L., Schmidt, S., & Walach, H. (2004). Mindfulness-based stress reduction and health benefits: A meta-analysis. *Journal of Psychosomatic Research, 57*(1), 35–43.

Section IV

Reflections on the Fruit

16

The Men's Spirituality Group: A Leader's Personal Narrative

Carl E. Thoresen

"God expects but one thing of you, and that is you should come out of yourself . . . and let God be God in you."

—Meister Eckhart

"Of all that is wonderful in the human being, our most glorious asset is the capacity to change ourselves."

—Eknath Easwaran

This story concerns a group of men I have been working with well over 15 years. Our focus has been, and remains, on trying to grow spiritually every day of our lives—no small project. I'm using a narrative style because I want to convey experiences, a perspective about what I have encountered in leading this group. Personal stories rarely appear in scientific or professional articles, but they allow for expressions of emotions and reflections not easily captured by questionnaires, physiological measures, and statistical reports.[1]

Why tell this story? First, an avalanche of books and studies on matters of the spirit has appeared since 2000. Findings suggest that participating frequently in religious attendance, for example, reliably predicts about 7 more years of life with other factors controlled. In addition, a clear majority of Americans (more than 80%) report wanting to grow more spiritually and find more meaning and purpose in life.[2]

Second, readers who may want to become members of a group on spiritual growth might like a taste of what it would be like. For many, church committees and Sunday sermons don't do it. One in-depth interview study described it this way.[3] Many Americans regularly attending religious services fit the category of spiritual "dwellers," who feel secure in the sanctuary along with visiting with friends, maybe serving on a committee. Others labeled "seekers" often rejected church doctrine or never have become church members. These seekers explore ways to grow more spiritually, but often not systematically nor consistently. A third but hypothetical group could be called "practitioners," those learning and using spiritual practices regularly. This third group could be identified as the "missing middle of Christianity." The lack of this group leaves us without people who have developed the needed spiritual skills to make major life changes, often needed in experiencing God.

Third, I hope to provide practical information for those who might want to lead such a group. When I started the Men's Spirituality Group (MSG), information was not available on structuring a group focused on spiritual growth. Having taught university courses on using groups to solve a variety of problems, I knew the needed processes. But I lacked experience in the "nuts and bolts" of leading a group to foster spirituality.

Fourth, students of all ages might be interested in ways I structured a group focused on spiritual skills. Hopefully readers will consider doing spiritual group work and even do research on it. The research surface has been scratched, but some clear impressions exist. Such groups can be successful.[4]

Coming to Terms: God, Spirituality, Religion, and Mystics

Some key terms deserve comment because they can be confusing and controversial. Karen Armstrong, noted scholar of world religions, observed: "all theology is poetry."[5] She could also have included *God*, *religion*, and *mystics* as terms involving poetic license. Most descriptive words fail to capture the essence or felt experiences involved. I'm reminded of

Michael Polanyi, a famous philosopher, noted for his work on tacit knowledge: "We know more than we can tell." The language of poetry, with its metaphors, parables, and analogies can, at best, try to convey our complex personal experiences involved in these words.[6]

The word *God* can refer to a Universal Spirit having literally thousands of names—a timeless transcendental reality pervading all of nature. Meister Eckhart, the 13th-century Dominican priest, spoke of God's eternal presence in all people using this metaphor:

> "The seed of God is in us. Given an intelligent and hard-working farmer, it will thrive and grow up to God, whose seed it is; and accordingly its fruits will be God-nature. Pear seeds grow into pear trees, nut seed grow in nut trees, and God seeds into God." (p. 12)[7]

The word *spirituality* comes from the Latin word *spiritus*, meaning something absolutely vital to life, such as breathing. William James's take focused on actions: "the feelings, acts, and experiences of individual men [and women] in their solitude, as far as they apprehend themselves to stand in relation to whatever they may consider the divine" (p. 32).[8]

Religion provides a vital social and cultural institution. It promotes a sense of community among those seeking to understand their relationship to the Divine, primarily through study of sacred texts, music, worship, and rituals. At its best, religion kindles the fires of spiritual experiences rich in community, offering support and reaching out with compassionate love to others. At its worst, religion as a social institution can foster ignorance, abuse, hatred, and violence.

Mystics have existed as parts of religious traditions for thousands of years. Why discuss them? Because mystics have supplied many examples of how they came to have a transcendent relationship with God. In telling their stories, they have described steps in their spiritual struggle. William James viewed the mystics with insight needed to discover the depths of truth unavailable by "discursive intellect." In trying to capture their experiences of God in words, they stand out as extraordinary spiritual exemplars or models.

A Bit of Background

In the 1960s, I started with others at Michigan State and Stanford to explore how emerging psychological methods (e.g., self-reinforcement, social modeling) could be help people make needed changes. These methods used a framework called behavioral self-control.[9] The possibility that self-control might play a role in solving health problems, such as chronic sleep problems and chronic fears, fascinated me.[10]

Over the years, I also sought to grow spiritually. I tried TM (Transcendental Meditation) and explored Zen Buddhism, including training at a Zen Buddhist temple in Japan. Our family attended Unitarian churches during these years. Late in the 1980s, we joined the United Methodist Church in Los Gatos, California, where we remain members. While being very active in church activities, I still felt detached. Was I missing in action amid all these activities, or were the activities themselves missing in their spiritual relevance? Looking back over these decades, two experiences stand out as seminal in my understanding of spirituality, especially spiritual practices: the Type A behavior pattern and the Blue Mountain Center of Meditation.

Type A, Heart, and "Mike" Friedman

One day in the mid-1970s, I answered a call from Meyer "Mike" Friedman, a cardiologist twice nominated for the Nobel Prize. He had discovered the Type A behavior pattern, mostly from observing how his heart patients behaved. Mike said, "I'm told you're an expert in behavior change. If that's so, I need help in changing Type A behavior in heart patients." Over the next several months, we worked on a research proposal designed to change Type A behavior and reduce the risk of another heart attack. NIH funded a 5-year study to treat more than 1,000 heart patients using a behavioral self-control framework. Results demonstrated that a small-group treatment approach could reduce heart attacks (by more than 40% compared to other treatments used). Type A behavior could also be changed.[11] Mike and I each led some of the small groups (there were more than 35). This direct experience proved invaluable.

One initial experience impressed me: using an invocation at the beginning of each group session. Jim Gill, a Harvard-based psychiatrist and Jesuit priest, suggested we create a ritual to set the tone for each group meeting. I felt uncomfortable about doing so and expressed my reservations, but to my surprise, the invocation proved very popular with participants. Here is Jim's invocation. Standing and holding hands, participants said in unison:

We are here because we realize that we need more help than we can give ourselves. We need each other. So may all our efforts together be of benefit to each and every one and may we bring enrichment to all our lives and to those whose lives are in our care. We acknowledge this gratefully. Amen.

Here are some major observations I have made in leading groups. Some of these characteristics often overlapped with men attending the MSG:

1. Most participants lacked awareness of their social behavior and its effect on others.

2. Few understood their own emotions and how feelings influenced what they thought and did.

3. Many experienced loneliness but were often perceived by others as social and outgoing; few had a close male friend they trusted enough to listen to their fears and failures.

4. Almost all were very inpatient, easily distracted, and poor listeners.

5. Many were hostile in many ways, quick to anger, and highly competitive with others.

6. Almost all seemed unaware of "self-talk," that is, what they said repeatedly to themselves.

7. Few were awareness of their "body language": facial expressions, body postures, gestures.

Jess: A Case In Point

One participant offers a snapshot. Jess seemed typical of participants yet unusual in his openness. After a few sessions, he asked, "Would it be OK if I started going back to Mass?" Raised a Catholic who left the church in his early teens, he expressed doubts about returning but wondered if it could be helpful. A few weeks later, Jess told the group that he'd been attending Mass before work each morning. Doing so brought back memories in church of the calm he felt as a young boy, "a place still with the spirit of God." A few months later, a member commented that Jess seemed to be almost "a reformed Type A." Follow-up evidence of Jess over a decade documented substantial changes in lifestyle, such as being much less hostile and quick to anger. He had made the decision while still in the group to take early retirement and became active in outdoor activities and volunteering in community services.

Why was Jess able to make these changes? Conjectures suggest he found solace in attending Mass, received consistent support from his Type A group, something he'd never experienced before in his life, and gained insight about how his emotions influenced him, especially positive emotions. I suspect Jess's "tipping point" was his decision to attend Mass every morning; that action set into motion several lifestyle decisions allowing him to outlive his medical odds by almost two decades.

Another experience in the 1980s altered how I thought about spirituality and religion. I discovered Huston Smith.[12] His study and actual experience with three major religions challenged common perceptions that religions offered different views of God. He shed clarifying light on the three bedrock beliefs of all major religions: humility, charity, and veracity, a kind of intuitive or absolute truth. What I did not know about Smith was his awareness of Eknath Easwaran, the founder of the Blue Mountain Center of Meditation.

"Just What You're Looking For"

The earthquake in 1989 in the San Francisco Bay Area marks the time I received a postcard from a former doctoral student, saying "Carl, I found just what you've been looking for: the Blue Mountain Center of Meditation (BMCM)." I contacted BMCM and attended a workshop. What a precious gift this student had given me. At BMCM, I discovered the work of Eknath Easwaran, a professor of English literature from India who came to the University of California at Berkeley as a Fulbright Professor in the late 1950s. Educated at Roman Catholic schools in Kerala, a state in India where the Disciple Thomas had settled, he offered a unique program called passage meditation (PM) consisting of eight spiritual practices (see Figure 16.1).[13]

Easwaran's perspective, that a Universal Spirit exists in all, was described by Leibnitz, a German philosopher in the 1600s, as the

Perennial Philosophy. Leibnitz criticized the common dualistic belief that mind and body were completely unrelated. Overlooked was the fact that the perennial concept existed in the ancient Sanskrit scriptures of Hinduism (e.g., Upanishads) and included spiritual practices. It was in his spiritual practices that I realized Easwaran's extraordinary contribution. He had articulated practices based on the direct experiences of mystics from major religions and wove them together based on his own experience. In attending workshops and reading the inspiring stories of spiritual mystics, I came to realize the wisdom they had discovered. Figure 16.2 presents my effort to frame the basic features of this universal wisdom.[14]

Figure 16.1 Passage Meditation: The Eight-Point Program of Spiritual Development

1. **Meditation**—Silent repetition in the mind of memorized inspirational passages from the world's great religions. Practiced for one-half hour each morning.

2. **The Mantram**—Silent repeating of a mantram or mantra—a word or phrase with spiritual meaning and power. It can be used whenever possible, day and night.

3. **Slowing Down**—Setting priorities and reducing the stress and frictions caused by impatience and hurry.

4. **One-Pointed Attention**—Giving full concentration to the matter at hand. Avoiding multitasking.

5. **Training the Senses**—Overcoming conditioned habits and learning to enjoy what is beneficial to inner peace and love; reducing excessive information.

6. **Putting Others First**—Gaining freedom from selfishness and separateness; finding joy in helping others.

7. **Spiritual Fellowship**—Spending time regularly with others to provide mutual inspiration and support in using these spiritual practices.

8. **Spiritual Reading**—Drawing inspiration from the writings by and about the world's great spiritual figures and from the scriptures of all religions.

Adapted from E. Easwaran (2005). *Strength in the Storm.*

Figure 16.2   Spiritual Wisdoms in Action

- Discover the Divine Self within you and within everyone.
- Work to transcend selfish attachments, including egoism.
- Become more compassionate in your actions with all.
- Strive to experience more positive than negative emotions each day.
- Understand thoughts and actions are influenced by your emotions.
- Seek stillness and inner peace each day.

Before describing the details of the MSG, I mention some features that attracted me to PM and its practices:

1. Open to all or to no religious frameworks.
2. Reliance on direct human experience, not theological dogma.
3. Use of writings of inspirational mystics from all major religions in meditation.
4. Eight spiritual practices in a form highly available to the modern reader.
5. Developed by a noted scholar whose life exemplified the effects of spiritual practices.

After using these practices for years, I decided to honor the saying: "If you really want to learn something challenging, try to teach it to someone else." Besides, I really missed being in a spiritually focused group. So why not create one!

Beginnings of the Men's Spirituality Group (MSG)

I approached the pastor at our United Methodist Church about starting a men's group focused on spiritual practices. He agreed and asked if he could be a member. I invited men in the church to my home for a presentation on PM. Nineteen men attended. I had copies of Easwaran's text called *Passage Meditation* on the eight practices.[13] I gave a brief overview. Nine agreed to attend, with seven showing up at the first evening meeting. In the initial meetings, I brought up some of my experiences with other groups, such as common behavioral characteristics associated with impatience, competiveness, anger, fear, and sadness (see earlier list of Type A characteristics). For example, members were typically unaware of the quality and quantity of their "self-talk" and its influence on their actions. Others were ignorant of how their verbal and nonverbal actions often conveyed messages not intended. Others lacked close, intimate friendships.

Initial Format of Meetings (Mondays, 7:30 to 9:00 p.m.)

The flow of each meeting at first was somewhat flexible, since I was not sure of sequence and specific topics. In the initial meeting, I mentioned some "rules for our spiritual road." First, conversations in this group are confidential. While topics could be shared with others, "who said what to whom in the group" was not. Second, we decided to function as an "open group," meaning that all men were welcomed to attend (church members and nonmembers). Any man was welcomed to attend ("drop in") any session. Over the years, about 20 men have dropped in to check things out. Roughly one out of three returned, some for a few months, some still attend. Of the initial group in the mid-1990s, three remain (others have died or physically cannot attend). Typical meeting attendance varied between 5 and 7, but as younger men have joined, the average ranges between 9 and 11. Most are college educated with careers in computing, engineering, or other professional fields, including teaching.

Initial Format of MSG Sessions

- Invocation (3 minutes): Leader signaling others to stand and recite Jim Gill's invocation (mentioned earlier): "We are here because we realize . . . "
- "In-Breath and Out-Breath" Practice (5 minutes): Each member was asked to pay full attention to his breath coming in and going out, helping focus attention directly on "being in the present moment."
- Hatha Yoga Postures (10 minutes): Each member was invited to lie supine on the carpeted floor to practice a few Hatha yoga postures to

Figure 16.3   Prayer of St. Francis of Assisi

Lord, make me an instrument of thy peace.
Where there is hatred let me sow love.
Where there is injury, pardon.
Where there is doubt, faith.
Where there is despair, hope.
Where there is darkness, light.
Where there is sadness, joy.
Oh Divine Master, grant that I may not so much seek
To be consoled, as to console,
To be understood as to understand,
To be loved as to love.
For it is in giving that we receive,
It is in pardoning that we are pardoned,
It is in dying to self that we are born to eternal life.

alleviate tension, especially in the shoulders, neck, and lower back areas.

- The Week's Experiences (10–15 minutes): Comments on the past week tied to one or more of their eight spiritual practices.

- Major Topic: (30–40 minutes): Discussed one spiritual practice, such as slowing down or training the senses, sharing comments about that practice. Initially, we used Easwaran's introductory book, *Passage Meditation*, along with *God Makes the Rivers to Flow* and *Words to Live By*.[13]

- Meditation Practice (15 to 30 minutes): All members initially use the Prayer of St. Francis (see Figure 16.3).[14] Each was asked to memorize and use St. Francis's Prayer for their initial passage for meditation. Later, each member selected other passages from *God Makes the Rivers to Flow*.

- Closing Prayer/Benediction (5 minutes): Initially, each member volunteered to lead a prayer, often selected from a passage in *God Makes the Rivers to Flow*.

Over the years, the format evolved. In the last several years, we've focused more time on spiritual practices. I came to realize that reading and discussing other books, no matter how worthwhile intellectually, became distractions from working on specific spiritual practices. The moral: Be wary of an activity that looks, sounds, or feels spiritual but could distract from working on specific practices.

Early on, we participated in some outside social activities, such as going out for dinner and taking in a film or a talk with a spiritual theme. We also tried to assist a needy family (e.g., provide dinners, presents, deliver Christmas trees). Sometimes we shared the joy of decorating the tree with children who had never had this experience. As the MSG became larger, our focus shifted more attention to Monday night meetings and assisting the church's Outreach Committee.

Contemporary Format of Sessions

- Listening to Sacred Music (5 minutes): Lights dim and sitting in a circle.
- Group Reciting Prayer of Saint Francis (3 minutes): Men standing and holding hands while reciting slowly in unison.
- Mantram Practice (5 minutes): Saying your mantram slowly to yourself or writing it in your mantram book.
- Early Check-In Needed? (5–15 minutes): Ask group if anyone needs to share a concern that otherwise would be distracting for him during the meeting. (Adding this check-in has greatly improved attention during the meeting.)
- Showcasing a Passage From *God Makes the Rivers to Flow* (5–10 minutes): Anyone may share part of a passage (or all of it if short) and comment on what attracts him about this passage.
- Selecting *Words to Live By* (5 to 10 minutes): Member chooses to read and comments on what this means for his practice.
- Discussing Topic (20 to 30 minutes): Topic announced in previous session (e.g., multitasking related to Slowing Down practice). Handout sometimes used.

- Meditating on a Passage (20–30 minutes): Each member uses a pas-
  sage(s) he has memorized, saying the words slowly and silently to
  himself.
- Closing Prayer/Benediction (3 minutes): Typically the group selects
  a short passage as a benediction. The benediction is rotated every
  few months.

What Would Success Look Like?

This question helps guide experiences needed to be successful. The goal of
MSG from the outset has been to grow spiritually by learning and using
spiritual practices on a regular basis, with the hope of experiencing more
of God's presence. The mystics' messages seem clear (see Figure 2).
First, make room for God within you. Second, making room involves suffering because you are breaking long established selfish attachments.
Third, spiritual practices are the means to overcome selfish attachments
and to direct more attention and energy to spiritual experiences.[15]

Some Evidence of Change

Evidence on hand blends qualitative reports with quantitative data. The
consistent 80% attendance over more than 40 sessions per year has been
encouraging. Asking members why they keep coming, spiritual fellowship
and support rank highest. Learning spiritual practices also ranks high as
another reason. Attending Sunday morning services has clearly been
viewed as distinct from learning spiritual practices. Most see attending
Sunday as offering other important religious activities, such as the sacred
music and connecting with friends in the congregation. Some would add
sermons. (Note: Some members are not church members.) One member
put it this way: "This group has become my church service." The fact several pastors over the years have been MSG members suggests that the
group has served their own spiritual needs.

The essential criteria of success, as already noted, have to do with
members' experiences, including their use of spiritual practices. Some
practices, however, are more difficult than others. Consensus exists on
the most challenging of the eight practices: Meditating first thing each

morning and Training the Senses. Sitting quietly, meditating on a passage for 20 to 30 minutes (let alone 5 or 10 minutes) in our 24/7 information culture, creates daunting challenges, yet they are possible to overcome, as members have proved.

Training the Senses is by far as the toughest practice. Why? Because just about everything we consume is involved: what we take in from the outside through all our senses. We also take in lots of information from our mind, such as memories, especially secrets, conflicts, and other "unfinished business." Yet almost all incoming information goes on outside of our conscious awareness but uses huge amounts of energy. The cost of "living in the past" or "fussing about the future" much of the time can be exorbitant. The Buddha long ago reminded us that taking charge of what we attend to presents one of the steepest paths to climb in experiencing the spiritual unity of all life. At least members have become very aware of what they're taking in and often discuss what works for them to reduce it.

"Hard it is to train the mind, which goes where it likes and does what it wants. But a trained mind brings health and happiness. . . . More than those who hate you, more than all your enemies, an untrained mind does greater harm." (p. 183)[16]

I have tried out different ways for group members to evaluate their spiritual growth. One assessment deals with rating daily emotions, comparing positive to negative feelings during the day. I ask them to take 2 to 3 minutes to rate a list of positive and negative feelings at the end of each day for a week or preferably two. Many seem to lack awareness of their overall "emotional tone." Out of 20 questions about your day, here are two: "What is the most angry, irritated, or annoyed you felt?" or "What is the most inspired, uplifted, or elevated you felt?" Range of how one felt today goes from: "Not at all, A Little Bit, Somewhat, Quite A Bit or Consistently" (see www.positivityratio.com).[17] Currently, I ask each member to conduct this assessment twice yearly. Discussing results in the group helps clarify how spiritual practices could boost positive and lower negative emotions.

Each member also rates twice a year how often during the past week the eight practices have been practiced. Ratings go from "Not at All" to "Consistently." Results of 14 members recently revealed three major patterns: Training the Senses practice had the lowest scores (from "Not at

All" to "Somewhat"); Putting Others First and Spiritual Fellowship yielded the highest pattern (from "Somewhat" to "Consistently"); and the other five practices (Meditation, Using a Mantram, Slowing Down, One-Pointed Attention, and Spiritual Reading) were spread out over all rating categories. One summary question asked about PM overall. Almost all indicated "Moderately."

Recently, I asked members to take 15 minutes during the group to write an answer to this question: "How have you changed related to your experience attending MSG?" Here are two selected examples followed by a list of themes developed by an impartial rater. Eight common themes were identified.

Have I Changed? Two Dramatic Examples

"I used to have a 'volcanic' temper. Driving especially was a literally gut-wrenching experience. Now I am calmer and kinder. Things in general irritate me much less, if at all. I start the day in a more serene mood, which I attribute to my morning meditation. Little irritations I don't notice as much. The feeling of God's immediate presence is now with me, and I look at others differently, conscious that God is in them too."

"I credit my life to the MSG. Driving home one evening from the airport in freeway traffic, I suddenly lost all feeling on my right side of my body (I was having a stroke). Suddenly the car started to accelerate wildly because my right foot was pushing down on the accelerator pedal. I immediately started to say my mantram and kept saying it nonstop and at the same time used my left arm to grab my right leg off the accelerator. I was able to move over to the slow lane and drive myself home. But I had to call 911 because I could not get out of my car."

Common Themes of How I Have Changed

- Understanding more about what has been happening in my life and having a vocabulary to talk about it.
- Experiencing my spirituality by using these practices.
- Having tools to slow my life down and feel calm.

- Supporting each other in the group and becoming good friends.
- Paying attention to my feelings about myself and others.
- Learning about other religions and what we have in common spiritually.
- Becoming more aware of the needs of others and trying to put their needs before mine.

Overall, the MSG could be deemed moderately successful. Self-reported spiritual experiences speak to gradual changes in positive feelings, thoughts, and actions. Also, changes in the overall tone in the group have occurred, something hard to describe but definitely felt: fewer critical comments, more eye contact when speaking to the group, and more focused attentiveness by members when someone is speaking. A good sense of humor, lots of smiling, and laughter have increased over the years.

Another encouraging change has been members taking emotions more seriously. The "I don't do feelings ..." attitude has diminished greatly. Some spouses have shared comments, such as "It's remarkable.... (he's) talking about feelings ... listening and actually hearing what I'm saying ... "

Finally, I know of changes in myself, due primarily to spiritual practices supported by working with MSG. I continue to be awed by the spiritual mystics. Their patient love and persistence, often when faced with suffering and persecution, offers much inspiration. A diminishing ego also makes more room in my heart to grow bigger.

Some Concerns and Convictions

Gaining knowledge can be viewed as a circle growing larger in circumference. As we come to know more about matters of the spirit, we also come to know more about what we don't know. Serving as group leader continually reminds me of what I have learned about processes of growing spiritually and what I have yet to discover. It makes for genuine humility.

The Automaticity Problem

Several years ago, I focused on research about how much of our lives happens outside of our conscious awareness, sometimes called the automaticity of human experience.[18] This work reveals that most of the time (more than 80%), our brain conducts millions of routine activities without our conscious awareness. Spiritual mystics were the first to recognize this "automated ignorance" and how it keeps us unaware of our own emotions and inner talk. They grew to understand the power of love, compassion, hope, and faith from their experiences in community and also consistently warned against relying solely on logic and reason.

> " . . . The Self cannot be known through the study of the scriptures, nor through the intellect . . . nor through hearing discourses about it." (p. 66)[19]
> Katha Upanishad (Hindu scripture

Instead, they counseled using spiritual practices to become aware of emotions and thoughts by calming the body and stilling the mind.[14] Also offered was a different way to think about oneself: not as independent, but as spiritual beings connected with each other and all of life.[14]

Fast forward to the 21st century and the explosive growth of neurosciences describing how the brain really works. For example, Timothy Wilson, a prominent neuroscientist, noted that at any one moment, the human brain can take in 11 million bits of information but, at best, can only be aware of 40 of these. His comments that some researchers believe the evidence to be strong enough " . . . to suggest that the unconscious mind does virtually all the work and that conscious will may be an illusion" (p. 24).[20] Spiritual practices work to reduce our "automaticity," allowing us "to lead an examined life" in order to experience God. Could it be that emotions determine the quality of our lives far more than our logical thinking and factual knowledge?

Positive Emotions: The Lifeblood of Spirituality?

Emotions represent a complex set of psychophysiological processes, ranging from awe and anger to worry and wonder. By and large, emotions, especially positive emotions, still suffer a bad rap, often seen as impulsive and anti-intellectual in nature. These views no longer dominate everyone's understandings.[17] But many continue to perceive emotions as quite distinct from thinking and reasoning. Yet it is spirituality that lives in our emotions.

A few years ago, George Vaillant, a Harvard medical scholar, authored a book on spiritual evolution.[21] Spirituality, to Vaillant, exists as an amalgam of eight positive emotions, those binding us to others and to our experience of God: love, compassion, hope, faith (trust), joy, awe, forgiveness, and gratitude. He argues these eight positive emotions serve as "the lifeblood of spirituality." I have found his description very helpful. Using the rating form of emotions mentioned earlier gives members a tool to reveal some "automatic" processes. In particular, this lifeblood metaphor of positive emotions can be used as a rough gauge for members to assess their spiritual progress. Still, it has been challenging for some members to rate their emotions daily, typically because it discloses more negative than positive feelings. Yet their expanding awareness of emotions has been very encouraging.

Suggestions for Group Leaders

Leading groups fosters humility. First, all groups differ, making generalizations questionable. These few suggestions might hold water: Resist the urge to talk unless what you have to say can pass the Three Sufi Gates: Is it true? Is it necessary? Is it kind? These ideas apply to both leaders and members. I've had good results with these questions in the MSG, and it's become a group norm. Often we talk when we would learn more by listening carefully.

Sometimes a leader needs to step in and redirect the conversation. Doing so can be challenging, but it is crucial if the group is to be effective. Some examples: a member "in mid-stream" shifts to a different topic, often without realizing it, or a member sharply criticizes the comment of another. One way of handling such criticism would be to ask the member to rephrase the comment without the negative tone or manner. I've found that many fail to recognize the negativity in how they talk with or about others.

I appreciate the wisdom in this epigram: "Spirituality is more caught than taught." Spiritual modeling has to do with the kinds of behavior that inspires change: The Buddha, Jesus, Moses, Mother Teresa, and Gandhi, among many others, offer compelling examples. I have found inspiration almost daily—sometimes even hints of wisdom—by spending even a few minutes reading and sometimes memorizing the words of spiritual models.[22, 23]

When it comes to using spiritual practices yourself and with others you lead, keep this message in mind: "Patience attains the goal." Try your best to be what you would have others become. Being hurried or distracted means being out of touch with the Spirit within you and in others. Finally, remind yourself of the significant role you and your group can play when dedicated to learning and using spiritual practices to the benefit of all.[24]

I thank Kay Thoresen for her persistent yet patient editing and encouragement when I really needed it. Thanks to Doug Oman for encouraging me to write this chapter and Tom Plante's invitation to include it. Ed Bridges deserves thanks for his careful reading and enthusiastic reactions. Members of the MSG over many years deserve my sincere appreciation for their patience, support, and friendship, plus their good humor! Finally, Eknath Easwaran will forever have my gratitude and love for his extraordinary contributions to my understanding of what it means to live a spiritually focused life and how one can do so.

Notes

1. McAdams, D. (2006). *The redemptive self: Stories Americans live by.* New York: Oxford Press. See also McAdams, D. (1993). *Stories we live by: Personal myths and the making of the self.* New York: Morrow.
2. McCullough, M. E., Larson, D. B., Hoyt, W. T., Koenig, H. G., & Thoresen, C. E. (2000). Religious involvement and mortality: A meta-analytic review. *Health Psychology, 19,* 211–222; Miller, W., & Thoresen, C. (2003). Spirituality, religion and health: An emerging field of research. *American Psychologist, 58,* 24–35.
3. Wuthrow, R. (1998). *After heaven: Spirituality in America since the 1950s.* Berkeley: University of California Press.
4. Oman, D., Hedberg, J., & Thoresen, C. E. (2006). Passage meditation reduces perceived stress in health professionals: A randomized, controlled trial. *Journal of Consulting and Clinical Psychology, 74,* 714–719; Oman, D., Shapiro, S. L., Thoresen, C. E., & Plante, T. G. (2008). Meditation lowers stress and supports forgiveness among

college students: A randomized controlled trial. *Journal of American College Health, 56,* 569–578.

5. Armstrong, K. (2010). *Twelve steps to a compassionate life.* New York: Knopf. Armstrong observes that "we are addicted to our egotism," depriving us of compassionate lifestyles.

6. Polanyi, M. (1966). *The tacit dimension.* London: University of Chicago Press.

7. Meister Eckhart, cited in Easwaran, E. (2005). *Words to live by: Short readings of daily wisdom.* Tomales, CA: Nilgiri Press.

8. James, W. (1902/1985). *The varieties of religious experience.* Cambridge, MA: Harvard University Press.

9. Thoresen, C. E., & Mahoney, M. J. (1974). *Behavioral self-control.* New York: Holt, Rinehart, Winston.

10. Coates, T. J., & Thoresen, C. E. (1977). *How to sleep better: A drug-free program for overcoming insomnia.* Englewood Cliffs, NJ: Prentice-Hall; Shaw, D. W., & Thoresen, C. E. (1974). Social modeling and systematic desensitization approaches in reducing dentist avoidance. *Journal of Counseling Psychology, 21,* 415–420.

11. Friedman, M., Thoresen, C. E., Gill, J., et al. (1986). Alteration of Type A behavior and its effect on cardiac recurrences in postmyocardial infarction patients: Summary results of The Recurrent Coronary Prevention Project. *American Heart Journal, 112,* 653–665.

12. Smith, H. (1958/1991) *The world's religions: Our great wisdom traditions.* San Francisco: HarperOne.

13. Easwaran, E. (1978;/2008). *Passage meditation: Bringing the deep wisdom of the heart into daily life;* Easwaran, E. (1982/2009). *God makes the rivers to flow: An anthology of the world's sacred poetry and prose;* Easwaran, E. (1990/2005). *Words to live by: Short readings of daily wisdom.* See www.easwaran.org.

14. I developed these spiritual wisdoms from reading world mystics and shared them with the MSG. Framing them in action terms seemed to relate them more to spiritual practices (e.g., "Become more compassionate in your actions with all" instead of "compassion").

15. Killingsworth, M., & Gilbert, D. (2010). A wandering mind is an unhappy mind. *Science 330,* 6006,932. DOI: 10.1126/

science.1192439. In more than a thousand people, 47% of the time people reported their mind was wandering, and that strongly predicted unhappiness. Also, positive thoughts did not predict happiness, but unpleasant or neutral thoughts predicted unhappiness.

16. Quoted passage from Easwaran, E. (2009). *God makes the rivers to flow.* Tomales, CA: Nilgiri Press.

17. Fredrickson, B. (2009). *Positivity.* New York: Crown. Introduces positive emotions and need to increase them to offset negative emotions with a "tipping point" of at least a 3:1 ratio of positive to negative emotions and www.positivityratio.com to assess them.

18. Bargh, J., & Chartrand, T. (1999). The unbearable automaticity of being. *American Psychologist, 54,* 462–479.

19. Quoted passage drawn from Easwaran, E. (2009). *God makes the rivers to flow.* Tomales, CA: Nilgiri Press.

20. Wilson, T. (2002). *Strangers to ourselves: Discovering the adaptive unconscious.* Cambridge, MA: Belknap Press. See Brooks, D. (2011). *The social animal: The hidden sources of love, character and achievement.* New York: Random House.

21. Vaillant, G. (2008). *Spiritual evolution: A scientific defense of faith.* New York: Broadway.

22. Oman, D., & Thoresen, C. (2003), Spiritual modeling: A key to spiritual and religious growth? *International journal for the psychology of religion, 13,* 149–165.

23. Oman, D., & Thoresen, C. E. (2007). How does one learn to be spiritual? The neglected role of spiritual modeling in health. In T. G. Plante & C. E. Thoresen (Eds.), *Spirit, science and health: How the spiritual mind fuels physical wellness* (pp. 39–54). Westport, CT: Praeger.

24. Questions about passage meditation? Go to www.easwaran.org. Also see Flinders, T., et. al., (2010). Translating spiritual ideals into daily life: The eight point program of passage meditation. In T. Plante (Ed.), *Contemplative practices in action: Spirituality, meditation, and health.* (pp. 35–59). Santa Barbara, CA: Praeger. Using mantrams? Borman, J. (2010). Mantram repetition: A "portable contemplative practice" for modern times. (pp. 78–99) in using mantrams in the same book.

17

Fruit of the Spirit: Next Steps

Thomas G. Plante

This book has attempted to bring together many different and thoughtful expert voices among academic professionals who specialize in the integration of spiritual and religious behavior and psychology. All are well-established and serious scholars who highly value and conduct quality empirical research and writing. In addition, they come from both Eastern and Western traditions. To our knowledge, no other book is currently available that has examined the evidence-based research findings of the qualities that are articulated in the sacred scriptures regarding the fruit of the spirit in both a scholarly and applied manner.

Overall, the chapters provide support for the notion that religious and spiritual practices, behavior, and engagement are associated with improved psychological, physical, and community functioning and well-being. Religion and spirituality can make us better. The fruit of the spirit can result in a better quality of life. However, we must be mindful of the need for future quality research as well as the downside of religious engagement, too. Intolerance, rigidity, and in-group/out-group conflict can be problematic and create a situation in which this type of religious engagement can lead to fruit that is not healthy but unhealthy. This fruit can lead to violence, bias, prejudice, and cruelty: a double-edged sword, perhaps.

This book project represents the fourth edited book that our team at the Spirituality and Health Institute at Santa Clara University has now published that brings together experts and students from the various spiritual and religious traditions in psychology, religious studies, public health, nursing, science, literature, and several other fields.[1-3] Our institute includes quarterly extended lunch meetings to discuss a wide variety of multidisciplinary and multifaith research, teaching, conference, and book projects as well as collaboration on many other related topics as they arise. We fondly begin our meetings with the question, "Where might the spirit lead us this time?" We are never disappointed at the end of our discussions. Our lunch table includes clergy, professors from many academic disciplines (e.g., psychology, religious studies, biostatistics, public health, engineering, philosophy, English literature) from several universities, students from a variety of disciplines, and community leaders in faith-based nonprofit social service agencies. Perhaps this institute and current book project could serve as a model of what could be done elsewhere in both professional and lay circles. We do a lot on a little lunch money.

The religious and spiritual traditions offer much. There is much to learn and celebrate when thoughtful and well-meaning people with skills and perspectives that are informed by their spiritual and religious traditions come together and learn from each other with an open, caring, and respectful manner. Having table fellowship around meals helps to enhance the working and personal relationships as well. We hope that our book project will be a contribution in the right direction for religious and psychological understanding that might stimulate further reflection, research, and application and, in doing so, make the world a better place.

Since this volume was not able to address all of the empirical and applied approaches from the spiritual and religious traditions, future books are clearly needed in our view. Future projects might continue to examine how religious and spiritual behavior and practices can be best understood and used in health promotion broadly defined. Further research may wish to expand in both the empirical and theoretical directions. Empirical research might examine how spiritual and religious engagement might be most effective with certain populations as well as what role belief in and practice of religious and spiritual activities could play in obtaining the greatest desired mental, physical, and community health effects. Future research may also investigate the effectiveness of these traditions from a cultural, socioeconomic, or religion-of-origin lens in order to determine how these factors might influence their effectiveness in daily life. As we could present but a taste of what the world's religions and spiritual traditions have to offer in regard to psychological well-being, future volumes may wish to examine traditions not discussed in this book (e.g., Sikhism, Jainism, Taoism, Confucianism, Shamanism, Paganism).

It is our hope that this book will serve as an enlightening and thought-provoking guide to those searching for a more thoughtful, mindful, spiritual, and contemplative path to healing, stress relief, and overall well-being, perhaps for themselves and for others with whom they live and work. We hope that this book has brought forth a way for individuals to experience the fruit of the spirit or provided some insight into how their traditions enhance well-being broadly defined. The fruit of the spirit perhaps leads to a better quality of life when considered and used thoughtfully and sincerely.

Notes

1. Plante, T. G., & Thoresen, C. E. (Eds.). (2007). *Spirit, science and health: How the spiritual mind fuels physical wellness.* Westport, CT: Praeger/Greenwood.
2. Plante, T. G., & Sherman, A. S. (Eds.). (2001). *Faith and health: Psychological perspectives.* New York: Guilford.
3. Plante, T. G. (Ed.). (2010). *Contemplative practices in action: Spirituality, meditation, and health.* Santa Barbara, CA: Praeger/ABC-CLIO.

About the Editor
and Contributors

About the Editor

Thomas G. Plante, PhD, ABPP, is professor of psychology and director of the Spirituality and Health Institute at Santa Clara University as well as an adjunct clinical professor of psychiatry and behavioral sciences at Stanford University School of Medicine. He currently serves as Vice Chair of the National Review Board for the Protection of Children and Youth for the U.S. Council of Catholic Bishops (USCCB) and is Past President of the Society for the Psychology of Religion and Spirituality (Division 36) of the American Psychological Association. He has authored or edited 15 books, including *Contemplative Practices in Action: Spirituality, Meditation, and Health* (Greenwood, 2010), *Spirit, Science and Health: How the Spiritual Mind Fuels Physical Wellness* (Greenwood, 2007), and *Spiritual Practices in Psychotherapy: Thirteen Tools for Enhancing Psychological Health* (American Psychological Association, 2009).

About the Contributors

Richard A. Bollinger, PhD, is a psychologist at the Hospital of the University of Pennsylvania.

Diana Corwin is a graduate student in clinical psychology at the PGSP–Stanford Psy.D. Consortium.

Don E. Davis, PhD, is an assistant professor in counseling psychology at Georgia State University.

Michele Dillon, PhD, is a professor of sociology at the University of New Hampshire.

Diane E. Dreher, PhD, is a professor of English and work-life balance consultant at Santa Clara University.

Robert A. Emmons, PhD, is a professor of psychology at the University of California, Davis.

David B. Feldman, PhD, is an associate professor of counseling psychology at Santa Clara University.

Aubyn Fulton, PhD, is a professor of psychology and social work at Pacific Union College.

Aubrey L. Gartner is a graduate student in counseling psychology at Virginia Commonwealth University, on internship at Catholic University.

Richard L. Gorsuch, PhD, MDiv, is a professor of psychology at Fuller Theological Seminary.

Peter C. Hill, PhD, is a professor of psychology at Rosemead School of Psychology, Biola University.

Joshua N. Hook, PhD, is an assistant professor of counseling psychology at the University of North Texas.

Cheryl Koopman, PhD, is a professor (research) of psychiatry and behavioral sciences, Stanford University.

Maximilian M. Kubota is a graduate student in counseling psychology at Santa Clara University.

Anjali Mishra is a graduate student in psychology at the University of California, Davis.

Doug Oman, PhD, is an adjunct associate professor in the School of Public Health, University of California, Berkeley.

Michelle J. Pearce, PhD, is an assistant clinical professor in the Duke University Medical Center Department of Psychiatry and Behavioral Sciences and an instructor for Duke School of Medicine.

John E. Pérez, PhD, is an associate professor of psychology at the University of San Francisco.

Leyla M. Pérez-Gualdrón, PhD, is an assistant professor of counseling psychology at the University of San Francisco.

Megha Sahgal is a graduate student in counseling psychology at Santa Clara University.

Steven J. Sandage, PhD, is professor of marriage and family studies at Bethel University.

Shauna L. Shapiro, PhD, is an associate professor of counseling psychology at Santa Clara University.

Len Sperry, MD, PhD, is a professor of mental health counseling, Florida Atlantic University, and clinical professor of psychiatry, Medical College of Wisconsin.

Jonathan J. Sperry, MSW, PhD, is a staff psychotherapist at the Center for Counseling and Psychological Services at Florida Atlantic University.

Carl E. Thoresen, PhD, is professor emeritus of education, psychology, and psychiatry/behavioral sciences at Stanford University and a senior fellow at Santa Clara University.

Loren Toussaint, PhD, is an associate professor of psychology at Luther College.

Daryl R. Van Tongeren, PhD, is an adjunct instructor in the department of psychology at Virginia Commonwealth University.

Amy Wachholtz, PhD, MDiv, is an assistant professor of psychiatry at the University of Massachusetts Medical School and the director of health psychology at UMass Memorial Medical Center.

Jon R. Webb, PhD, is an associate professor of psychology at East Tennessee State University.

Kathleen Wall, PhD, is an associate professor of psychology at the Institute of Transpersonal Psychology.

Paul Wink, PhD, is a professor of psychology at Wellesley College.

Everett L. Worthington, PhD, is a professor of psychology at Virginia Commonwealth University.

Caifang Jeremy Zhu, PhD, is senior counselor at Beijing Yu Xin Yuan Psychological Counseling Center, guest research fellow at the International Center for Buddhist Studies, Renmin University of China, and adjunct associate professor of English at Beijing International Studies University.

Index

CPSIA information can be obtained at www.ICGtesting.com
Printed in the USA
BVOW01*1003151114

375062BV00008B/45/P